The Danes
of SEND MANOR

The Life, Loves and Mystery of Gordon Stewart

Best Wishes
Bob Akal

WILLIAM GORDON STEWART (1885–1952)
William Gordon Stewart with his aging Champion Midas of Send,
owned by Prince George, Duke of Kent. Circa 1935.

The Danes
of SEND MANOR

The Life, Loves and Mystery of Gordon Stewart

R O B E R T   H E A L

The BOSTON
MILLS PRESS

Cataloging in Publication Data

Heal, Robert, 1929-
The danes of Send manor
The life, loves and mystery of Gordon Stewart

ISBN 1-55046-355-1

1. Stewart, Gordon, 1885–1952. 2. Great Dane. 3. Send Manor (Ripley, England).
4. Kennel owners — England — Ripley — Biography.
5. Businessmen — England — Biography.   I. Title.

SF429.G7H42 2001   636.73   C201-930130-8

05 04 03 02 01   1 2 3 4 5

Published in 2001 by
BOSTON MILLS PRESS
132 Main Street
Erin, Ontario
Canada N0B 1T0
Tel 519-833-2407
Fax 519-833-2195
e-mail books@bostonmillspress.com
www.bostonmillspress.com

Distributed in Canada by
General Distribution Services Limited
325 Humber College Boulevard
Toronto, Canada M9W 7C3
Orders 1-800-387-0141 Ontario & Quebec
Orders 1-800-387-0172 NW Ontario
& other provinces
e-mail cservice@genpub.com

An affiliate of
STODDART PUBLISHING CO. LIMITED
895 Don Mills Road
#400 2 Park Centre
Toronto, Ontario
Canada M3C 1W3
Tel 416-445-3333
Fax 416-445-5967
e-mail gdsinc@genpub.com

Distributed in the United States by
General Distribution Services Inc.
PMB 128, 4500 Witmer Industrial Estates
Niagara Falls, New York 14305-1386
Toll-free 1-800-805-1083
Toll-free fax 1-800-481-6207
e-mail gdsinc@genpub.com
www.genpub.com

THE CANADA COUNCIL | LE CONSEIL DES ARTS
FOR THE ARTS | DU CANADA
SINCE 1957 | DEPUIS 1957

We acknowledge for their financial support of our publishing
program the Canada Council, the Ontario Arts Council,
and the Government of Canada through the Book Publishing
Industry Development Program (BPIDP).

Design by Gillian Stead
Printed in Canada

Contents

Acknowledgments

MY SINCERE THANKS. There were hundreds of people who contributed to and helped with this book. I'll only mention a few of you here, so if I leave you out, it's not through lack of appreciation but because of my limited intelligence, and I apologize to you.

In England, canine historian and dog judge Eric Bailey was just super, always willing to help when I called upon him. Jean Lanning, a long-time breeder of Great Danes and a friend, all-breeds international judge, member of the committee of the Kennel Club and author of many Great Dane books, gave great suggestions and advice.

In Surrey, England, Andrew Montgomery and his wife, Maureen, dug out his father's and mother's records and photos to be used. Andrew's father, Robert Montgomery, was the extraordinary head of training at Send Kennels, and his mother, Audrey Field, trained the dogs.

In New Zealand, Gordon Stewart's nephew, Gordon V. Stewart, had invaluable family records and supplied many photos for the book. He would direct me and answer many of the questions that puzzled me.

My old pal Bill Siggers gave me the original idea and insight into what this man Stewart was all about and started all my curiosity.

Les Bowerman is the present owner of Send Manor, where I visited and chatted with him about the history of that wonderful old house. Les was a great help.

There were four kennel maids still available for me to talk with. As eyewitnesses, their memories, photos and background data contributions were invaluable. Win Leake lives in Surrey, England, and Phyllis Hill (nee Hudson) near Bournemouth, on the coast. Then there was Nora Napoliello (nee West), who lives in the United States, in

Colorado, and Margaret Fife Failes (nee Tracy) from Norfolk, England. What grand, dear, wonderful ladies you are! A great big hug and kiss to each of you, with my very sincere thanks. I couldn't have written the book without all your help.

John Osborne, now of South Africa, did original digging for early motor-car history. Thank you John.

Feffie Somerfield of *Dog World* dug through old files of her newspaper with great results, as did Bill Moores of *Our Dogs*, who arranged photos.

For searching out old research on Gordon Stewart's safety crusades, I want to particularly thank Elizabeth Osborne, my head of research for Ashtead, Surrey. Researching the eccentric artist Augustus John was a real lark. Great help came from author Michael Holroyd, whose excellent biography, *Augustus John*, by Random House, is a must read for all of you.

The National Portrait Gallery of London, the National Gallery in Ottawa, the Lord Beaverbrook Museum in New Brunswick, the Washington National Gallery, the National Portrait Gallery of the Smithsonian Institution, and the collection curators for the royal family also helped out.

When I was researching the members of the Royal family who had been associated with Gordon Stewart, Miss Pamela Clark of the Royal Archives at Windsor Castle responded to every question over several years and dug out invaluable information for me.

Helping me through the motor-car years was Morris-car historian Harry Edwards, who supplied most of the background data and photos of those early years.

Stewart's aviation years, long ago (1910), were tough to research. But bit by bit I pieced together that chapter with the help of the RAF Museum, the Royal Aeronautical Society, *Aero* and *Flight Magazine* archives.

When I got into his purchase of the Strand Theatre, the Theatres Trust and Theatres Museum in England opened their archive information to me to provide what I needed for those exciting years.

Even Dame Vera Lynn wrote me personally when I was researching Gracie Fields.

John Pulford and John Granger of Brooklands Museum in Surrey had pictures and historical articles on Sir Malcolm Campbell.

From the Kennel Club in London, Barbara Walker (librarian) and Philip Robinson went back years, with massive research on pedigrees etc. for Send Kennel. What a great job they did.

Vicar Tony Shutt of St. Mary the Virgin Church in Send, Surrey, supplied the history for his church, where Gordon Stewart is buried.

Ron Dickenson with his trusty computer and word processor, as usual, was always ready to pitch in. Everyone I wrote and talked to helped out gladly — people who knew Gordon Stewart and many who didn't know him at all. You all contributed immensely to this tale of adventure.

To all others, my very sincere thank you.

Bob Heal,
January 2001

LEFT TO RIGHT: *Champion Seanymph's Brutus of Paarldane, Bill Siggers, Shirley Heal, Champion Minka of Clausentum (bred by Jean Lanning). I was slow setting my camera, and Bill had just finished the punch line of his joke when I snapped the picture. "There were two nuns crossing the plaza in Rome, when a tourist asked if he could take their picture. While he was fiddling with his camera, one nun asked, 'What's he trying to do?' 'Focus,' said the other nun! 'Both of us?' asked the shocked first nun."*

PHOTO BY THE AUTHOR

Preface

I love any and all Great Danes! So does my lovely wife, Shirley, my best friend, critic sometimes when I deserve it, and mother of our three really fine children, Wendi, Scott and Stephen. At least I think she must — they chew up her socks, dig up her petunias from the flower boxes, and steal the toys from her white Persian cat, Jeepers, who is the love of her life.

Yet I see her cuddled up with them on her bed, healing and comforting them when they're ill and scolding when they've been naughty. Understanding, when there's been an accident in the house by an old, dear friend in the later years of life.

She's sat patiently by my ringside as I've judged Great Danes around the world. And when I'm done, she'll sometimes gently question me on my selections. Shirley has typed many hundreds of research letters for this book, struggled through my lousy handwriting to type the manuscript, and always is there to help and advise.

I well remember one time at our farm in Rockwood, Ontario, Canada, when we were trying to shoot some promotion pictures of our great Champion Diplomat. My old pal Bill Siggers was over visiting us from England, and he was the "director" of this hilarious event. Come to think of it, every event with Bill was hilarious.

Mat didn't feel like posing—after all, he was a star resting at home, not on the road at a dog show. He was off duty.

Shirley was rolling on the ground, meowing like a cat (or something) to get Mat's attention. Bill was roaring with laughter at her crazy antics. Mat was indignant. The photographer said to hell with it and went home.

So I dedicate this book to my two dear friends. I don't think Shirley will mind sharing the spotlight with Bill Siggers. She loved him too!

But for Bill, I probably wouldn't have known anything about Gordon Stewart in the first place, or have met so many great friends all over the world who have shared their Danes with Shirley and me.

It's been a wonderful journey knowing and loving you both, Shirley and Bill. So I dedicate this book to you Shirley, and to Bill, wherever he may be.

Bob Heal
January 2001

Foreword

I t gives me great pleasure to write the foreword to this much-wanted book, which fills an important gap in the history of Great Danes between the two world wars.

It must be some forty years ago that Bob and Shirley Heal started to purchase Clausentum Great Dane show stock from us. They were shipped to Barbados, and in those days the only way was on the Fyffe banana boats, which was a journey of some weeks. The Heals are Canadians, and Bob, a highly successful international businessman, kept homes in both countries, regularly commuting between the two.

Bob is a connoisseur in all aspects of his life, and one of his hobbies has been to own and breed, in a small way, the finest of Great Danes. Only the best of British, American and German bloodlines were used in his plans. His greatest pride was to own the top-winning American and Canadian Champion, Dinro Diplomat.

Well known in the UK as a championship show judge of Great Danes, he also judges the breed worldwide, and the zenith of his career was when he judged the breed at Crufts Dog Show in 1998.

His book on Great Danes will be read with great enthusiasm by students of the breed. But it will also be of interest to people outside the breed and even outside the dog game itself. Gordon Stewart was a self-made man extraordinaire, probably one of the richest men in the world and a Richard Branson of his time.

Bob realized after writing his book *He Whacked the Bloody Lot*, about his friend Bill Siggers and the history of the illustrious Ouborough Great Danes, that there was a great void left, in that the equally famous Send Great Danes and their owner had a tale that should be told. He decided that when he updated the Bill Siggers book, he would write a couple of chapters on the Send Danes. Now it has actually become an interesting, exciting and detailed book in its own right.

I remember well a very wet evening in June, when Bob, Shirley and yours truly went tramping around the little churchyard of the ancient parish church of Send, to find the grave of Gordon Stewart.

Then there were whistle-stop journeys with Bob, Eric and Gina Bailey and me, to interview octogenarians Win Leake and Phyllis Hill, kennel maids who were so happy to co-operate.

This book is a treasure trove of the golden history of the Great Dane. We also learn a great deal about Gordon Stewart, the man himself — complex, ruthless, and one of the most highly successful businessmen of his time. He was the main driving force behind Bill Morris (later known as Lord Nuffield) in the launching of his first cars.

Enjoy reading this fascinating book. Thank you, Bob, for bringing it to us.

Jean Lanning

THE DANES OF SEND MANOR

Perfectly trained Send Danes. Left to right are Mona, Karan, Meg, Lancelot, Ulana and Egmund. Circa 1933. PHOTO COURTESY NORA WEST

❖

Introduction

THIS STORY TAKES PLACE IN ENGLAND EARLY IN THE TWENTIETH century, and my original interest was in Send Kennels and the Great Danes. But I soon discovered that Gordon Stewart's life was a kaleidoscope of colourful bits and pieces that intertwined and connected into a marvellous picture of the adventures of a truly amazing and interesting man.

All his papers, photos, records, trophies and personal information seemed to vanish when he died in 1952, which made the research job difficult indeed. There were no children to consult after his wife, Irene, who might have had family records, died. But then I found his nephew, Gordon V. Stewart in New Zealand.

I had to research through the back door as it were, contacting hundreds of sources not personally connected to Gordon Stewart throughout his life, then following up lead after lead. Doors would open, then shut! There were many dead-end streets. But eventually I found myself having to sift through the thousands of scraps of information I'd collected.

I don't like to do puzzles. But in this case, each little irregular piece had to be fitted into each little hole before the whole picture developed. And what a marvellous picture it is — a series of stories and events with more human interest, intrigue and substance than *Coronation Street*.

It's a story of elegant aristocracy, royal princes and the King of England, knights and their lovely ladies, powerful cars and powerful men, the early days of flight, the wonderful world of the theatre, glamorous actresses and actors, five hundred Great Danes, *The Hound of the Baskervilles*, the early days of the motion picture industry, and *The Pied Piper of Hamelin*.

Wondrous personalities such as Sir Malcolm Campbell, William Morris (Lord Nuffield), Dame Gracie Fields, famed artist Augustus John and many others are also a part of it all.

This is the story of a great man, his life and his loves. For Gordon Stewart had an eye for a pretty young lady, and that led to discreet affairs and mistresses. But that's understandable too — he was a man of power. His marriage to his only wife, Irene, was distant and cold, but he never abandoned her and was generous with her and with everyone else who stuck by him.

Amazingly, had Gordon Stewart and Bill Morris not met accidentally in 1913, this story might not have happened. Everything stems from that meeting: the beginning of the empire and the wealth that made all else possible.

Photos will vary in clarity — remember that some go back over one hundred years. These are rare insights into remarkable events, and I'm gladly sharing them with you. Few photos are more recent than forty-six years. What started out as a history book is now another story, full of adventure and romance, yet a true story. It's an intriguing tale of success and failure, sadness and joy.

The heady stuff of life — and of death.

Grandfather Edwin Smith left a family trust (1832–1911).
PHOTO COURTESY GORDON V. STEWART

Gordon Stewart's mother, Eleanor Sophia Stewart (nee Smith)
(1861–1932). PHOTO COURTESY GORDON V. STEWART

CHAPTER ONE

The Early Years

Theere are wonderful stories hidden in history, and one of the most remarkable is the story of Gordon Stewart. It's true what they say — fact can be stranger than fiction.

Some might tell you he was born with a silver spoon in his mouth, and they're partly right. His family of doctors, lawyers, sea captains and astute businessmen were all upper middle class in England. But any silver and gold Stewart amassed was surely earned, through cunning, intelligence, ambition and plain old hard work. He dreamed big dreams, made big plans and took big, calculated risks. His uncanny ability to see into the future meant he was there when it all happened.

Most things he did were never accomplished by other men, perhaps because he'd try anything new, and in the first half of the twentieth century a lot was happening and a lot was new.

His story begins in England, in 1885. He was born near Epsom, Sutton, on May 13, to Eleanor Clifford Stewart (nee Smith), and was named William Gordon Stewart. Later he would drop the first name William and use only Gordon Stewart, as everyone called him Willie and he hated that.

His father, Raynham Vivian King Stewart, was a tea merchant. Hard and severe, he was not at all close to or loving with his family. There were two sisters, Madeline and Dorothy, and four brothers, Raynham, Arthur, Walter and Vivian.

The maternal grandfather, Edwin, played a large role in Gordon Stewart's early years. He wanted all the grandsons to join the Royal Navy and follow a career at sea. Whatever for, I can't tell, as Edwin certainly kept his feet on dry land and built a sizeable fortune doing it. He was a tough businessman; an estate agent and auctioneer in London. He also invested heavily in English and American railway stock.

Edwin looked after his daughter and the children financially because Eleanor and Raynham's marriage was shaky and finally ended in separation at the turn of the century.

He lived well, at the Coburg Hotel in Mayfair, and always spent his holiday time at the Grand Hotel in Brighton, the same hotel the IRA bombed in 1985 trying to kill Prime Minister Margaret Thatcher.

Edwin also paid for Gordon Stewart's schooling at Eastbourne College, on the south coast of England, near Worthing. Grandfather Edwin pleaded with Stewart to join the Royal Navy, but he'd have none of that. He knew what he wanted even as a teenager — to go to London and earn his fortune in business. The morning he was to leave, he and Edwin had their final row. Stewart told him once and for all he would not join the navy, and that he wanted to learn about the new motor cars being developed. That was the last straw for his grandfather.

Edwin plunged his hand into his pocket and came up with a small coin. It happened to be an American ten-cent piece. "I'll bet you this dime," Edwin thundered, "that the motor car will never replace the horse on the streets of London."

The bet was on. Stewart took the coin, packed his bags and started out. He didn't know where to go or what to do, but now he had to show his grandfather that he would succeed. The world was waiting for Gordon Stewart, and by God, he wouldn't disappoint that world.

At ten his father had bought him a puppy, his first Great Dane, and oh, how he hated to leave his old pal behind. But never in his wildest dreams did he imagine that one day he'd own five hundred Great Danes and the largest kennel the world would ever see — in any breed of dog.

From a friend, Stewart learned that a company called the Wolseley Sheep Shearing Machine Company was hiring young men. It had transferred its business from Australia to Birmingham in 1889, and Herbert Austin was general manager. Years later he would found the Austin Motor Car Company.

The Wolseley company initially made bicycles which, along with horses, were the main mode of transportation at that time. In 1901 it re-registered as the Wolseley Tool and Motor Car Company, to manufacture the early Wolseley motor cars. They had produced the first one in 1896.

As fate would have it, Stewart's first job was working for Herbert Austin, making Wolseley cars. Then he'd go on to befriend William Morris. Gordon Stewart was obviously destined for a place in the world of motor cars in Britain, and grandfather Edwin would soon lose his bet and his dime. Stewart was a true entrepreneur, and everything new and different caught his eye. The British papers were full of new developments in England, on the Continent and in America. Young bold men were actually trying to fly. The Wright brothers, who also made bicycles in America, were getting their designs in the air.

Herbert Austin had designed two aeroplane engines for this new market, so Stewart set out to design an aircraft to use them. The Mulliner Coachworks liked what they saw, and built Stewart's Mulliner 1 Monoplane, which he showed at the first Olympia Aero Show in London in 1910. He was then only twenty-five years old, and it was there that he met a man who would be a lifelong friend — Malcolm Campbell.

At twenty-six, Stewart felt he knew enough to make his move. In 1911 he joined forces with another young man named Ardern, and his first company, Stewart and Ardern, was born. In 1912 Stewart travelled to the North of England Motor Show at Manchester. There he met Bill Morris, and that meeting would forever change their lives.

Those two young men, bold and ambitious, took a chance on each other that would make them multimillionaires and close friends for life. By 1912, at age twenty-seven, Gordon Stewart had really begun his life — Great Danes, motor cars, aeroplanes. And what next?

In his wildest dreams he could never imagine what lay before him — that he'd befriend the King of England, produce motion pictures, build a huge business empire of many companies and own the Strand Theatre in London's West End. There'd soon be affairs of state with Britain's aristocracy and affairs of the heart with some of the most beautiful stars of England's stage and screen.

CHAPTER TWO

From Sheep to Motor Cars

Frederick York Wolseley was the third of four sons. He was born in County Dublin, Ireland, in 1837. His older brother later became Field Marshal Viscount Wolseley. Frederick went to Australia before he was thirty, as a sheep-station manager in Victoria.

An engineer of sorts, he began tinkering and developing methods for mechanically shearing sheep. He took out his first patent on the equipment and then bought a large sheep station near Walgett to try out his inventions on his own sheep. The next year he registered the Wolseley Sheep Shearing Machine Company, because by then he had over forty patents. But he wound up this company in Australia and transferred it to England in 1889, where it became the Wolseley Sheep Shearing Machine Company of Birmingham.

Herbert Austin had been recruited to work with him in Australia and went to England with the new company as general manager. But the sheep-shearing machinery business wasn't all that good, so Austin switched the company focus to bicycle manufacturing and motor cars. Bicycles were the most common mode of transportation in those days, along with horses. Wolseley himself resigned from the company in 1894 and died in 1899.

In 1901 the company became the Wolseley Tool and Motor Car Company. Herbert Austin had made the first prototype Wolseley in 1896 and improved it in 1897. Production cars came off the line in 1899. One of these competed very well in the Thousand Miles Trial of 1900, around England.

Austin-designed Wolseleys were made for the next six years, and by 1901 Wolseley was among the biggest of the British car manufacturers. They sold three hundred and twenty-seven cars that year, increased to eight hundred in 1903, and by 1914 were producing three thousand a

Frederick York Wolseley (1837–1899). Wolseley himself never built cars, but he had the foresight to choose Herbert Austin to run his firm, which later built them.

PHOTO COURTESY
BROOKLANDS MUSEUM

year. Austin was a clever promoter and featured the Wolseley in any race he could find. But the company directors and Austin had a falling out. He went to Deasy in 1909, and Wolseley never quite made it much further without him.

By 1921 they had made twelve thousand plain, conventional cars, and when they went bankrupt in 1927, the company assets were scooped up by Sir William Morris. William Morris was, by then, called Lord Nuffield. The company pioneered a small car that resembled the Morris Minor, and by 1939–40 they had a comprehensive range of models.

In 1953–54 the Nuffield-Austin merger meant a new design, and by 1958 the Austin-engineered Wolseley was an attractive compact design that was basically an expanded Morris Minor. By 1975 the long decline of Wolseley came to its end with the Princess models, and soon the company was no more.

Wolseley went from sheep shearing in Australia to making motor cars in England. Sir William Morris (Lord Nuffield) took them over, and Herbert Austin, who had been Gordon Stewart's boss (having left Wolseley to start his own company), later merged with Lord Nuffield.

*A 1917 Sopwith Camel fighter, used by
the Home Defense Squadron for Zeppelin defence.*

*The German Zeppelin L-12, damaged while raiding England
August 10, 1916, was towed to Ostend and dismantled.
Note the two machine gunners at the top.*

CHAPTER THREE

Men Can Fly

In March 1998 I was sitting in a Boeing 747 at thirty thousand feet, just leaving the coast of Labrador to fly over the Atlantic into London's Heathrow airport, with my wife beside me. We were off to judge the Great Danes at Crufts. I couldn't help thinking about Gordon Stewart, in 1909, trying his hand at designing aeroplanes at twenty-four years old, and I marvelled at how far aviation had come in just ninety years or so.

In 1909 the English, European and American aeroplanes looked like flimsy, metallic birds — all wings and little else — while around me on that 747 were hundreds of people, tons of cargo and fuel in a massive flying machine that looked, and indeed was, sound and substantial. It took you from Toronto to London in about six hours. I thought back to the First World War, when reconnaissance aircraft spotted for the troops, and peppy little fighters like the Sopwith Camel successfully battled the huge Zeppelin airships as they silently carried incendiary bombs from Europe to drop over London.

That was only about six years after Gordon Stewart and other young men his age were doing their first plane designs. It was understandable that Stewart would become interested in aviation — it was the new idea, that men could fly. He was young, adventurous and visionary, and he worked at the Wolseley Tool and Motor Car Company of Birmingham at the time. The manager, Austin, saw an opportunity to get in on the act, as all kinds of firms had begun building these early planes.

The first requirement was a light but powerful engine to drive the wooden propellers. Austin designed, for Wolseley, both a 60-horsepower, 8-cylinder, V-type engine weighing three hundred and forty pounds and a new (in 1909) 30-horsepower, 4-cylinder vertical that weighed two hundred and ten pounds. The Wolseley eight-

The Mulliner 1 Monoplane, 1909.
PHOTO COURTESY GORDON V. STEWART

*Simplified sketch of the Mulliner 1 Monoplane
designed by Gordon Stewart in 1909.*
PHOTO COURTESY GORDON V. STEWART

*Gordon Stewart used this 8-cylinder, 35-horsepower JAP engine
in his Mulliner 1 Monoplane instead of a Wolseley engine.*
PHOTO COURTESY GORDON V. STEWART

cylinder was popular, well known everywhere and particularly desired for the aircraft being built in France. Good results were being achieved by both of these engines.

So Stewart began sketching designs for the airplane he envisioned could use the Wolseley engine, and the Mulliner Company liked what he designed. But for some reason along the way he changed his mind about the engine. In 1909 he designed a plane called the Mulliner 1 Monoplane, which was the first monoplane to be built by Mulliner Coachworks of Long Acre, London, and Northampton. It was a single-seat tractor, but he fitted it with a 35-horsepower, 8-cylinder, JAP engine, built by a competitor of Wolseley. His design had a six-foot-three-inch Spencer propeller, a thirty-three-foot wingspan and a length of twenty-seven feet, weighing a total of four hundred and twenty pounds empty and six hundred and five pounds loaded. It was listed at a maximum speed of forty miles per hour, and cost four hundred and fifty pounds.

Now I'm a little leery about the listed speed, because I have no record of anyone trying to fly it — certainly not Gordon Stewart. And sometimes he'd be known to stretch a point. Later you'll read how he advertised his first new Morris Oxford motor car in *Auto Car* magazine as doing fifty miles per hour on the road. By then it only had a dummy wooden engine, and Stewart had yet to see or drive a manufactured prototype on any road at all.

His monoplane was written up in aeroplane magazines at the time as having "clever design and irreproachable workmanship." So the design was not panned by the critics. It was actually noted as quite original, not following the lines of other well-known planes.

Stewart displayed his monoplane in 1910 at the first Aero Show at Olympia, which is a huge exhibition hall complex in London. Although well received by the aeroplane enthusiasts, I don't know how the venture went commercially. I can only surmise not so well, as Stewart did not continue designing aeroplanes, and in 1911 he left Wolseley and branched out on his own with his first company. Perhaps the move was hastened when he switched his monoplane engine to a JAP instead of a Wolseley.

Rear view section of the Mulliner 1 Monoplane, 1909.
PHOTO SUPPLIED BY GORDON V. STEWART

Wing-frame section of the Mulliner 1 Monoplane, 1909.
PHOTO SUPPLIED BY GORDON V. STEWART

It was, however, at this time that he met another twenty-five-year-old who wanted to fly. Born in 1885, the same year as Stewart, Malcolm Campbell designed, in 1909, his first aeroplane, then built it and crashed it. He rebuilt it and recrashed it. After doing this a few times, he figured out that maybe he was cut out for another line of work and sold the scrap aeroplane for twenty-two pounds.

The Mulliner Coachworks shop. In the foreground, the fuselage frame of the Mulliner 1 Monoplane is being assembled, 1909.

PHOTO COURTESY GORDON V. STEWART

Campbell and Stewart would meet again at Brooklands track around 1914, where Campbell was racing and Stewart was promoting the Morris Oxford, and they chummed around again. They both went their separate ways but stayed in contact, and then joined up in 1932 for Safety First films. By now his friend was Sir Malcolm Campbell.

Stewart did not venture into aviation design work again, but he did stay in touch with flying through the Royal Flying Corps, and was still in their reserve during the Second World War. In an interview with a reporter in the thirties, he confirmed that he and a small group of enthusiasts (including Claude Grahame-White, the famous aviator of that time) had designed and built the first Hendon Aerodrome, south of London.

I can find no authority to confirm that statement! The Royal Aeronautical Society, the Royal Air Force Museum at Hendon and Brooklands Museum all checked their records for me, to no avail. However, that doesn't mean the statement wasn't true. As one Hendon historian, Bill Firth, put it, "There were a lot of early pioneers, but the interest was in the planes, not in the aerodrome, so little is known about these men."

William Morris behind the wheel of his 1913 Morris Oxford at the Stewart and Ardern showroom, 18 Woodstock Street, London.

PHOTO COURTESY HARRY EDWARDS

CHAPTER FOUR

The Morris Car

The Birmingham North of England Motor Show in 1913 was held February 14–22, at the old Exhibition Hall, Rusholme. It was here that Gordon Stewart's business life would begin.

A young man named Bill Morris showed a model of his new Morris Oxford, along with his engineering drawings for the proposed motor car. It was yet to have a motor, however, as the parts hadn't arrived in time for the show. So Morris showed the mock-up model with only a dummy wooden motor in it. Stewart really liked the look of that car, even though it couldn't run, or be started for that matter.

These two men had nothing to lose — Morris didn't have a car and Stewart didn't have a showroom.

They made their deal on speculation alone, as ambitious, gutsy young men will do. Stewart gave Morris an order for the first four hundred cars that he could produce, and Morris, with this order in his hand, could get his company going. It was located at the Old Military College at Cowley. Stewart was able to obtain the funds for the order from grandfather Edwin's trust fund, so everything was set to go if they could get a Morris Oxford on the road. "Come and get it," Morris said excitedly as he called Gordon Stewart. "Our number one is ready."

So Stewart set out for Cowley.

"I pray to God the car will run," he mumbled as he boarded the train. His neck was out a foot. He'd rented his first showroom for his new company, Stewart and Ardern, in a little space at 18 Woodstock Street, just off Bond Street in London. On one side was the tailor Steadman and Sawyers and on the other side, a small office. If you put them end to end you could get two cars on the floor. His parts stores and repairs bay were in the basement.

As the train rattled through the countryside he remembered that this week his ad was appearing in *Auto Car* magazine. It read that the new Morris Light Car could do forty-five to fifty miles per hour on the road. The trouble was it had never been on a road.

"Bloody 'ell," muttered a worried Stewart.

This took the guts of a true car salesman, as all he'd seen in Birmingham was a dummy car model with a dummy wooden motor.

As Stewart climbed into the first Morris, Bill Morris and the factory crew watched apprehensively. He drove a few hundred yards and there was a loud crack. The cast iron universal joint had snapped. They replaced it with another, and he got a few miles further and that one cracked again.

Back to the drawing board for Morris, and back to London for Stewart — a very worried man indeed.

Morris made the next universal joint of phosphor bronze, and Stewart went to Cowley to try again. This time William Morris, his Morris Oxford and Gordon Stewart were rolling gleefully down the road to an outstanding future.

Back in London, Stewart talked Harrods into displaying the car of the future in their store. That year, 1913, it was placed in Harrods stall number nine at the motor show at Olympia, and huge crowds flocked to see the new car.

Soon Morris and Stewart had three models to show. The standard model was known as the Morris Light Car, and in 1914 they added a deluxe chassis, a two-seater torpedo, the coupe and a light delivery van to the market. To promote the cars, Stewart and Morris put them in the eight-hundred-mile London-to-Edinburgh road trial. This was a large event, only for motor cars, organized by the Motor Cycling Club in 1914. Six Oxfords competed, driving four hundred miles up to Edinburgh and four hundred back to London. Bill Morris and his passenger, Henry Golpin, drove in business suits in one, to show the advantages of a closed car. Gordon Stewart drove another. The Morris entries all did well — they won gold medals and a special trophy, the Light Car Cup.

William Morris behind the wheel of his Morris Oxford in 1913. His accountant, Varney, is beside him. Gordon Stewart stands by the bonnet. Outside the first Stewart and Ardern showroom, 18 Woodstock Street, London. PHOTO COURTESY HARRY EDWARDS

Gordon Stewart never missed a chance to promote the Morris Oxford. Here Champion Lancelot of Send clears the car while Audrey Field, his trainer, looks on with delight. Circa early 1930s.

PHOTO COURTESY ANDREW MONTGOMERY

Note hire purchase terms, even then, and driving lessons included, 1928.
COURTESY HARRY EDWARDS, MORRIS HISTORIAN

Stewart and Ardern's early ad, 1913.
COURTESY HARRY EDWARDS, MORRIS HISTORIAN

Stewart and Ardern did not have exclusive distributor rights for the car; H. W. Cranshaw of Manchester had rights for the north of England, W. H. M. Burgess had the south and Stewart had London and its surrounding area. But London had all the action, the huge population and head offices of England's best companies. It was, without a doubt, the best territory.

The Morris was an outstanding success, and Stewart and William Morris grew up together very quickly. By 1923 Stewart and Ardern had to move to much larger premises on Bond Street. It was agreed that Morris would stick to building the cars, and Stewart would do the selling through a solid distributorship with experienced salesmen, offering credit facilities, driver training and efficient service depots.

The theory was sound and instantly successful. Sell them a Morris and offer outstanding service with available parts, and the customer would come back for his or her next car.

Stewart soon had convenient service centres at Gatliff Road and Ebury Bridge Road, Victoria. Later he would circle London, with

Whether your business is big or small . . .
it's better business to deliver with a
Morris Light Van

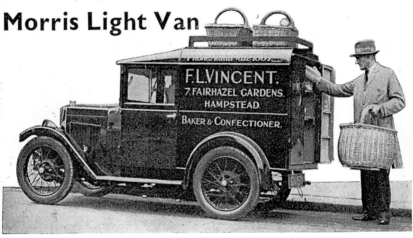

❖ A pound's a pound and a minute's a minute—whether you own a chain of shops or are just starting up on your own. No one these days can afford to be careless in the matter of overheads. That's why you find that both famous firms and "one-man" businesses are running Morris Light Vans—the vans that look after your time and money. They're cheap to buy and cheap to run.

They're fast and they're utterly reliable. There's lots of room inside for your goods and lots of room on the outside for your name and an advertising message. As for goodwill—well, which would *you* prefer? Your bread and pastries arriving along a dusty road via a boy on a bicycle at five miles an hour, or arriving in a dustproof Morris Van, spick and span and punctual to the minute?

THE 1933 8-10 CWT. VAN WITH NEW BODY, STILL SMARTER AND ROOMIER

MORRIS 5-cwt. VAN - - £110

4-cylinder 8 h.p. engine.

❧ Equipment includes Triplex glass single-panel windscreen and door-windows, Dunlop cord tyres, Lucas lighting, starting and coil ignition, chromium finish. Internal measurements: height 3 ft. 6 in.; width 3 ft. 4½ in. Length behind driver's seat, 3 ft. 4 in. Cubic capacity 38 cubic feet, with doors at back.

Price ex Works

MORRIS 8-10 cwt. VAN - - £160

4-cylinder 14/32 h.p. engine.

● Equipment includes Dunlop cord tyres. Lucas lighting and starting set. Triplex glass single-panel windscreen and winding windows, chromium finish. Internal measurements: height 3 ft. 10 in.; width 4 ft. 3½ in.; length 4 ft. 6 in. Cubic capacity 70 cubic feet.

Price ex Works

Write for full particulars and detail specification of Morris Light Vans. Our generous terms for deferred payments will also be sent. Morris Motors Ltd., Cowley, Oxford.

MORRIS LIGHT VANS

The British Baker *magazine, 1933.*

modern, convenient locations at Croydon, Sutton, Harrow and Southend. They were all manned by experienced technicians, with the latest service equipment and the best sales force in England.

By 1924 the Morris Commercial Vehicles Division was operating. This was a great plus for Stewart and Ardern, as London was the commercial centre for all of Britain. In 1926 they opened a huge display and service centre at the Vale, Acton; this would be Stewart and Ardern headquarters for the next fifty years. The floor area totalled one hundred and seventy-seven thousand square feet.

Stewart wanted a prestige showroom in London's prosperous West End and found a site at Berkeley Square. It had been the home of the Marquis of Lansdowne. He demolished Lansdowne House, with its famous garden, and built Morris House. (Sir William Morris had been honoured along the way and was now known as Lord Nuffield.) Bill Morris opened Morris House for Stewart at an official ceremony in 1934. It cost four hundred thousand pounds and had forty thousand square feet of floor space.

In 1939, the Metropolitan London Police took delivery of a large fleet of Morris vans for transporting prisoners. Great publicity for Stewart and Ardern!

By this time the company was the largest car distributor in Britain, with the finances for the finest service areas and the best equipment. New engine-tuning equipment cost one hundred thousand pounds alone. The company just grew and grew and seemed unstoppable.

Then, in 1939, all hell broke loose — war was declared.

While all this was happening, Stewart was amassing the fortune to do other things. In the early twenties he bought Send Manor in Surrey, south of London, and proceeded to build the biggest kennel in the world. He also established the British Poultry Development and Send Grist Mills companies, so he was a busy entrepreneur indeed.

But never forget the importance of his meeting Morris. That motor-car empire he built and the fortune that flowed from it made all else possible.

CHAPTER FIVE

Dream...
and It Might Come True

L ieutenant-Colonel C .E. W. Beddoes had come out of military service after the First World War and opened the Dog's Bath Club in Beauchamp Place, London, in 1925. It started out as a grooming, handling and training parlour for dogs and soon caught on with the elite, members of the Royal family and the titled gentry of England.

As many of these patrons chose to wait for their dogs to be done, Beddoes and his wife would serve light refreshments and tea. This branched out when he added an elegant lounge and full bar service. The Dog's Bath Club was registered, and one had to be invited to become a member.

Later in 1925, Beddoes was invited (by James Voase Rank, who established the Ouborough Kennel with my close friend Bill Siggers) to become secretary of the Great Dane Breeders Association that was just forming. After one of these meetings, Beddoes was approached by Gordon Stewart, a member of that association, and also a member of the older Great Dane Club. They had a long chat, and Stewart told him about his very real dream to establish the best Great Dane kennel in England, and if possible, the world.

His father had bought a Great Dane for him when he was ten years old, and they had become devoted pals. From that day on Gordon Stewart vowed he'd own a kennel of Danes.

"Beddoes," he said, "I'd like to bring you down to my home at Send Manor in Surrey tomorrow. I'll send around my man to pick you up. I'll tell you what I want to do."

By 1925 Stewart had only a handful of Danes. In 1922 he'd bought Professor of Falklands and Rufflyn Rouvia. Then in 1925, he added two

*Colonel C. E. W. Beddoes helped Gordon Stewart plan
the Send Manor kennel development. Circa 1925.*

more from England: Champion Wolfram of Sendale, who sired a number
of good dogs (including the harlequin dog, Champion Danilo of Send
and the black bitch Champion Rakie of Send), plus Alanie Sendale.

Beddoes agreed to come, and Stewart outlined his plan. He showed
him drawings of the proposed kennel, to be developed on about fifty
acres of the Send Manor grounds behind the great house. He'd establish
an ultra-modern facility and, by careful scientific selection, breed a line
of Great Danes not only with elegance, grace and beauty, but with the
mental qualities to prove a theory that Stewart had.

He strongly believed the Great Dane had the character, stamina and
prowess to equal any breed, such as Alsations, used for special
obedience duties. Stewart explained that his operation would equal or
better anything in the world. He'd have his own veterinary staff, a
completely equipped dog hospital, a modern commercial kitchen and
a cold-storage plant. And all food would be made on the premises, with
special recipes formulated by recognized experts on canine dietetics.

"My word," stammered Beddoes, "that'll cost a fortune!"

"Don't you worry about that," shot back Stewart indignantly. "I'll handle all the necessary financial details and will personally see that the job's done right. Now what do you think of these dogs I have?" he asked Beddoes.

"To tell you the truth," Beddoes replied, "they're good, but not good enough for what you intend to do."

"I rather thought you'd say that, so here's my proposition for you. I want you to help me plan the entire facility and buy me the best Danes we can find in the world. What do you say?"

I should interject here that Stewart had already approached Bill Siggers to try to take him away from Rank and Ouborough, but Siggers turned him down.

Beddoes said he'd have to think it over for a couple of days, as he had the Dog's Bath Club to worry about. He talked it over with his wife, and she urged him to go with Stewart for awhile. She could handle the business.

So, for the next six months of 1926 he travelled with Stewart all over Europe to buy first-class stud dogs and brood bitches to build the Send line. They bought scores of dogs, particularly in Germany, Holland and Italy, and paid high prices to get the best they could find. Draftsmen and craftsmen were hired to plan and build the kennel facility the way Stewart had dreamed it would be.

Reg Giles, a carpenter in Ripley who later worked for Send, personally filled in some of the story in an article for the Ripley Historical Society years ago. He related that his uncle, Harold Giles, went to work with Stewart as the foreman in about 1925. There was no electricity then in the Send Marsh area, so Stewart had his own electric generating plant installed to serve the house, workshop, offices and kennel buildings. All they previously had were paraffin lamps for lighting.

Giles continued, "That Stewart really helped the village of Ripley with employment during the economic slump in the twenties and thirties."

He hired twenty-five building and maintenance men, under his father Harold Giles, for constructing kennel runs and chicken houses. There were three gardeners, with a butler, a cook and a maid in the house. He also employed two chauffeurs, ten kennel boys, five cook-house and kitchen staff, thirty kennel maids, two office girls, three dog trainers and eight managers for the various sections of the operation. Add it up — it took a staff of ninety-one to help Stewart fulfil his dream.

He also bought two Morris fire engines, keeping one for the kennel grounds and giving the other to Ripley Village.

"Only one person, Vernon Grave, could drive it for a long time," said Reg Giles, "and he was half mad. We had a lot of fun watching them practise on summer evenings. The horses that drew the other fire equipment were scared of the thing, and old Sam Brown got slung off it rounding Challons Corner!"

Stewart bought up an existing grist mill business, which he renamed the Send Grist Mills. At first it had a baker, salesman and other staff and was organized to sell animal feed throughout England. This flourished through the Second World War. It would supply the wheat, flour and other ingredients to his Send Manor kennel cook-house for the Danes, and his poultry feed.

At the back of the property at Send Manor, he built a thriving poultry operation housing thousands of chicken stock and pigeons. It was named British Poultry Development and eventually had a huge egg and chicken market, which included many of the fashionable London hotels. This company would also supply the eggs he used in the feed for the hundreds of Send dogs in the kennel.

He later held poultry and pigeon shows at Send Manor, with breeders and manufacturers exhibiting, thus building up the reputation of his company throughout the country.

So there you have it — the beginning of a marvellous dream that Gordon Stewart first had in 1895, when he was ten years old and played and walked with his first Great Dane. It was an endeavour he felt would allow him the relaxing contrast he needed, away from his heavy business commitments in London.

Send Manor House in 1998.
PHOTO BY THE AUTHOR

Champion Midas of Send with Gordon Stewart in Send Manor.
Circa 1931. PHOTO COURTESY GORDON V. STEWART

CHAPTER SIX

Send Manor

G ordon Stewart was about thirty-six when he decided to buy Send Manor in Ripley, Surrey, in 1921. This was just after his marriage to Constance Ethel Irene Russell in 1919. Irene, as she was known, was born January 9, 1893, so was eight years younger than he was.

It stands to reason that he bought Send Manor for his new bride. But sadly enough, in about ten years they were living apart, although they never divorced.

He then bought an apartment building on Wellbeck Street in London, which he named Gordon House. Irene had a flat there where she would spend most of her time, only appearing at Send for special functions for distinguished guests or theatre people. Stewart's sister Madeline also had an apartment there and was still there at the time of his death in 1952.

By this time, he'd had eight prosperous years building Stewart and Ardern, after taking delivery of his first Morris Oxford in 1913. Send Manor had been owned by a wealthy farmer before Stewart bought it; the house was old and grand, with exposed, old, oak beams and huge fireplaces to heat the rooms.

The construction of Send Manor had begun in 1628, and the completed first section dates to around 1670. Victorian additions were made to the building in 1870. Research indicates that the house once belonged to Queen Margaret of Richmond, mother of Henry VIII. She used it when visiting her son, who was educated at the monastery at Newark Abbey, near Pyrford.

Send Manor and the lands that Henry inherited from his mother passed from him in a way typical of that period. A great tournament was held at Woolwich, at which the estate was offered as a prize. So it went into the hands of Count Tregoz, then through various owners until Stewart bought it in 1921.

The manor had about fifty acres of land, on the outskirts of Ripley village, and was already named after the nearby village of Send when Stewart bought the property. With the help of Colonel Beddoes, he built a kennel facility that was the finest in England, or anyplace in the world for that matter.

Phyllis Hill, a kennel maid whose maiden name was Hudson, still recalls the layout of Send Manor and the kennels. She married Leslie Hill, the assistant dog trainer to Bob Montgomery. Reproduced here is her memory of the layout and how she drew it for me in 1998. It is quite remarkable in detail, as she had left Send Manor over sixty years before.

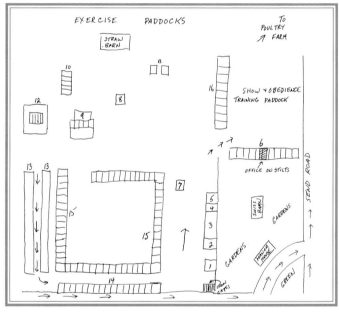

Phyllis Hill's layout plan of Send Manor.

1.	GIRLS' CANTEEN	9.	HOSPITAL WITH RUNS/KENNELS
2.	BAKEHOUSE AND ROOM TO CRACK BISCUITS	10.	WHEELING KENNELS AND BATH HOUSE
3.	KITCHEN/KELVINATOR ROOM/BOILERS FOR HEAT	11.	TWO INCINERATORS
4	STOREROOM FOR GROOMING EQUIPMENT	12.	QUARANTINE KENNELS INSIDE HIGH FENCE
5.	COVERED SHED FOR FEED BARROWS	13.	GENERAL KENNELS
6.	SHOW RANGE WITH SMALL OFFICE ON STILTS	14.	GROWING STOCK KENNELS
7.	MAIN OFFICE ON STILTS	15.	GENERAL KENNELS
8.	FIRE ENGINE IN GARAGE	16.	GENERAL KENNELS

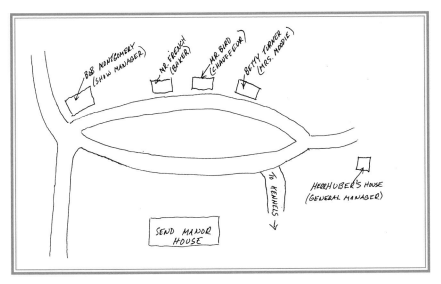

Cottages built by Gordon Stewart for special staff.
DRAWN BY KENNEL MAID NORA (WEST) NAPOLIELLO

The manor house faced a village green. On both sides and at the rear were manicured gardens tended by three gardeners. Just behind the gardens, Stewart rebuilt a barn into a remarkably beautiful building that had a tennis court on the floor. It would be used for exhibitions of obedience and dog races and had quite a large open area.

You will see on the plan that a girls' canteen was built to the left of the manor house gardens. Down from that were the bakehouse, kitchen and cold room, food stores area and a utility shed. The architectural beauty and excellence of the facility was due in large part to the fact that all the buildings were designed in a theme, in the style of an authentic Swiss village.

They all looked like Swiss chalets, and the interior decorating carried through this concept, with mountain-scenery paintings and wood carvings and crests on the walls.

The tree-lined lanes between the buildings were lovely and landscaped beautifully as avenues, each with its own name. The show fields, or ranges as they were called, behind the manor house gardens, had a row of kennels with an observation office on stilts, where Show

Stairs leading up to a corner of the main office building constructed on stilts. PHOTO COURTESY NORA WEST

Front view of the Swiss-style Karinda Hut, where the shows and indoor exhibitions were held. PHOTO COURTESY NORA WEST

Heated winter quarters at Send Kennel for whelping bitches.
PHOTO COURTESY NORA WEST

Manager Robert Montgomery watched the training progress. His office overlooked a large grassy area used as the show and obedience training paddock.

And this was not the only building on stilts; there was also a much-larger main office that housed about five office staff and all the files and records. Stewart also built other smaller units on stilts, where he housed his prized birds and pigeons. One of these bird houses on stilts still survived as a derelict building on the grounds in 1998, as you can see in the photograph on page 49. To the left of the training facilities were long kennel buildings for the adult dogs, with whelping kennels and a bathhouse in a separate building. Inside the kennel ranges was another large, grassy training area. There was a separate, long block of kennels nearer the roadway for the puppies and growing stock and a heated section for in-whelp bitches and litters in winter.

Every kennel block had outside runs for each kennel. Each kennel usually housed two dogs — dog and bitch — and each had a wire-fenced run for exercise. All these kennels were in long rows, making up the kennel blocks or sections. There were about two hundred and ninety individual kennels and outside runs to house around five hundred dogs. Then there were individual sections such as the dog hospital, and the large main office on stilts you'll see in photos in this chapter and elsewhere. There was also a small building that housed the Morris fire engine.

Stewart built an isolated quarantine building off by itself behind a high fence. This was out of bounds to all staff except those who worked in that section. British regulations required that all dog imports be quarantined for six months in government-controlled facilities when entering Britain. Stewart was allowed his own facility because he imported a lot of dogs. As a result of these precautions, Britain remains rabies free today. (These restrictions were revised early in the year 2000.)

An area at the rear was for two incinerators to burn refuse to control disease. There was also a barn for storing the wheat straw used for bedding in the individual kennels.

*Gracie Fields with a team of fawn Great Danes in front of
one of the exotic bird lofts at Send Manor, early 1930s.*

The same bird loft where Gracie Fields posed, as seen in 1998.
PHOTO BY THE AUTHOR

As a hobby, Stewart raised varieties of exotic birds and pigeons, and held poultry and bird shows at Send, as well as dog shows. Win Leake, a former kennel maid, remembers, "He had a beautiful collection of Jacobean pigeons that he raised to show at exhibitions throughout England. He also supplied pigeons to experimental labs for research purposes."

At left is a photo from the early thirties of Gracie Fields in front of a bird loft built in the Swiss style and on stilts. Above is that same building as it stood over sixty-five years later — a pitiful, derelict sight. You'll see other bird lofts connected to other buildings in the backgrounds of pictures throughout the book.

At the very rear of the fifty acres, Stewart established two other companies, his British Poultry Development and the Send Grist Mills. These companies grew to be important and prosperous commercial ventures and will be described in other chapters. They were essential as food sources for his kennels, but grew to serve food markets throughout England. They both prospered during the Second World

*Gordon Stewart with his movie camera in
the early thirties.* PHOTO COURTESY GORDON V. STEWART

War, supplying tons of food weekly to the home front and troops
overseas.

Now that the buildings were taking shape, Stewart needed a large
staff — always about ninety to a hundred people when the kennels
were in full swing. Send Manor and the kennels were indeed a
complete village, beautifully designed and maintained and organized to
run as an efficiently structured operation.

As always, Stewart planned well, then hired the best management
available for the various kennel departments and functions. This would
become the most remarkable kennel operation that the world had ever
seen.

Left to right: Mrs. Gordon Stewart, Sybil Church, Margaret Tracy and Mrs. Beddoes, in the Karinda Hut.

Always lots of puppies to exercise at the puppy range at Send Kennel. PHOTO COURTESY ANDREW MONTGOMERY

◆ 51 ◆

The puppy range building. PHOTO COURTESY NORA WEST

The home kennel building. PHOTO COURTESY NORA WEST

Front of the Karinda Hut in winter.

PHOTO COURTESY NORA WEST

In front of one of the pigeon lofts. At right is Bob Montgomery.
Second from right is trainer Miss Ecob, with a cropped-ear import.

Training with dumbbells for races. See Bob Montgomery's office and
observation post on stilts in the centre of the kennel range overlooking the
outside training grounds. Background right, other kennel maids watch
these skilled trainers in action. These girls here were the "special six"
from the training section of Send Kennel. Left to right are Vic Allfrey,
Miss Bond, Sybil Church, Margaret Tracy with Bernard, Phui May,
and Audrey Field with Champion Lancelot on the far right.

Prized Jacobean pigeons at the fountain at Send Manor.
PHOTO COURTESY GORDON V. STEWART

Watering the chickens at the huge British Poultry Development owned by Gordon Stewart. It operated at the rear of the Send Manor grounds. PHOTO COURTESY GORDON V. STEWART

A sample promotion folder for British Poultry Development.

In front of the large main office building on stilts — a team of harlequins. Left to right are Nora West, Betty Turner (Moodie), Sybil Church, Miss Bond, Audrey Field, Margaret Tracy with Draga, Phui May, Vic Allfrey, an unidentified girl and, on the far right, Flo Webb. PHOTO NORA WEST

Inside the Karinda Hut. Front row, left to right, the first kennel maid is Vic Allfrey, second from her left is Gordon Stewart, and Mrs. Stewart is on his left. Next to her is Sybil Church with two fawn Danes, and in centre is Audrey Field. Margaret Tracy is in front of the vicar, fourth from the right is Mary Ryde with Phui May on her left, second from right is Colonel de Pinto, and Bob Montgomery is at far right. Note the numbered wheel at top left, used to spin out the number of spaces a dog would move in the races. PHOTO COURTESY ANDREW MONTGOMERY

Outside the Karinda Hut. Obedience trials between Alsatians and Send Great Danes. In front row, fifth from left, is Captain Radcliffe. Seventh from left is Mrs. Gordon Stewart in fur collar, and next to her in a large fur hat is Mrs. Charles Cruft. In centre with cigar is Gordon Stewart; Charles Cruft, who originated Crufts Dog Show, is on Stewart's left; and next to Charles Cruft is Colonel de Pinto, a trainer at Send Kennel. Then Margaret Tracy with Mona and Karan; Sybil Church with a harlequin; Bob Montgomery, the training manager at Send; and on his left hand, Mary Ryde. Next is Audrey Field with Champion Lancelot and a harlequin. On the right end is Phui May with Champion Egmund (the Hound of the Baskervilles, see Chapter 18). Behind Audrey Field in the second row at right is Herr Eickenbauer, the Send trainer from Germany. Circa 1932.

Win Leake at feeding time.
A fully grown Great Dane ate two pounds of meat
and two pounds of biscuit and other food each day.
PHOTO COURTESY WIN LEAKE

CHAPTER SEVEN

A Thousand Meals a Day

A t Send Kennel a staff of five prepared over one thousand meals a day for the dogs and kennel staff. There were over four hundred of them, plus puppies and quarantine imports, so that at the height of operation there were about five hundred Danes at any time. Different menus were needed for puppies, sick dogs, fat dogs, thin dogs, stud and show dogs, in-whelp bitches and for many other conditions requiring special food care.

The regular adult dog menu was two pounds of raw meat and two pounds of biscuit with a bit of "soup" on top, fed once a day. One day a week they were fed boiled rice and wheat flakes, with stock made from the marrow bones saved from the beef and horse carcasses that the butchers cut up every day in the kitchen. All stud dogs, in-whelp bitches and juniors also had two raw eggs a day with their meal. These came fresh from the poultry farm Stewart established at the rear of the grounds of Send Manor.

Young puppies were fed six times a day with such things as boiled rice, then raw eggs, lime water and calcium phosphate. Just think of the thousands of gallons of fresh water pumped every day in the kitchen and butcher shop for the kennels, staff facilities and washing down.

If a dog was very thin, it was fed again that day. Fat dogs got the meat but not the biscuit. Tons of meat came from cattle and horse carcasses delivered to the kennel by huge vans. These horse carcasses came mainly from the same contractor who supplied quality high-protein horsemeat to the horsemeat shops so popular then in England and Europe. The horsemeat vans delivered twice a week — on Tuesdays and Fridays — but the kennel maids tell me that a lot came from Sandown Race Track as well. The carcasses were stored in a large Kelvinator refrigerated room that led off the kitchen.

Mr. Reginald French, the baker, with a biscuit slab to be broken up in the cracking machine in the bakery.

The butchers cut up the meat from these whole carcasses, saved the bones for soup stock and used a large commercial electric mincer to grind the raw meat for the daily meals. The tiled kitchen also had large copper cookers to cook meat and boil rice. To keep meat production going on a twenty-four-hour basis, the night watchman doubled as a butcher at night.

Phyllis Hill (nee Hudson), a kennel maid, remembers well a really impressive young local lad named Jimmy Souter, whom Bob Montgomery, the show manager, had originally hired to be a clean-up boy around the kennels. Jimmy was promoted to help the butchers and would do anything well to please his managers. He could barely read or write and came from a large, poor family. He hardly had clothes or shoes to wear, but he was so well liked by the staff that they all chipped in to help him get along — with clothes and food for the family.

Mr. Reginald French had come from a commercial bakery and baked large slabs of biscuit with a special recipe Stewart developed

Nora West on left and Betty Turner (Moodie) at right feeding a young brindle Dane. PHOTO COURTESY NORA WEST

Feeding time at the puppy range. A wild scramble.
PHOTO COURTESY WIN LEAKE

The avenue in front of the food-service building. The chart below shows how the various operations were laid out in this building.

THE AVENUE IN FRONT OF THE FOOD BUILDING.
IT WAS LAID OUT LIKE THIS:
from right to left

1. Room for cracking biscuit slabs
2. Bakehouse
3. Kitchen with cookers and Kelvinator room for meat
4. Storeroom, grooming equipment, etc.
5. Covered shed for feed barrows/trolleys

with a group of nutritionists. He had his own efficient bakehouse, with large ovens and an electric cracking machine to break up the biscuit slabs. The biscuit was dried and then broken up into different sizes according to the ages and needs of the dogs. Smaller bits went to the puppies, larger for the grown dogs and the left-over crumbs were cooked up for the sick dogs. Nothing was wasted.

The kennel maids loved Mr. French. He cooked up delicious currant buns for the girls as a special treat and sent them over to their canteen, about fifty yards away from the bakehouse.

A picture of the building used for this food service is shown here. On the right end was the bakehouse; next on its left was the kitchen and cold room, on its left was food storage and a large room used for grooming equipment etc. Left of that, on the end, was a covered shed for food barrow and trolley storage.

The storeroom held rice, wheat flakes, cod liver oil, Parish's Chemical Food and wheat germ, all used in various diets for the dogs. Mealtime was an amazing study in organization. Each kennel maid was responsible for her own dogs in her range section. She had large trolleys on wheels, each with a stack of shelves that held her dogs' food bowls. She pushed the trolley to the kitchen.

Each kennel in a range held a dog and a bitch together, and one was fed in the kennel house and the other fed in the wire run, so each got the correct meal, according to its needs or age. An upright stand held the bowl so these huge dogs need not bend down to eat from the ground.

You can imagine the waste left from this operation, so two incinerators were built near the rear of the property to burn up all garbage and maintain strict sanitation for the kennel.

The mammoth job of feeding all these dogs is hard to imagine. Needless to say Stewart approached the many problems of organization with the same professionalism he used in any of his companies. No expense was spared, and only qualified, reliable staff were hired, directed by the best management he could find.

Nowhere in the world, then or today, has any kennel fed one thousand meals a day, seven days a week, year after year.

The dog ambulance of Send Kennel. The crest says Royal Veterinary College. Bob Montgomery is at the left and Mr. Mitchell in white duster at the right. PHOTO COURTESY ANDREW MONTGOMERY

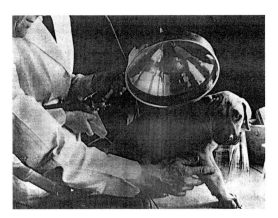

Mr. Elliott, the manager at Send Kennel after Herr Huber left in 1934, demonstrates the infra-red equipment at the kennel hospital.

CHAPTER EIGHT

The Hospital

I had the opportunity in 1998 to personally interview two kennel maids who had actually worked in the veterinary hospital that Stewart built on the grounds at Send Manor. Both Win Leake and Phyllis Hill (nee Hudson) are mentioned in other chapters, and here are some of the things they remember about this medical facility.

It was wonderfully equipped with the most modern equipment Stewart could buy. It had its own testing laboratory and infra-red and ultra-violet units for treatment of skin problems. Its surgery would have been the pride of any vet. Attached to the hospital building were indoor and outdoor runs for the animals under treatment, who were not returned to their kennels until totally well.

A veterinary came two or three days a week from Woking in Surrey and was always on call twenty-four hours a day. There was a resident canine nurse and a hospital staff of five at all times. Professor Hobday of the Royal Veterinary College was a consultant vet as well. Stewart designed a Morris dog ambulance loaded with first-aid equipment. It was kept on the grounds and accompanied the dogs to the shows, prepared for any emergency, accident or problem with the dogs or the show kennel maids.

Win Leake recalls that Mr. J. H. Huber, the overall kennel manager, first gave her a job in 1934 in the hospital, exercising and grooming the patients and boiling instruments. Phyllis Hill had to do the rounds every day of two hundred and ninety individual kennels to check for any sick dogs. There were always the usual sore elbows, boils between the toes, and bumps, scrapes and bruises. She also remembers quite a number of third-eyelid problems, and I've covered this in another chapter.

"If we had a bloat problem at night," says Leake, "we usually lost the dogs because they'd go undetected too long. During the day, we'd give them ginger or chunks of washing soda to make them bring up food and gas. Then the vet would jab a needle into the stomach to relieve the gas and we usually saved them."

Hill says the Danes were amazingly brave, and they usually were able to stitch up a gash without a muzzle.

Once, they had a bad outbreak of mange, which she thinks came from an imported dog. About fifteen of them had to be completely covered in old railway train oil. "The smell was horrible, but it seemed to do the job," she recalled. Another time they had a terrible outbreak of leptospirosis, which was attributed to escaped rats from filming *The Pied Piper of Hamelin*. They got into the stored rice and grain and left the disease in the food.

I well remember when my wife Shirley and I lived in the Caribbean, we had to raise kennel water off the ground on stands. The rats loved to urinate in water and leptospirosis was rampant in the islands both for dogs and humans. A terrible, dangerous disease. The leptospirosis at Send was treated with intravenous drips for all the dogs, twenty-four hours a day, much as we do today. But the death count was high.

Send Kennel had an ingenious way of communicating with the hospital staff on their rounds if there were any problems. Each kennel door had a small wooden square that slid in a grooved holder — white on one side and with a single green line on the other. When all was well in that kennel the white side showed, but if a kennel maid noticed a problem with any of the dogs in her section, she would turn the square around, showing the green line in a horizontal position. This meant "something's wrong, better have a look." The hospital staff doing daily rounds would check out the dog and either take it to the hospital or treat it for minor problems. Once that was done, the hospital kennel maid turned the green line to a vertical position which said to the dog's attendant, "We've got your message and are taking care of it."

Naturally, for immediate, serious problems, the kennel maid rushed her dog to the hospital herself or got the hospital staff or dog ambulance at once.

Stewart was always mindful of trying to develop new canine health treatments. Because distemper was then such a problem in England, as well as at his kennel, he developed tests for field distemper vaccine in his own hospital lab. Taking one hundred and eighty young dogs from six to eighteen months old, he divided them into sections of thirty-six and placed them in new kennels never before used. Special kennel maids were used, and they were not allowed near any other dogs.

Two weeks prior to the actual test, every dog had its own temperature chart and diet record made up, and food intake, degree of appetite, bowel movements and other information were recorded several times a day. Only those in perfect health were allowed to take the test, which was inoculation with the new field distemper vaccine that had been developed in the laboratory. Only two of the hundred and eighty had any ill results — one had pneumonia and the other took fits, from which she fully recovered and later grew to become a show Champion. And there were no distemper cases in the entire lot, while before, a number of dogs would come down with distemper in any group like that of one hundred and eighty dogs. By 1931, Send Kennel had no distemper cases, as of course all Stewart's dogs were inoculated.

Today, distemper has been eradicated in England.

The ultra-violet-ray equipment at the hospital was used to treat skin diseases, bites, wounds and sprains. Any dog with a tendency to rachitic conditions was also treated. Stewart allowed others to use this equipment, and the girls remembered noted breeder Muriel Osborn bringing her dogs over to the hospital at Send Kennel for ultra-violet-ray treatment. Stewart also installed cinder tracks at the kennel to harden his dogs' pads.

So you can see that Stewart advocated a hands-on treatment for his dogs. He contributed money and time for the experimentation and tests for new canine and other health measures that eventually benefited all dogs in England. I know of no other kennel in the world or kennel owner who did so much!

German and American Champion Etfa von der Saalburg.

At left, Reichsieger Etfa von der Saalburg, owned by Mrs. Margaret Hostetter of Ridgerest Kennels. At right is Champion Ozelot von Birkenhof, owned by E. E. Ferguson of the United States.

CHAPTER NINE

The Third Eyelid

E very dog has a third eyelid. The upper and lower ones can be seen clearly but there's an inner eyelid that unfolds from the corner of the dog's eye (to cover the eyeball under the upper and lower lids) towards the outer corner of the eye. When a dog is dosing off or even asleep, this membrane can often be seen.

Sometimes a birth defect will occur and skin-like tissue will grow on that third eyelid. Sometimes with hair. Consequently this growth causes discomfort and suffering for the dog when the eyelid opens and closes across the eyeball.

This defect is quite uncommon today, but in the first half of the last century the problem was known to and experienced by breeders at one time or another. This tissue can be removed surgically and the defect corrected.

* * * * * * *

We were walking across the lawns of Picton Mount in Surrey and through the lovely gardens towards the tennis courts as my friend, Bill Siggers, who had developed and managed Ouborough Kennel for J. V. Rank from 1922 until 1952, talked to me about the various ailments and treatments of the Great Danes in the 1920s and 1930s.

"We began having more incidents of a third-eyelid condition in our Danes at Ouborough," Siggers said. "And when I checked back through pedigrees of our dogs, it seemed to me that the ones most affected came through our importation of Essma von der Saalburg from Karl Farber in Germany.

"Now I can't be sure, because English breeders had been importing dogs from the Continent before I started buying there. But all signs pointed to my conclusion.

"I well remember my first visit to Karl Farber in Bad Homburg, Germany...the beautiful fawn dog Champion Bosco von der Saalburg and his young brindle son, Dolf von der Saalburg. I really wanted to buy those dogs, but Karl Farber was the most honourable man I'd ever met as a breeder of Great Danes. He told me, 'No amount of money could ever buy either of those dogs.' And he stuck to that.

"Dolf, in my opinion, was going to be greater than his father Bosco, but Farber wouldn't part with him either. In my letter to James Rank after my visit, I told him about Dolf's eyes. He'd had an operation for eyelids and it gave his expression a rather odd look. But all else about that dog was just perfect in my view. He was a dream come true to see in a Great Dane.

"Farber had turned me down when I offered him two thousand Deutsche Marks and our Rolf of Ouborough, for Dolf."

Rolf was a famous fawn German dog Siggers had imported to Ouborough Kennel. Born on June 10, 1921, his sire was Champion Famulus Hansa, sire of Dolf's dam Fauna Moguntia, out of a bitch named Hella. He was imported into England in 1923 and was an important foundation sire for Ouborough. So you see, Siggers's offer of his Rolf carried considerable value.

Dolf was by Bosco ex Fauna Moguntia, and Farber had two sisters to Dolf — Essma and Etfa. Etfa was sold to the United States, and Siggers bought Essma and took her to Ouborough in 1927 to build bloodlines to Farber's Bosco and Dolf.

If you will refer to Siggers's letter to J. V. Rank from Ludwigshafen (reproduced in Chapter Eleven), you will see his own description of his visit to Karl Farber and his mention of Dolf's third-eyelid operation.

The connection to Dolf in the United States is very strong indeed. Etfa von der Saalburg was imported into the United States and was owned by Mr. Joseph Eigenbauer when she went Best in Show at the Los Angeles Kennel Club show in 1928. She was whelped in Germany on May 17, 1925, and was a German Champion by 1927. Then in December 1928, Margaret Hostetter of Ridgerest Kennels purchased

Champion Baldo von Nordstern of Erin Dale (brindle son of Dolf von der Saalburg); owners Mr. and Mrs. Charles A. Harris of Marion, North Carolina.

Reichsieger Riese von Loheland, centre, with his younger brother and sister, Vassall and Vacca von Loheland.

Ozelot von Birkenhof Loheland, imported to the United States by E. E. Ferguson.

Oerlang von Loheland, imported to the United States by E. E. Ferguson.

the now German and American Champion Etfa von der Saalburg from Eigenbauer. She showed Etfa at Westminster in 1929 and the bitch went Best Great Dane and thereafter won seven Best in Shows in her illustrious career in the United States.

Mrs. Hostetter also bought two lovely sisters, bred by Mr. Eigenbauer, out of Etfa, by Harold Lloyd's Champion Lloyds Titan Boy, a brindle. They were Princess Barba and Betty of Ridgerest.

In 1931 Mrs. Hostetter took Champion Etfa and Betty to Germany and bred Etfa to Helios Hexengold. She also purchased Irmin von Odenwald and then bred Betty to him. In Germany, she also bred Little Sister of Ridgerest, out of Etfa and by Titan Boy, to Elch Edler von der Saalburg. The bitch Ozelot von Birkenhof, the mother of Oerland von Loheland by Kalfdan von der Rhon, a Dolf grandson, was a product of this mating.

So you see that, not only did Etfa originally go to the United States in 1927 and spread her blood around, she went back to Germany and was line bred again to Karl Farber's von der Saalburg line, with Bosco and Dolf bloodlines in particular. Etfa and Betty went back to the United States with more and more Saalburg blood to spread around.

It is interesting for Dane historians to know that Ozelot was bred to Mary A. Davis's Champion Etfa von der Saalburg's Boy Brion, but tragically died two weeks before the litter was due because of infection from a nail injury from her crate on the voyage from Germany back to the United States.

When you think of the many major American breeders who were touched by the Etfa bloodlines from Karl Farber's von der Saalburg kennel, you can easily see how the same third-eyelid condition that Bill Siggers suspected, might also cover the Great Dane breed in the United States. Siggers had imported Etfa's sister Essma.

The lines of early breeders J. Eigenbauer, Mary A. Davis, Harold Lloyd, Margaret Hostetter, Laura O'Day, Ruth Martin and Suzanne Daniel Hawkins of Planetree Kennels, Stanley Coates of Oakdane and William Gilbert, just to name a few, will be found in a very large number of later pedigrees in North America. Therein lies the Saalburg legacy.

Back in England, Gordon Stewart of Send Kennel, at the same time, was buying scores of German dogs, with many going back to the Saalburg lines. He too had tried to buy Bosco and Dolf but was rebuffed.

At the beginning of their relationship, Stewart and J. V. Rank of Ouborough were certainly friendly and talking, because Rank gave German Dane statues to Stewart, and the two of them were in constant contact through their membership in the Great Dane Breeders Association. Stewart also used Ouborough stock. But later on, the competition to buy and breed the best Great Danes took its toll on that friendship.

Stewart tried to lure Bill Siggers away from Rank, but Siggers refused to go. And competition in the show ring was fierce indeed, with Ouborough always running slightly ahead of Send. In all my talks with Siggers, never once was there a mention of him breeding to Send dogs. Stewart thought his Danes more refined than Ranks's, and Siggers never thought much of Stewart's dogs — he said it was all quantity and no quality.

Mrs. Phyllis Hill, the wife of Leslie Hill, who was assistant show manager to Bob Montgomery of Send Kennel, met with me, Jean Lanning, and Eric and Gina Bailey at her home near Bournemouth in March 1998. I was in England to judge the Danes at Crufts on March 5 that year. Phyllis worked as a kennel maid at Send before marrying Leslie Hill. She was principally assigned to work with the hospital section of the kennel, to look after ailing dogs.

"Did you have any third-eyelid problems when you were at Send Kennel?" asked Jean Lanning.

"Oh yes," replied Phyllis, "quite a lot, really. The vet would come in and take off a section of the eyelid, stitch it up and the dogs recovered quite nicely."

So is there an obvious connection?

From Germany to Ouborough and Send Kennels in England. From Germany to the United States. And what goes around comes around, because the breeders in the United States then bought dogs from Ouborough and Send, and English breeders bought from the United States.

You certainly can't blame it all on Karl Farber. He obviously got his problem from breeding to other dogs. But was he the funnel that spread the problem with the third eyelid throughout the world?

A wonderful team of Send harlequins with Gordon Stewart handling. Far left is Win Leake. On his right hand is Nora West and on his left hand is Betty Turner (Moodie), later to inherit a good part of his fortune. Early 1930s. PHOTO COURTESY NORA WEST

Nora West with Champion Ulana and a litter of her puppies. Note the main office building on stilts in the background.
PHOTO COURTESY NORA WEST

CHAPTER TEN

Five Hundred Great Danes

At the peak of Stewart's Send Kennel development they ran on around five hundred Great Danes. Historical articles through the years will vary the numbers between three hundred and five hundred, and that may confuse you. But the interviews I had years ago with Cynthia Young, and recently with the four former kennel maids, Win Leake, Phyllis Hill (Hudson), Nora (West) Napoliello and Margaret (Tracy) Fife Failes, will confirm that there were always about four hundred dogs in various stages of training and rearing in the kennel in the peak period. And at any given time there would be scores of puppies and dogs still in quarantine, which must also be taken into account. There were two hundred and ninety individual kennels in the long ranges to house the dogs, each of which usually held two Danes.

The rest of what I'll tell you in this chapter stems from chats and letters with these four wonderful eyewitnesses.

Win Leake was at Send Kennel from 1934 until 1952, when Stewart died. Then she continued to work in the poultry company at the rear of the property. She now lives in Surrey, England. Nora West came in the early thirties when she was sixteen years old. She married in 1950 and moved to the United States, where she now resides in Colorado with her daughter. Her married name is Napoliello.

Margaret Fife Failes was Margaret Tracy before her marriage. She joined the kennel staff as a handler/trainer in 1929 and left in 1934. Now in her nineties, she lives in Norfolk, England, and her mind, humour and fond memories of Send are remarkable.

Phyllis Hill (nee Hudson) joined the kennel operation, in the office, in 1934, and then worked in the hospital. There she met Leslie Hill, the assistant show manager and trainer. They married, left about 1937 and joined up with Show Manager Bob Montgomery. He had gone

A newspaper clipping from the early 1930s. Gordon Stewart had a tennis pro give free lessons in the Karinda Hut to the kennel maids. Front dogs left to right are Mona, Bernard and Ulana of Send. Kennel maids left to right are Margaret Tracy, Betty Turner (Moodie) and Audrey Field.

COURTESY MARGARET TRACY

Crossing the training field. At rear right is Show Training Manager Bob Montgomery and partially hidden is his assistant Colonel de Pinto. At front left, handler Audrey Field, and front right, Nora West. Note the white jackets with Send Kennel maroon crest on collar, breeches and knee-high socks. PHOTO COURTESY NORA WEST

to develop a large boarding and training kennel near Guildford in the mid thirties, which belonged to Audrey Field's mother. Bob and Audrey (who was a first-class trainer and handler) met at Send and married. Phyllis Hill now lives near Bournemouth, on the south coast in England.

Bob Montgomery's name will appear often in this book because of his remarkable talent for training dogs; he must have been a kind and patient man to accomplish what he did. He and his first wife (who looked after the welfare of the staff and puppies at Send) divorced when Robert fell in love with Audrey Field, an instructor in the show and training section. Field will also be seen and mentioned many times throughout this book.

By the mid thirties, Stewart was reducing his kennel operation, so the Montgomerys set off to build up the family kennel, where Bob specialized in training dogs for the blind. Many of the lovely, invaluable photos in this book came from Bob and Audrey's records. They are deceased now, but their son Andrew Montgomery and his wife, Maureen, have allowed me to use their wonderful family photo collection. I will be forever grateful to them.

The four kennel maids mentioned above also delved back into their closets and came up with many other photos that I use throughout the chapters. Their minds were remarkably clear on the detail of Send Kennel — the people, operation, events and dogs, and best of all, they actually saw and experienced it all.

They all say that they loved working at Send, that Gordon Stewart was kind and considerate, and that those years left wonderful memories for them all.

There were usually about eight managers for the Send operation in the heyday of the kennel. Mr. J. Huber of Austria was hired by Stewart to be the overall general manager. He also did extensive travelling, buying Danes in Europe in the twenties and early thirties. Huber left Send in about 1934.

Robert Montgomery was the show and training manager, and under him were assistants Leslie Hill, Colonel Lionel de Pinto, and Herr

Leslie Hill.

Eickenbauer from Germany, whom Huber had recruited to assist in obedience and show training. There were also managers for the office, hospital, bakehouse and kitchen staff.

Of the two chauffeurs at Send, Mr. Bird (whom the girls nicknamed Dicke), did most of the driving of the show van. He took the dogs and kennel maids to dog shows, obedience trials and demonstrations, and to the midnight cabarets at the fashionable West-End hotels in London — I'll describe those events later. Bird lived across the green from Send Manor in one of the many cottages Stewart built for his management staff.

Girls were always hired to handle the dogs, but Stewart hired boys to do the cleaning up and general work; the boys never worked with the dogs. Most of the time there were about twenty-eight to thirty kennel maids proficient in operating the various sections of the kennel organization.

Stewart ran the kennel with the precision of a military operation, dividing it into the dog show and training section, hospital, food service, quarantine sections, etc. Staff did not cross over into other sections unless promoted to do so. The girls seemed to have a wonderful time, and Stewart did everything he could to make them comfortable. Every week he had a tennis instructor come down from London to give the girls free lessons.

There was great camaraderie amongst them.

When at work, they were all addressed formally and only by their last name — Miss Leake, Miss West, Miss Tracy, Miss Hudson, and so on. But some had nicknames given to them in fun and affection. For

Trainer Leslie Hill, right-hand man to Show Manager Bob Montgomery, schooled the Danes for demonstrations, shows and movie appearances.

PHOTO COURTESY PHYLLIS HILL

Training for the races. Left to right are Audrey Field with Lancelot, Margaret Tracy with Bernard, Phui May, Sybil Church with Rafe, Nora West with Donna, and Vic Allfrey with Midas.

PHOTO COURTESY NORA WEST

Left to right: Phui May with unidentified brindle, Audrey Field with Wotan, Sybil Church (nicknamed Squib) with Egmund (the Hound of the Baskervilles). PHOTO COURTESY NORA WEST

May 5, 1932. Bath Championship Show, Bath, Somerset. Nora West is at left with Betty Turner (Moodie) on her left. Vic Allfrey is the handler at far right.

PHOTO COURTESY NORA WEST

example, Sybil Church, whom you see identified in many photos, was nicknamed "Squib." Miss May was called "Phui."

"It was a German word that meant a bad smell," recalls Margaret Tracy. "So when the dogs had an accident or just plain old wind, all the girls would say Phui. Miss May could never pronounce it right," she added, "and that's why we gave her the nickname Phui May."

With Herr Huber from Austria and Herr Eickenbauer from Germany as their trainers and daily companions, I can well imagine the girls picked up quite a few German words. Most of the bad ones, anyway!

Their canteen was the hub of activity during the work day and a lively scene on the weekend for dances, fun and socializing with each other. There was many a romance, and weddings occurred between staff members at Send, with Stewart often providing the food and beverage for these events.

Nora West (Napoliello) is the girl you always see in the photos with the big smile. Her humour has stayed with her, as the stories she tells are always touched with her laughter. "The office had a siren on the roof," she recalls, "that had a wartime all-clear call. At twelve noon on Saturday, the siren blew and we'd assemble for our pay cheques. When that siren sounded, all the dogs would start to howl — all five hundred of them. So you can imagine the noise. Heard for miles around!" And with fondness for her friend Win Leake, she says, "Leaky used to make delicious coconut ice and bring it to sell us at the kennels."

I have never heard a disparaging word from any kennel maid. They all thought Stewart a generous, kind man.

He had started with only a couple of English Danes in 1921, and ten years later had about five hundred at the kennel. Large numbers were imported; in 1926, Kennel Club records in England show twenty-seven Send imports registered — six in 1927, six in 1928, four in 1929, two in 1930 and six in 1931, most from Germany, Holland and Italy. I will deal with the actual names and pedigrees of almost one thousand Send Danes in an appendix at the end of the book.

Winter sleighride on the frozen pond. Circa 1932.
Champion Ulana enjoys the ride. PHOTO COURTESY NORA WEST

Not all Send dogs are listed there, by any means. You can imagine that with five hundred Danes, breeding puppies, importing and trading, the overall numbers of Send dogs over the years would be staggering — probably in the thousands.

Ouborough Kennel and Bill Siggers were already importing by about 1922, so Stewart was behind. Send never really did equal Ouborough in overall show wins and Challenge Certificates when they competed head to head in the twenties and thirties. But the real thrust at Send was in obedience training, with unique demonstrations, dog team trials, steeplechase and hurdle races, agricultural show displays, film and theatre productions.

Ouborough never could equal that!

Three of the most famous names from Send Kennel were Champion Midas of Send, Champion Lancelot of Send and Champion Ulana of Send. You'll see and read a lot about them in the following chapters.

*Trainer Audrey Field
with Champion
Lancelot of Send,
a blue Great Dane.*
PHOTO COURTESY
ANDREW MONTGOMERY

The kennel maids worked hard, for little money, and the hours were long. Win Leake recounts, "I cycled seven miles to work each day and seven miles back at night. Rain, sleet and snow. I always took my own dog duster back home and washed it out every night, so my dogs were always shiny and groomed just right every day.

"We started work each day at 8:30 A.M., so I had to leave home very early. Stayed 'til 6:00 at night. In winter we sometimes went home earlier because it got dark earlier. At 10:30 A.M. we'd have tea and then a lunch break.

"I was paid one pound sterling a week, but six pence went for insurance. We alternated, with every other Tuesday afternoon and every other Sunday off.

"But I loved every minute of it," Win continued, "and could hardly wait to get to work each day. Where else could you get a job outdoors, with lovely dogs and really fun girls working with you?"

The girls each had a few dogs to look after. There were some hours of organized exercise and training every day, with grooming and then rest before the meal. The show and training section usually had five to eight girls. The kennel boys put sawdust down in the runs, and wheat straw was used for kennel bedding. In the winters, in-whelp bitches and their litters were housed in heated winter quarters, but the rest of the dogs had no heat in the kennels, so they snuggled up in their straw beds in the wooden kennels. Winters in England, of course, are not that severe compared with some other countries.

Says Phyllis Hill, "Gordon Stewart did not allow staff to argue with him and was accustomed to getting his own way. Jobs were hard to get, so we didn't argue." And sometimes, relates Phyllis, "when his dogs weren't pulled out first at shows, he would storm into the ring and snatch the lead from the handler, thoroughly upsetting the dog and removing all chances of it ever winning."

Reg Giles, the early carpenter and later foreman, remembers that "Gordon Stewart would fire someone on the spot. He had the habit of marching the person to the front gate and closing it after him. It was not a pretty sight to see!"

Phyllis Hill also laughingly says, "Mr. Stewart always had his chauffeur pick him up exactly at 9:00 A.M. to drive him, in his big Daimler, up to London to his office. The chauffeur put a fresh flower in his buttonhole every morning.

"The boss had lured this chauffeur away from one of the prominent upper-class families," said Phyllis. "If they were attending a function where there were royal family, politicians or other important people, the chauffeur was instructed to always see that Stewart's Daimler was first in line behind the VIP cars. That way he'd be seen by them and often photographed by the press as being with them.

"Well, this one time," continued Phyllis, "the chauffeur got into a card game with other chauffeurs and missed his first place in line. Stewart was furious and would have fired him straight away except for the man's prominence with upper-class titled families. He would have been hired at once by someone else."

Under the mistletoe. Kennel maid at left is Margaret Tracy and receiving her yuletide kiss is Sybil Church. PHOTO COURTESY WIN LEAKE

Everything about the kennel and dogs was first class. The girls wore grey dusters over their clothes for daily duties, but at shows and demonstrations wore crisp white jackets with maroon trim on cuffs and collars with the S. K. emblem (Send Kennel). The show van, ambulance and other vehicles accompanying the dogs and handlers to shows were smartly colour-coded in maroon as well. Everything matched, and everyone was clean and smart.

*At the Great Dane Club Open Show, Hillside School Playing Field,
Reigate, Surrey, August 2, 1933. At far left is Phui May, Flo Webb
next and then Sybil (Squib) Church. To far right is Nora West.*

PHOTO COURTESY NORA WEST

*Having a break. Left front is Vic Allfrey, behind her is Margaret Tracy.
At rear, kneeling, is Audrey Field with Lancelot the blue Dane,
then Phui May, Nora West hidden behind the dogs, and Sybil (Squib)
Church at far right. Early 1930s.* PHOTO COURTESY NORA WEST

A perfect Christmas gift basket from Send Kennel.

PHOTO COURTESY WIN LEAKE

*A mixed team of fawns, harlequins, blacks and blues waiting
to perform an obedience demonstration at a horse show.
A wonderful picture of dependable Great Dane temperament.*

PHOTO COURTESY ANDREW MONTGOMERY

On August 18, 1929, Farber sent this postcard to Siggers showing the aging Grand Champion Bosco von der Saalburg, then eight years old (right), and his famous son, Champion Dolf von der Saalburg.

Champion Prinz Mephisto. See the letter from W. Kunitzer.

CHAPTER ELEVEN

The German Influence

In my book, *He Whacked the Bloody Lot*, on Bill Siggers, J. V. Rank and Ouborough Kennel, published in 1986, there is a chapter on the hardships of seeking out and buying dogs in Europe in the 1920s and 1930s. That chapter contains many references by Bill Siggers to Gordon Stewart, who was hastily buying up any good Great Danes he could find. And, according to Siggers, a lot that weren't so good. A lot of garbage was offered to the unwary buyer.

Siggers and J. V. Rank began buying German stock in the early 1920s, but in 1921 Stewart was just buying Send Manor and building the kennel facility, so he had a lot of catching up to do. Here is that same chapter, which gives you a marvellous background into the trials and difficulties of travelling to Germany to seek out Great Danes, then haul them back to England by tram, train and boat.

It wasn't just the money. Finding good stock was tough. Negotiating was a problem because these two competing kennels drove up demand, and the crafty breeders, naturally, played one buyer against the other to boost prices. Then, as often as not, when they got them home, some dogs wouldn't breed and some bitches wouldn't conceive, so they'd have to start all over again.

Here's that chapter that I wrote for the other book years ago. I've updated it here and there. It contains a lot of good meaty stuff on the Danes of yesterday, who influenced the breeding in England and in the United States as well.

There is no one Germany.

Germany is a million things to millions of people, I thought, as the Mercedes cut through the wooded countryside towards Munich that day in 1975.

Whatever the Kaiser and Adolf Hitler had set out to do, they accomplished but one thing, and that was to leave Germany in bits and pieces forever — different images to different men.

My wife, Shirley, and I had flown to England from Barbados and picked up Bill Siggers in Surrey. I was over to judge Great Danes at the Great Dane Breeders' Association Show in London. We had flown to Stuttgart the day after the show to see the Bundessieger, Germany's world-famous dog show.

At the show, I looked up Annaliese Maier of Eremitage Kennels near Munich, and we'd been invited to go up to visit her kennels. I was looking for a bitch to take home. Rose Robert, of Dinro fame in the United States, had asked me to look out for a good blue Dane for her, and I had been firmly instructed by Rose on what a good blue Dane should be.

So here we were, once again, in Germany that November to buy Great Danes. To Bill Siggers, who had first gone to do just that in the early twenties, it seemed to be an exciting safari once again.

As the dark-green sedan chewed up the miles on that country road, I realised that Germany, to me, was beautiful countryside. Deer seemed to be everywhere, grazing quietly in the fields between the dark forests and the snow-dusted roadway. Venison was served in every quaint village inn when you stopped for lunch. There were oompah bands in nighttime cafes as you strolled the cobbled streets, huge steins of ale, big-boned men, and frauleins with ruddy complexions and loud talk.

But to others, Germany was different. The memories were bad — of friends gone, a leg or arm left behind, the suffering always overshadowing the beauty of that country.

From the moment we arrived at Stuttgart airport, I knew Germany meant a great many things to Bill Siggers.

He changed. His bitterness showed and he never lost it. It was quite evident he didn't like some German people no matter who they were. The transformation from the gentle, thoughtful friend I knew was profound and complete.

The chauffeur driving the Mercedes had introduced himself many times to Siggers by another name, but Siggers always called him

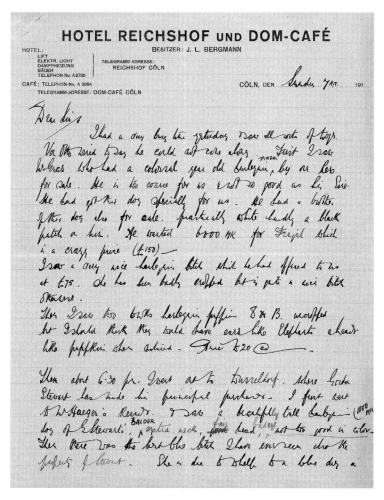

Front page of letter to J. V. Rank from Siggers.

"Adolf." And the coldness I felt come out of Bill towards some we met reached the point of embarrassment many times.

To Siggers, Germany represented his twice being wounded in France in the First World War and the huge bomb crater from a V-2 rocket at his Ouborough Kennels during the Second World War. Cities like Stuttgart, completely flattened by the bombing, were now rebuilt and bustling, not a scar to be seen, while his beloved London still showed the ruins of war.

Front page of a letter dated June 4, 1926,
to J. V. Rank from Heinrich Grass.

Rolf of Ouborough, 1926.

"It pays to lose a war," he mumbled as we travelled along.

And as we motored through the early-morning mist, I thought of another time with Siggers, at Picton Mount in Surrey. We walked through the woods with his Great Danes, Mark and Chloe.

"Over there," he pointed. "That great dip in the land where the magpies are darting about is a bomb crater, and here's the outside entrance, near the tennis court, to the bomb shelter that Henry Orpen built.

"The other entrance is under the stairs near the downstairs loo. It's closed up now. We were right on the path as the V-1 rockets came over towards London, and every now and then, the buzzing sound would stop and you'd wait to hear where it crashed down. It was a frightening experience," he said, "you never knew where the damn things would drop!"

And then he began. Bill Siggers was one of the best storytellers I knew. We went up to his bedroom where all his old records were stored. He pulled out the files and photos so I could see his Germany then.

Deutscher Doggen-Zwinger „v. d. Saalburg"

Bes.: Karl Färber

Bad Homburg v. d. H., Löwengasse 11a

⁂

den 28. Dezember 1938

Dear Mr. Siggers & Family!

Besten Dank für freundliche Übersendung des schönen Calenders vom Oberough-Kennel! Wir wünschen Ihnen und Ihrer werthen Familie ein glückliches Neues Jahr. Wir dachten immer Sie dieses Jahr wieder bei uns zu sehen aber Sie waren sicher nicht auf der Reichssieger-Ausstellung in Köln sonst hätten Sie uns doch mit Ihrem Besuche beehrt! Zur Zeit haben wir noch Bruno und Filly und eine gelbe Tochter und einen gelben Sohn von bei Die Jungtiere sind jetzt 19 Monate alt. Leider konnte ich nicht nach Köln gehen es war mir zu teuer mit 4 Hunden. Auf der Schau in Offenbach bekamen die beiden Jungtiere die Nte Vorzügliche Lege eine Aufnahme der Hunde bei. Die junge dunkelgoldgelbe Hündin mit schwarzer Maske ist noch abzugeben. Im Sommer war ein Mr. J. ILLINGWORTH aus England Hier der Herr ist Mastiff Züchter und sagte er würde Sie kennen und auch wahrscheinlich bald in England auf einer Ausstellung

Die 3 Gewinner des Goldpokals des D.D.C. Fauna, Champ. Dolf u. Champ. Bosko. Ausgezeichnet mit: Staats-, Kartell-, Club-, Zucht- u. Ehrenpreisen: Besitzer des Goldpokals des D.D.C.; der goldenen Kartellmedaille für hervorragende Leistung; der silbernen Kartellmedaille; der goldenen Bundesmedaille für besten Champion aller Farben 1927; des silbernen Kartellbechers; der silbernen Baron von Gingins Gedächtnismedaille; vieler Züchtergruppenpreise; der Italienischen Vermeille-Medaille, Sociéta Italiana Aliani; zweimaliger Gewinner des Züchterwanderpreises des D.D.C.; Besitzer des Züchterwanderpreises des S.W.D. Doggen-Clubs und des Zuchtwanderpreises des Doggen-Bundes 1926.

A letter from Karl Farber, dated December 28 1938.

THE CAPTION UNDER THE PHOTO AT TOP LEFT OF FRONT PAGE:
The three winners of the Deutsche Doggen Club: Fauna, Champion Dolf and Champion Bosco. Distinctions: State, Associate, Club, Breeder's and Honorary Prizes. Holder of the Gold Cup of the Deutche Doggen Club, Association Gold Medal for Special Achievements; Association Silver Medal; Federal Gold Medal for Best Champions of all Colours, 1927; Association Silver Cup; Baron von Gingins Memorial Silver Medal; many Breeders' Association prizes; Italian Vermmeille Medal, Societa Italiana Aliani; twice winners of the Breeders Challenge Trophy of the Deutche Doggen Club; holder of the Breeders' Challenge Trophy of the South-West Deutche Doggen Club and of the Breeders' Challenge Trophy of the Doggen Federation 1926.

Translation of Karl Farber's letter
to Bill Siggers, dated December 28, 1938

Deutche Doggen - Kennels
"v.d. Saalburg"
Karl Farber
Bad Homburg

Dear Mr. Siggers & Family,

Thank you very much for sending the beautiful calendar of the Ouborough Kennels. We wish you and your dear family a Happy New Year. We had always hoped to see you here with us this year, but you possibly were not at the State Champion Exhibition in Cologne otherwise you certainly would have honoured us with your visit. At the moment we still have Bruno and Zilly and a yellow daughter and son of both. The young animals are 19 months old now. Unfortunately I could not go to Cologne. It would have been too expensive with 4 dogs. At the show at Offenbach both young animals received the grade: Excellent. I am including a picture of the dogs. The young dark goldish-yellow female with the black mask is still available.

Last summer a Mr. F. Illingworth from England was here. The gentleman is a Mastiff breeder. He said he knew you and would probably get to see you at an exhibition in England.

In the hope of hearing from you soon, we greet you and your dear wife and family.

Yours very sincerely,
Karl Farber and Wife

Please give our best New Year wishes to the Rank family.

[Author's Note: See page 100 for a photo of Karl Farber's Bruno.]

In 1926 Karl Farber sent this postcard to Siggers. Farber holds (left to right) Fauna Moguntia, Dolf von der Saalburg and Bosco von der Saalburg.

The building of the Ouborough line was a plan and a philosophy. Siggers's boss, James Voase Rank, approached it as if it were one of his industrial companies. It became evident in the first years after the war ended in 1918 that there were not enough good Great Danes left in England to use. But there were dogs in Germany, and the Rank and Siggers team set out to buy their foundation stock. Rank had the cheque book and complete confidence in Siggers's eye for a dog. He never interfered in Siggers's judgement, and Siggers never betrayed that trust. He was a tough buyer, sometimes critical beyond reason. He set his sights high and the standard of Great Dane he wanted was always of prime importance.

Siggers had many trips to Germany, sometimes successful and sometimes not. The early dogs he bought were beautiful, but heartbreaking because they failed miserably to produce puppies. The dogs wouldn't breed and the bitches wouldn't conceive.

Rolf of Ouborough, 1926.

Dolf von der Saalburg in 1926.

Mrs. Morgan at Richmond Championship Show in July 1926, with Plaza of Ouborough (right) and Vivien (left), who won the Challenge Certificate. Daily Mirror *photograph.*

Stuttgart, October 1975, at the Bundessieger Show.
The author on the left, with his wife, Shirley. Siggers doing the pouring.

On one trip, Siggers and a Dane he'd just bought were thrown in jail. It was hard to travel in Germany in the early twenties. "You bought a dog," Siggers said, "and then took it with you on the train to go back to the channel boat and across to England.

"I'd bought this brindle dog, about a year-and-a-half old. He didn't understand my language but seemed to know what I wanted. I didn't understand his language either and that's where the trouble began."

"We were both standing on the train platform in Munich, signs all about us that I couldn't read, when all of a sudden he relieved himself. He'd hardly finished when two huge policemen showed up, frantically yelling at me and my dog.

"Neither of us knew what the hell was going on! The next thing I knew, we were trundled off down the street into a police station, and there the dog and I both spent the night in a cell. It's hilarious now but it wasn't then. Apparently it was against the law for a dog to foul a train station, even though they were allowed to travel by train.

Farber's yard behind the shop, with the brindle Bruno, bred by him.

"All the times I went to Germany, I never got used to the lingo and always got myself in all kinds of trouble," Siggers mused.

The trip in 1926 was memorable indeed, because it was on that trip that Siggers met Karl Farber and the royal family — Bosco and Dolf. I won't go into the history of those two dogs here. Every serious breeder of Great Danes knows them and other books have covered that.

But Siggers was the only person I ever knew who had personally known Karl Farber and his dogs, and in these pages I have reproduced a letter and card from Farber and the documentation of the trip in 1926 that you'll find interesting.

Each trip had a plan, and Rank's instruction was discussed and followed. Siggers reported regularly every day on his progress.

Siggers recruited German men to assist him as translators on his trips. One of these was Ernst von Otto, a brilliant sculptor and author on German dogs. The cropped, bronze Great Dane model bequeathed

Rolf von der Saalburg at the age of fourteen months.

by Siggers to the Kennel Club in England at his death was one of Bosco von der Saalburg and sculpted by von Otto. In my library I have a book written by von Otto (and given to me by Siggers in 1973), entitled *German Dogs in Words and Pictures*. It was published in 1928, in English, and had been commissioned by the German Kennel Club, dedicated to "His Highness the Maharaja Dhiraj of Patiala."

To better understand what Siggers was offering Karl Farber — the sum of two thousand Deutsche Marks and Rolf, for Dolf von der Saalburg — you had better know who Rolf was.

Rolf was a fawn dog, quite famous in Germany, purchased by Siggers for the Ouborough Kennels. Born on June 10, 1921, his sire was Champion Famulus Hansa, sire of Dolf's dam Fauna Moguntia, out of a bitch named Hella. He was an important foundation sire for Ouborough in their early breeding plans and was imported into England in 1923.

In all the history I have read on Great Danes, Karl Farber is always referred to as having "kennels." In fact, Siggers told me, he lived above a small shop in Bad Homburg, Germany, with only a small yard. He had four dogs: Bosco von der Saalburg, Fauna Moguntia, Dolf von der Saalburg (at the age of fourteen months, bred by Bosco ex Fauna), and Dolf's sister Essma.

Karl Farber and Siggers remained friends, and they exchanged letters afterwards, which are reproduced here from Siggers's files that I now have.

It is hardly surprising that certain hereditary problems in Great Danes are the same in the United States and England when you read Siggers's letter to J. V. Rank, written after first visiting Karl Farber in 1926. He wrote that Dolf "has had an operation to improve eyelids."

Two bitches by Bosco out of Fauna Moguntia form an important part of the history of Danes both in America and in England. Dolf's sister Etfa von der Saalburg was imported into the United States, and in 1927 Bill Siggers bought Essma (who was to prove an important foundation bitch for Ouborough Kennels in England) from the same litter. To this day, both countries suffer from the appearance of third-eyelid problems in litters from time to time.

When Siggers quotes prices to J. V. Rank, such as six thousand Deutsche Marks, equal to about one hundred and fifty pounds, it is easy to see that good dogs were not cheap then. In 1926 one hundred and fifty pounds represented a lot of money, so men such as J. V. Rank and Bill Siggers must be remembered for the tremendous contribution they made to Great Dane breeding by buying and importing such dogs to England.

The buying trip to Germany that I will document and lead you through here was not an easy one. Time was short, and distances vast when you had to travel by tram and train, dragging along puppies and dogs purchased, alone in a strange land with a strange language.

Siggers's job was made all the more difficult as he was third man in. Gordon Stewart of the famed Send Kennels in England, which ran up to five hundred Danes at one time, and W. Hertel from Glasgow, always seemed to be one step ahead of Siggers when he travelled from town to town.

Siggers bought Essma von der Saalburg (centre) from Karl Farber and imported her in 1927. Left is the young brindle, Dolf von der Saalburg, and right is Bosco von der Saalburg. Karl Farber is handling in Bad Homburg, Germany.

In the summer of 1983, Siggers and I had our final chat about Karl Farber. It was a pleasantly warm, blue-sky day in Blackpool, England. I had judged the Great Danes that day at the Blackpool Championship Show, while Siggers did various breeds. He judged the lovely snow-white Pyrenean Mountain Dogs while I watched. When he finished and the crowds that always came to him after he left a ring had gone, we sat alone together on a small bench in the city showground.

Bosco hiding Karl Farber. At left, reclining, is Dolf, and at centre is Fauna Moguntia. A postcard sent to Siggers from Karl Farber.

On the left of Karl Farber, sitting, is Dolf. At the right, standing, is Bosco. At the left, reclining, is Fauna Moguntia, and at the right, reclining, is Essma von der Saalburg. Postcard sent to Siggers from Karl Farber.

Dolf von der Saalburg with two children.
A postcard sent to Siggers from Karl Farber.

"I have tried to teach you all I know about judging Danes," said my eighty-seven-year-old friend. "I've tried to leave you my eye for my favourite breed."

"I doubt if you've accomplished that," I replied, trying to break the seriousness of the discussion. I was probably the only one whom he had told about his cancer and the fact that he was to go into Guy's Hospital for the first time that next week for tests. It was a sad time for both of us.

"But I have one more thing for you," he continued. "Try not to ever fault judge.

"Always remember our talks of Karl Farber in his little flat above that shop in Bad Homburg.

"When I saw those few dogs I knew then what a Great Dane must look like, and I've told you what that is. Never fault judge except your own dogs. Fault the hell out of those or you'll never improve the breed.

*Ador Viktoria, mentioned in Max Grass's letter
and bought by Gordon Stewart.*

Max Grass's Citroen Camphausen, 1926.

"But don't overlook the good points in another man's dog and put it down for a small point. Karl Farber's Dolf had a disturbing look to his head because he'd had his eyes fixed, and my Rolf, bred by Karl's Fauna Moguntia's sire, Champion Famulus Hansa, had a bit of a mismarked head too. But those dogs in conformation and temperament had what I dreamed of in a Great Dane."

Today, after I write this and Bill Siggers is gone, articles are appearing in magazines and books about Karl Farber and "the royal family" of his dogs. It is easy for all of us now with the twenty/twenty vision of hindsight to sing Karl Farber's praises, because the record shows unarguably that Farber's dogs had an immense impact on the Great Dane breed all over the world.

Alexander von Ferberturm. Owner Max Grass. 1926.

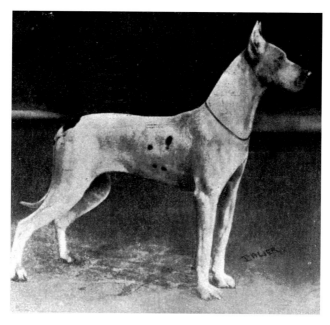

Violet II Camphausen. See Max Grass's letter, dated June 4, 1926.

Imperial Champion Bosco von der Saalburg.

After their first meeting in 1926, Karl Farber and Siggers became close friends and saw each other several times a year for many years until the Second World War. Farber would never part with his dogs, and Siggers held him in high esteem. In 1931 Farber gave Siggers this original terra cotta sculpture of Bosco. It was the sculpture used for casting models by a famous German china company.

Its plinth is engraved "Doppel Champion Bosko v.d. Saalburg '4584,'" and carries the French sculptor's name. It is dated 1929. On presenting it to Siggers, Karl Farber said, "This is the nearest thing I can give you, my English friend, to my great dog Bosco. The elegance of his neck and head are all here in this simple sculpture of clay."

When Bill Siggers knew he was dying, he passed this beautiful clay model on to me.

As I run my hand over it now, my greatest thrill is knowing that Siggers's close German friend, Karl Farber, lovingly held this model. And my great friend was kind enough to pass it on, for me to do the same.

But Siggers knew it then, without the aid of Farber's history of good breeding. Siggers was a man of vision, and he based his line breeding on Bosco and Dolf and Fauna Moguntia from the day of that first meeting in 1926. Few of the Ouborough dogs did not carry the line.

But for Bill Siggers's eye for a dog, I wonder where the Great Dane would be today.

Now here's what happened on that one-week trip in July 1926, which covered Munich, Dresden, Bad Homburg, Cologne, Frankfurt and Dusseldorf.

Item One

Prior to the trip James Voase Rank writes to Bill Siggers:
"SUGGESTIONS TO BE READ OVER EACH DAY
ON MR. SIGGERS' TRIP"

First you are going out there to get all the information you can about our competitors and to buy anything that is outstanding as regards quality and something which no-one has in this country as we want something better than what we have or anyone else has, and anything which is bought must be good as regards height, for instance, taller than Rex, clean in neck and excellent quality.

I suggest that if we could exchange Rex, which the whole of Germany knows, by getting something infinitely better than him — doing an exchange deal on a basis of Rex at £150 and we put another £100 down for a dog, we should probably get the finest dog in the country for £250.

The next thing you want to do is try and exchange some of our big stud dogs on a part exchange basis; there is Jock and Marcus, which we should be willing to let go at part exchange, and give cash for something else. We first want to try and do everything possible in the way of part exchange and cash for the balance (because the Germans not only like to get an exchange, but they like to get some cash, and you want to bear this in mind all through your trip).

My suggestion is that you should have a good look round before fixing up definitely with anything unless of course you saw something absolutely outstanding as it is no good buying and then seeing something better which you would like to have bought. We are not like Gordon Stewart — out to buy 20/30 dogs — we only want to buy 2 or 3 which suit our kennels and therefore you want to have a good look around and take Mr. von Otto round with you and pay his expenses and when you have had a look round, go and pick out the best one you can. You can take the firm offer of anything you think interesting, but we do not want to be burdened with anything unless it is absolutely outstanding, and we want to do as much part exchange business as we can, with Rolf, Rex, Jock or Marcus.

When you see Mr. von Otto I want you to ask where the bronze of the English type Dane is. I am waiting for that to send him a cheque for the lot.

I should like to exchange Rex for a big dog. Gordon Stewart showed me a photograph yesterday of a dog he paid £150 for, but after he bought it, the man wrote him begging him to let him off as his wife was so upset about it that she was creating a disturbance in the home.

The photograph was taken by our friend Dauer, therefore you will be able to go to his place and see it — a very fine dog, but of course you cannot really tell because Dauer can make you imagine anything. He is nearly black on one side, right through the middle of his body, but it is a dead clear black and the white is dead clear white, the whole of his front is white, and three-quarters of his face is black and the rest white. Naturally the best side was taken but Dauer will be able to tell you which dog it is. Gordon Stewart seemed very disappointed he had not got the dog.

What we want to do besides importing 3/4 puppies at reasonable prices (and these would want to be all bitches unless you had something exceptional as a dog) is to exchange Rex and put some money down and get a much better harlequin dog than him and also buy a wonderful brindle dog and brindle bitch. You will have to keep me closely in touch with things by sending night wires off which you can do at cheap rate. Our cable address in London is: James care "Millocrat, London."

I should be willing to exchange Marcus, Jock and Rex to get something really good and put down so much money — or to put so much money down without the exchange. Gordon Stewart is importing 27 dogs besides starting a kennel in Dusseldorf which I understand is for breeding puppies. This of course you will want to see.

J.V. RANK

Item Two
MAX GRASS LETTER OF JUNE 4, 1926:

TO J.V. RANK

Dear Sir;

Your address has been indicated to me by Mr. Ernst von Otto, Bensheim. You require 2 to 4 first-class spotted D. dogs not broken. I am one of the best known breeders of spotted dogs in Germany. I have bred for 20 years, the German champion Rex Lendor of the Zeltner Castle, which you have. It is a small dog. I knew Rex when it was six weeks old. It has inherited a very bad colour. No doubt you will know Mr. Gordon Stewart, Send Manor, Ripley. This gentleman visited me a few days ago and bought through my medium two dogs, the Grey Tiger Ador Vicktoria and the spotted bitch Nerolie Camphausen. This Ador Vicktoria has not a very nice colour. It is bad, but his offspring is pure white and varnish black. Please do not mention this to Mr. Gordon Stewart that I have written to you, otherwise I cannot obtain for you any first-class material. I may also inform you that I am the first secretary of the German dog club (Cologne branch), and I am not allowed by the Club to act as an intermediary for selling D. dogs in England. I am in a position to obtain for you the best large hound, pure white and varnish black, ideal, spotted, which is for sale in Germany. The dog is guaranteed 90 cm. high up to the shoulder. It has a first-class model head, long dry neck, heavy full mouth, and no trace of stiffening. It is 3 years and 9 months old, and most in demand in Germany for breeding purposes. This giant dog will be the best you can obtain for breeding purposes. It is true that the price is 6,000 Marks, but it is a dog which you have never seen before. If Mr. Gordon Stewart comes again to Cologne in July, he will no doubt pay me 10,000 Marks for the dog. Unfortunately I have no photograph, but I can give you my guarantee. The dog is actually twice as much as your Rex. I enclose the photograph of a female offspring of the dog whose photograph I enclose. The female dog is 18 months old, 80 high, and the best spotted in Germany. Both have dark eyes and organs like a horse. This dog will be ready for covering in 14 days, and could then be covered. The female dog is actually worth 4,000 Marks, I am prepared to let you have it for 3,000 Marks. Both animals are very well brought up, absolutely sound, without any defect. I know exactly how the dogs have to be sent to England. If you are prepared to pay this price, please remit the full amount, when I shall dispatch the animal at once, and advise you by telegram of the dispatch. I also have three first-class spotted young animals, whose father is Ador Vicktoria, which Mr. Stewart bought in Cologne. These animals are only 14 days old and cost 400 marks each. I should leave the animals not cut, and send to you when they are 3 months old.

I hope that you will have every confidence in me.

Yours faithfully,
Max Grass
Proprietor of the above firm
4, Rheinaustrasse,
Koln a/Rhein

P.S. I must ask you to treat this matter in strictest confidence.

If you are not interested, please return the photographs. I also have a sister of Citroen. It has a wonderful mouth and very narrow upper head, model head, which is so popular in England. It is a very fine dog, first-class built, only less spots. It has a very noble look. It will be a very good match for the Ador Vicktoria of Mr. Stewart. Mr. Stewart bought the sister. My Violett II Camphausen is, however, a hundred times better, and I can offer you same free Cologne at the lower price of 1,200 marks.

Item Three
BILL SIGGERS WRITES MAX GRASS:

Max Grass, Esq.,
Rheinaustr. 4,   June 19th, 1926,
Koln a Rhein

Dear Sir,

We are greatly obliged to you for your letter offering us various swarze gefleckte Dogge. It is in the intention of the writer to be in Cologne on July 2nd or 3rd and I shall be glad to hear whether it will be convenient for me to call and see the dogs you kindly offer and also any young uncropped puppies you may have that are of tip top breeding and of good colour. You are right in assuming we only want the best and it is only wasting our time looking at anything that is not first class.

You are not right in Grand Ch. Rex Lendor has developed a bad colour — on the contrary — he is a little better marked than was his sire Champion Prinz Fuchs who was purchased by us from Brunner in 1921. We have perfectly marked puppies by him. However, we are always open to buy anything of outstanding merit and shall look forward to do business with you. We have had business dealings with the late Mr. Wetz and Rembold of Mannheim etc. and have full confidence of a square deal when dealing with your countrymen.

I shall hope to hear from you by return.

Yours truly
W.G. Siggers

W. KUNITZER WRITES J.V. RANK

Dresden 8/6/26

Hohestr 110

Mr. J.V. Rank Esq.

Barn Ridge

South Nutfield, Surrey

Mr. E. von Otto, Bensheim, begs me to offer you some of my Great Danes. I can offer you a young bitch, Fauna of Asgard — 9 weeks with ears not cropped, with dark eyes and beautiful spotted. She is daughter of my Prinz Mephisto von Brennhof, the international conqueror. Mother is Ionna von der Burg Freipack, a granddaughter of Champion Prinz Fuchs and Champion Sperberg. In Fauna's genealogical table are eleven champions in the last 5 generations. Price is £75 off Dresden. A photo of her I enclose.

Further I can offer you a beautiful bitch of 9 months — Hexe — ears already cropped and 73 cm. high for 450 marks off Dresden. She will be a future star.

And last I offer you my celebrated Champion Prinz Mephisto von Brennhof 4 years. He is father of a great deal of the best German spotted black and white Great Danes. His ancestors are all spotted black and white — no yellow. Therefore he is the best husband of spotted or black bitches.

He is gainer of the titles

German Champion 1922

Great Champion of Berlin 1922

International Champion 1924

Victor of Czechoslovakia 1925

No other Great Dane has so many great and international victories as my Champion. I will sell him because I intend in July a brood of him off my bitch Bertha. From this brood I will bring up a young pup with my kennel name. Mephisto is healthy. He is greater than Rex Lendor.

Thereupon I will advise him and sell against highest offer, not under 7,500 Marks off Dresden.

The pictures I beg you to return as soon as possible.

I breed black and white spotted Great Danes since 1917. My kennel is one of the most famous of the whole of Germany.

In attention your answer I am.

Yours
W. Kunitzer

Item Five
BILL SIGGERS WRITES KUNITZER:

June 19th, 1926

Dear Sir,

We are greatly obliged by your letter offering Fauna and Hexe. I hope you have not had the Inna litter's ears cropped as I think one of these will suit us. I am proposing coming to Germany in the first days of July and should hope to be in Dresden on the 4th or 5th. I shall be glad to hear whether you hope to be home on these days as I should like to see what you have in the way of Deutsche Dogge, preferably uncropped, with a view to purchase. I should like to see Mephisto.

Please write to me by return of post.

Yours truly,
W.G. Siggers

Item Six
KUNITZER WRITES RANK:

Dresden, June 24th, l926
Hohestr. 110

J.V. Rank, Esq.,
South Nutfield

Dear Sir,

Having received your letter of June 19th I must write you, that Fauna is already sold. Hexe is very beautiful, she will be a star in future. My older bitch Bertha shall litter in the first days of July — Father of this litter is my Champion Prinz Mephisto, whose spotted daughter Asra was Champion at the Conqueror-Exhibition in Berlin last Sunday. She remained triumphant over the last spotted Champion bitch Aspe von Amalienborg.

If you should not purchase Hexe or Mephisto I can offer you one or some of these puppies of my Bertha. These puppies can rest uncropped and can deliver in September.

With pleasure I await your visit on the 4th of July. I am at home in the afternoon 2–6. In coming to my lodgings please take the tram Nr. 1 till end-station Dresden-Plauen and from there mount the Hohestr. only 7 minutes till Nr. 110.

Yours truly,
Willy Kunitzer

Item Seven
BILL SIGGERS REPORTS TO RANK:

Hotel Leinfelder Munchen
Munchen (Munich)

Thursday

Dear Sir,

It was a long journey from Mannheim to Munchen and raining very hard so I was not able to see much on my arrival here last night. However, I looked Brunner and Swarzmuller up and made early appointments for this morning.

Brunner showed me about 10 harlequins, a messy lot, some were not cropped but quite unsound, fair in head, some good for colour. Prices round about £50. He has a man from Glasgow buying here at the moment. This man Hertel is a little in front of me and asks for an option on all he sees — I am wondering who he can be.

He is welcome to any and all I have seen here. They are all more of Ch. Raluka of Braewood type colour. I did see one beautiful bitch this morning. Her name is Freya, could be a little clearer in colour but she is better than say Marcus — 5 months old. Her sire is Caesar von Zobtenberg who is little brother to our Cisca. I have not seen Caesar. I then went to see the dam of this bitch and found a heavily marked sort, very good size, fair good head, good neck, excellent body. The real good brood bitch. She is *the pet* of the whole neighbourhood, remarkable disposition, such a neck. They do *not* want to sell but if 3,000 to 4,000 marks were bid (£150 to £200) they might sell. This is far too big a price for a *bitch* and she is not better than Rex. I asked them if they would entertain swapping and they said no. If they did part with Freya they could have no other dog. They are poor people.

I then went to see Metzger from whom we had Serta. He had rubbish = Ador von Riesenfeld — Dog, 16 months good colour, coarse head, weak in legs. Hilda von Riesenfeld a big coarse sort. 1 year 10 months, Raluka the second describes her. 3,000 to 4,000 Marks.

I also saw a smart harlequin dog but too small, Apton von Siegerton (8624) 20 months. Sire: Tyras. Dam: a daughter of Prinz Fuchs.

I saw 5 litters of puppies — not a decent one, colour bad and really unattractive. It was most disappointing after all this journey.

Before coming away we had correspondence with a man named Swarzmuller who offered us a harlequin bitch "Betty." She is very nice bitch indeed but not quite our class, Price 3,000 Marks.

It is amusing here the breeders ask the same price for a bad as for a good specimen.

Betty is not anything like as good as this man claims. She is due to whelp in a few days but will have a little air probably! She is mated to a rotten dog.

While writing this letter Dauer had called to see me. I have had difficulty to get hold of him as he seems a busy man. I have got much very useful information from him.

He thinks the brindle dog at Bad Homburg, Dolf von der Saalburg, a very excellent dog. I asked him if he was better than our Rolf and he said "perhaps a little." He thinks Rolf very very good. I feel anxious to see Dolf although Renbolt would lead me to believe the owner will not sell. I think Stewart has had a go at buying this dog.

I am sorry I do not get on quicker with this trip but it takes so long getting about to the various places where they are which has to be by taxi — I made Brunner spend half the taxi fare this morning and he said he would pay all if I bought from him. So far I have spent £35 in expenses. It seems dreadful but everything is a little dearer than England and it is possible to get only 20 marks to the pound although today I did manage to get 201 marks 50 pfennig for a ten pound note.

Dauer tells me of a very good show dog here and he will drive me in his auto in the morning. He would take me tonight but we have had 14 days of rain, lightning and thunder something awful. My word, it does rain here, the streets are like rivers.

I shall then take the train to Dresden and travel through the night getting there about 7 a.m. Sat. See what is possible there and then go to either Bad Homburg or Ludwigshafen. At the latter place I pick up two puppies — fawns. If they develop like their dam I shall consider the trip worthwhile.

I have cabled you today asking for £70 and saying I have bought 3 fawns and 1 brindle and see no harlequins any good. I realise my errand is chiefly to swap and procure harlequins but I know you do not want any dud stock so I am reasonably critical without being too exacting as all dogs have faults. Stewart has put the prices right up! Some say he has given 10,000 Marks for one or two! Of course, the sellers have exaggerated and all else add a little to it.

It will be impossible for me to get right round and be back by Monday as I shall do Dresden Sat. — travel to Bad Homburg or Ludwigshafen to arrive there Sun. a.m., try to do both Bad Homburg and Ludwigshafen Sunday and get on to Cologne Monday then I am almost sure I cannot leave until Tuesday and come over by the night boat getting to Harwich Wed. a.m.

I shall do better if I can and if you wire today to say leave out Dresden or Homburg I can get home Monday night I hope.

I have not cabled you from various places as there has been nothing to cable about really and moreover by the time the day's running about has been done the post offices have been closed. Here, of course, it is different as there is an excellent big Post Office.

I shall not be sorry to get back as I'm sick of this lingo and the dogs are disappointing. I hope all the dogs are well and that Mrs. Morgan and yourself are not being caused too much bother. We need not sell any of our stuff cheaply after the selection I have seen here.

If Chloe and Thor are done with Kurmange the day before Richmond it will improve their coats. Do not show any Danes in the same classes as Stewart's dogs, leave ours outside in the lorry! Look at the catalogue and if you are satisfied take them into the show. Otherwise leave them outside and show the Wolfhounds only.

Always move Monarch quickly, if he walks slow he goes like a cow!

If Mrs. Morgan shows then we cannot do better and I do hope she will be able to do so if I am not back.

Yours obediently
W.G. Siggers

PS. A letter might catch me c/o Thos. Cooke and Sons near the Dom, Cologne (to be called for) as this will be my definite call Monday. It is no use giving the other addresses as I can't tell the hours I shall be there. I have just to get on as well as possible.

[Author's note: Indeed, Mrs. Morgan did show the Danes at Richmond Championship Show in 1926. See photo, page 98 with Vivien and Plaza. Vivien won the Challenge Certificate.]

Item Eight
BILL SIGGERS REPORTS TO RANK:

Ludwigshafen
Sun. night

James V. Rank Esq.

Dear Sir;

I got to Bad Homburg this morning and called on Farber's Kennels. He has 4 dogs Ch. Bosco, Dolf, Fauna and Essma. Bosco is 5 years old and easily the greatest fawn I have ever set eyes on, big and beautiful. Then Dolf is a son of Bosco and Fauna and he is of similar colour to Javar. Now 2 years old he will be at his best soon and then should be greater than Bosco. Dolf is the dog I went specially to see. He owns a high class head, extra deep and long in foreface with square lips, good skull. He has had an operation for improving eyelids which makes his eyes look houndy just now. Otherwise he is well nigh perfect and is a really big sort. Stewart has nothing to touch either of these dogs and their pedigree is the best possible. I asked Farber to name a price and he said he would not sell. I offered to exchange Rolf and 2,000 marks for Dolf but he ridiculed the idea, "not for all the marks in Germany" he said. The same remark applied to Bosco — This is the only man I have met who is really honest and sound about his dogs. He has a pretty fawn (Essma) bitch much like our Ayli only perhaps a little better, 1 year old by Bosco ex Fauna and yet he only asks 300 Marks! We will talk over to see if we can do with this bitch. Anyway we can always remember Farber as a real lover of his dogs and breeder of the best! Essma is qualified V and has won 2 firsts. I saw Rolf's old home in Hamburg. His Dam is alive still. She is a fair size fawn bitch with black marks.

Of all the dogs I have seen I like Ch. Bosco von der Saalburg the best — 6,000 Marks has been refused from U.S.A. for him I learn.

I got along to Frankfurt from Homburg as soon as possible and arrived here 10 p.m.

I shall leave here as soon as I can get a train after breakfast Monday morning with the two puppies I told you I bought here to go on to Dusseldorf which I shall not reach until late to-night.

I am to see in Dusseldorf an uncropped harlequin. I have two puppies to pick up there. I shall look up the train to come home when I get to Dusseldorf and get straight along from there.

I shall cable you to-morrow.

Yours obediently,
W.G. Siggers

Item Nine
BILL SIGGERS REPORTS TO RANK:

Hotel Reichshof und Dom-Café
Cologne Sunday 7 a.m.

Dear Sir,

I had a very busy time yesterday and saw all sorts of dogs. Von Otto wired to say he could not come along. First I saw W. Gras who had a colossal year old harlequin, Pingal, by our Rex for sale. He is too coarse for us and not so good as his sire. He had got this dog especially for us. He had a brother of this dog also for sale. Practically white, hardly a black patch on him. He wanted 6,000 Marks for Pingal which is a crazy price. (£150)

I saw a very nice harlequin bitch which he had offered to us for £75. She had been badly cropped but is quite a nice bitch otherwise.

Then I saw two 6 wks. old harlequin puppies, dog and bitch, uncropped but I should think they would have ears like elephants and heads like pumpkins when matured. Price £20 each.

Then about 6.30 p.m. I went out to Dusseldorf where Gordon Stewart has made his principal purchases. I first went to W. Haegar's Kennels and saw a beautiful tall harlequin (1,000 Marks) dog of G. Stewart's, Balour, extra neck, fair head, bad eye, not too much colour.

Then there was the best blue bitch I have ever seen also the property of Stewart. She is due to whelp to a blue dog in a few days and any puppies over 5 are Stewart's property but the first five belong to Haeger. I saw three puppies about 5 weeks out of a beautiful brindle bitch that Haeger is keeping. I asked him to put a price on her but he would not. Then I asked the prices of the puppies and it appears the three are Stewart's! He seems to have cornered the market. Woe betide him if he wants to unload. I like one in the litter, a dark brindle bitch, the other two are dogs. However, these puppies are nothing like the standard of our own.

W. Haeger then took me on to Stewart's chief source of supply, W. Burmann. The brindle dogs and brindle bitches we saw at Spratt's were bought from this man. He says Stewart buys no dogs in Germany without him and when I asked him about Stewart's kennels in Dusseldorf he said it had been mentioned in course of conversation but nothing had been arranged.

Burmann showed me a nice cropped fawn dog 10 months. And a promising little bitch cropped. Also the dam a lovely golden brindle for which he asked 1,200 Marks. She is 2 years. They promised to get appointments for me to see some puppies today so I am going by first train to Dusseldorf and if possible night train to Bersheim.

W. Siggers

Bob Montgomery watches Champion Ulana clear a row of dogs. At one trial she cleared a record jump of twenty-two feet. At far left is Champion Lancelot and at far right is the black bitch, Inga of Send, who loved to ham it up at the hotel cabaret shows. PHOTO COURTESY PHYLLIS HILL

Side view of the custom-built Morris show van. Champion Lancelot is the blue sitting in the centre of the row of Danes. PHOTO COURTESY PHYLLIS HILL

CHAPTER TWELVE

A Born Showman

Gordon Stewart thought back on one of the few kind acts his father had ever done for him. "He gave me my first Dane at the age of ten and I've always felt their mental abilities would make them outstanding as guide and police dogs, in obedience trials and demonstrations. So I'm going to set out to prove my theory is right. They're equal or better than any breed!"

Besides hiring Herr Huber from Austria to manage his kennel over-all, he hired the finest dog trainers in England, then brought over Herr Eickenbauer from Germany, who was a skilled dog trainer in Europe.

If his plan was to win dog shows and Challenge Certificates, he'd have done what J. V. Rank at Ouborough did — hire someone like Bill Siggers. But Stewart was a showman through and through. He wanted to attract more attention than just winning at dog shows. There are obvious reasons for this, and I think he had a hidden agenda, but I'll deal with that in the last chapter, where I discuss some conclusions I've drawn while researching this book.

Now, let's see what he actually did.

He hired Bob Montgomery and Leslie Hill, who, because of the results they achieved, had to be the finest dog trainers in England. Granted, there were other assistants like Colonel Lionel de Pinto, but these two Englishmen did it all, working tirelessly to put on the greatest shows on Earth with Great Danes.

The best five kennel maids were selected to work in the training section with these men. Under their direction, the girls set up daily training routines with their groups of dogs. The novelty was that all colours of Danes were used. Even groups of the same colour would perform together against other colours.

Champion Lancelot clears the stick held by two Alsatians (German Shepherds). The famed Crystal Palace Exhibition Hall is in the background. The Alsatian at right drops his end of the stick as this bloody big Great Dane flies over him. The Danes and Alsatians were always competing in obedience and the Send Danes usually won the competition.

PHOTO COURTESY
ANDREW MONTGOMERY

For those of you not familiar with the Great Dane breed, there are five colours recognized by the English standard — fawn, brindle, black, blue and harlequin.

Send Danes took on the Alsatians (German Shepherds) to prove they were equal or better than that breed for intelligence and prowess, and they usually won in those obedience demonstrations. They performed for royalty at Send Manor and at horse and agricultural shows. They were wildly applauded at fund-raising events, at the fashionable West-End London hotels and before the titled aristocracy of England. They were in films and in the theatre.

The hotels usually used for the cabarets, which began at midnight, were the Park Lane, Grosvenor House and the Dorchester. The film studios, Gainsborough, Pinewood and Gaumont-British, all used Send Great Danes in their movies.

Champion Egmund of Send had the lead role in the 1932 Gainsborough film, *The Hound of the Baskervilles*. (See Chapter 18.)

The Send dogs hobnobbed with the royal princes and future King of England, Sir Malcolm Campbell, Dame Gracie Fields and many other famous leading actors and actresses of the time. All that magical world of show business will be explored in later chapters. Stewart built

Champion Ulana leaps through the hoop attached to Lancelot's back.
Lancelot won't perform properly unless he has his box to stand on. 1930.

PHOTO COURTESY ANDREW MONTGOMERY

The "steeplechase with jockeys" race was hilarious.
The girls had to be in shape, as they had to run with the dog
and hang on to its lead. Vic Allfrey is pulling up the rear.

PHOTO COURTESY ANDREW MONTGOMERY

the most remarkable scene for his frequent shows at Send Manor, which would equal many of our theme parks today.

Now, let's look at how it was all done.

The Swiss "barn" was the focal point for all indoor shows at Send. It was large, like a community hall. The concrete painted floor was marked as a tennis court, and Stewart brought a tennis pro up from London once a week to give free tennis lessons to any kennel maid who wanted them.

The photos you see in this chapter will give you a better idea than I can, in words, of how that wonderful building looked. Remember that the whole Send Kennel area was like a beautiful Swiss village, with tree-lined avenues, each with its own name, and all the buildings designed in the Swiss style.

The Swiss barn was called the Karinda Hut and was of Swiss design inside and out, as you can see from the photos, with carved panelling for walls and wall crests, ornate balcony railings and other interior decor.

Stewart had one of the most popular artists in Britain, a Welshman named Augustus John, paint wonderful large canvases with beautiful Swiss mountain scenes. Those would be worth a fortune today, as John became quite famous. His paintings hang in the National Portrait Gallery of England, and his portraits are displayed on the walls of the titled aristocracy and in art galleries throughout the world.

Many games, trials and demonstrations were held in the Swiss Karinda Hut. There, Mrs. Stewart entertained the actors and actresses of the London stage. They were invited on the weekend to see the exciting dog shows and races.

"A great many famous stage and film stars were often at Send," recalls Margaret Fife Failes (nee Tracy). "I well remember among them were Gracie Fields, Vivien Leigh, Diana Wynyard, Gerald du Maurier, Conrad Veight, Jessie Matthews, Florence Desmond, Richard Tauber and Binnie Barnes coming out to the manor to attend the shows. Some stayed the weekend."

Binnie Barnes recently died, on July 30, 1998. She had become a great film star in England and the United States, after being born in

Andrew Montgomery's mother, Audrey Field, with a wonderful team of fawn Danes. The Send Kennel buildings are in rear. Note mesh bird cage at rear right.

PHOTO COURTESY
ANDREW MONTGOMERY

Send trainer Colonel de Pinto judges an obedience class show for the "come and sit." Lancelot sits and watches while Ulana strolls back to her handler with a ho-hum, lazy attitude. For the tricks she could perform this was boring stuff.

PHOTO COURTESY
ANDREW MONTGOMERY

Audrey Field with Champion Ulana explains dog training to a group of schoolgirls visiting Send Kennel.

PHOTO COURTESY
ANDREW MONTGOMERY

Last-minute instruction for the race. This is a class of all brindles.

Awaiting their start in the relay, a brindle team race.

North London in 1903, when Stewart was eighteen. Alexander Korda starred her in 1933 in *The Private Life of Henry VIII*, with Charles Laughton. She was so poor, the story goes, that she would smuggle home food used in the movie banquet scenes to heat up on her one-ring stove.

Noel Coward had cast her in a minor role in the 1930 film *Cavalcade*, and in 1931 she appeared with Stanley Lupino in short comedies and then starred in *A Night in Montmartre*. In 1932 her five-year contract with Fox Studios was spotty, and she left Hollywood.

Back in London, Binnie Barnes played opposite Douglas Fairbanks in *The Private Life of Don Juan* in 1934. Before 1939 she had made a score of films in Hollywood, including *The Last of the Mohicans* in 1935 with Randolph Scott, and *The Three Musketeers* in 1939. In 1938 she was in England to star for Korda in *The Divorce of Lady X*, with Laurence Olivier and Merle Oberon.

Although never really making top billing, Binnie continued in films throughout the forties and retired in 1955 to settle in Beverly Hills with her second husband, Mike Francovich. She had met Frank while she was playing poker with Clark Gable. They married in 1940 and lived next door to Elvis Presley.

She made a comeback and starred as a nun with Rosalind Russell in 1968 in *The Trouble With Angels*. Her last film was in 1972, playing Liv Ullman's mother opposite Gene Kelly.

Binnie was a great star who was a familiar young face at Send Kennel and very special to Stewart. Margaret Fife Failes says, "She seemed to be there more than the other stars, making a fuss over the dogs."

And, it appears, over Gordon Stewart as well.

Mrs. Stewart had a flat in London where she usually stayed. So often the young, beautiful, aspiring actresses stayed over the weekend as Stewart's guests at Send Manor, and his chauffeur drove them back to London on Monday.

A favourite show in the Karinda Hut, enjoyed by all, was the dog racing. Here's how that worked. Posts were set up on the floor and white tapes attached to them to form long lanes. Equal spaces were marked on the floor for each racing lane. Six lanes for six Danes. The

*Clearing the hurdles. Champion Ulana, at front,
always wanted to be first.* PHOTO COURTESY GORDON V. STEWART

A steeplechase race at Send Kennel.
PHOTO COURTESY ANDREW MONTGOMERY

Danes each wore a different numbered vest, and they lined up at the starting line in their individual lane with a handler.

There was a large numbered wheel (shown on page 148) on the balcony of the Swiss Hut, and it was spun for each dog in succession. Whatever number came up, the handler moved her dog that number of spaces down the lane, and then it was the next dog's turn.

The dog that reached the end first had won the race. Sometimes dice were used — one die rolled indicated the dog that was to move — lane numbers 1 to 6. No skill required, just the luck of the wheel or dice.

These races were attended by hundreds of lords and ladies, actresses and actors and prominent business friends of Stewart. They crammed the floor and spread up the stairs and along the balcony; heavy bets were placed on the numbered dogs. Those who had bet on the winning number split the pot, and there were actual betting totes with bookies there.

Refreshments were served, of course.

The kennel staff were kept away, except for the girls from the show section handling the dogs and those serving the guests. Nora West, Audrey Field and Margaret Tracy were kennel maids in the show section, so they got to attend these shows.

"I only saw the races once at the Swiss Hut," says Win Leake, "but I sure had to make a lot of sandwiches for that lot." Win didn't go on the show and training range section to join Nora West until 1937, and by then these Swiss Hut events and races were ending.

They also held a lot of obedience trials and indoor hurdle races in the Swiss Hut, with relay teams of dogs, plus any other event Stewart could devise to promote social contact with the upper crust of England.

Another favourite show they'd put on was headlined "Can Dogs See Colours?" This display was not only performed at the Swiss barn, but at fashionable West-End London hotels such as the Grosvenor, in Park Lane. These cabaret shows usually raised money for charity and were held at midnight after the theatre got out. Twelve lovely Send Great Danes were trained, all with perfectly matched black masks. They looked like clones except that some were dogs and some were bitches.

Without any lead, each dog was marched onto the ballroom floor by a pretty, smartly groomed kennel maid. Each dog wore a different-coloured silk handkerchief around its neck. They took up positions facing the centre, in a wide circle, and were given the signal to sit-stay.

I must mention here that Bob Montgomery's obedience training was far beyond what we see today with large groups of dogs. There were no audible commands — everything was done by hand signal and handler's body language.

The kennel maids left the area, but as they went out, each took from her pocket three coloured handkerchiefs the same colour as the neck piece for her dog. These were piled and mixed up in the centre of the circle. So you had thirty-six hankies in twelve different colours all heaped together on the floor.

Bob Montgomery would explain to the crowd that most people thought that dogs were colour blind, but he'd show that this might not be true!

He would ask someone to call out a colour, and voices would ring out, shouting different colours. When the noise stopped Montgomery would call out, "Red — get the red one, Blue — find the blue one, Yellow — find the yellow one, White — fetch the white one," in a sequence.

The dogs would trot out, pick up their colour of handkerchief, return to their place in the circle, turn around and drop their handkerchief in front of them.

Bob alternated colours and mixed up the call to the twelve Danes, but finally all thirty-six hankies would be back in front of the right dogs — three of each colour of kerchief on each dog. Montgomery had one character of a dog in the group, who would cause howls of laughter and great applause, adding even more interest to the show. He'd not been taught to do so, but sometimes, not always, he'd run out and pick up the wrong colour. No one knew why.

Bob would smartly command, "Stop Blue, that's not your colour. You jolly well know it's not." And that dog would go back, drop the wrong colour in the pile, pick up the right one and go back to his place

These next three photos show the training for the hotel cabaret show
"Are Dogs Colour Blind?" and are explained in this chapter.
The coloured kerchiefs have the scent of each dog's handler.

Here the Danes train to
find their own "colour"
of kerchief. Note part of
the office on stilts in the
background as Audrey
Field, left, and her
future husband Bob
Montgomery, centre,
look on.

The Danes have found
their proper kerchief
and return it to their
handler/trainer.
PHOTO COURTESY
NORA WEST

A close-up of the
harlequin handled by
Vic Allfrey (see above)
with its coloured
(scented) kerchief.
PHOTO COURTESY
WIN LEAKE

in the circle. Sometimes he'd do it twice in the show. Just a mischievous showman — but a hilarious addition to the program.

Of course, the trick was that a kennel maid carried her three coloured kerchiefs around on her person for days, making sure her scent impregnated the cloth. Her dog selected the correct kerchief by smell, not colour. Your vet will tell you that everything appears to dogs in shades of black and grey.

You'll see a photo on page 124 that shows Bob Montgomery doing an outdoor trick with Champion Ulana of Send jumping over five dogs. The blue Champion Lancelot of Send is at the end on the left closest to you. Now see that little black bitch down at the far end at the right of that picture? She has a white blaze on her throat and her name is Inga of Send.

"Inga was a real character," says Phyllis Hill with a laugh. "A real extrovert! During this show, Bob Montgomery would tell her to stand and stay in place at the end of the line while he positioned the other dogs. Once, Inga glanced around at the audience and saw all the smiling, friendly people. So she broke her position and did a complete turn around the ring as if to take a bow. No one knew why she did it.

"The crowd loved it, laughing uproariously.

"So from then on," Phyllis says, "Inga did this every show, and Bob Montgomery let her do it, as the crowd loved her so!"

Champion Ulana could jump twenty-one feet over small hurdles or sometimes twenty-two dogs lying down in a line. That's probably some kind of distance record. Champion Lancelot jumped great distances too and liked to be first in the steeplechase and hurdle races outdoors. But this big blue was always the macho male. When he was in the middle of a line of dogs, he insisted on standing or lying on his box. He'd not perform properly until his box was brought to him.

Stewart always tried to impress the elite of England and would do anything for them in order to gain favour. At one Ladies Kennel Association show, held at Crystal Palace, a duchess mentioned to Stewart that she was worried about the safety of her valuables at the hotel that night.

So Stewart told her about "Lance's box."

Often at the dog shows Bob Montgomery and Leslie Hill would sleep in the benching area with the dogs as they overnighted for the next day's show. The staff all knew that they could put their valuables in Lance's box, and no stranger could approach that box without Champion Lancelot going wild.

So the duchess left her jewels safely overnight in Lance's box, and all was well. Another point scored for Stewart with the gentry, by one of his beloved Great Danes.

Another popular game at the cabaret shows was the "Hand of Whist." Margaret Tracy says it was played by four Danes each, with about eight cards if played outdoors, and if indoors, about six cards. The large cards were placed on a stand in front of each dog, and four kennel maids guided the dogs, by quiet voice if outdoors, and if inside, by teaching the dogs to recognize the numbers 1 to 6.

The girls would indicate a number to each dog, and the dog would go to the stand and lift out the right number.

"Then there was the 'Round-about' that was so popular," Fife Failes recalls, "that the famous Bertram Mills Circus begged Stewart to let the circus use this Dane act. And Cunard wanted to have the dogs entertain first-class passengers on their ocean liners. But Stewart wouldn't have his dogs leave home."

The Round-about had eight pairs of Danes stand spaced out round a big circle with one dog of the pair in front of the other. There were eight kennel maids standing spaced apart, in the circle centre. The maids had four Danes jumping clockwise over the inner circle of the eight standing dogs and four counterclockwise over the outer circle of the eight standing dogs. You can imagine the action of all this performance and the noise and applause of the crowd.

All of the eight jumping dogs in the one circle were stopped by a whistle to either stand, sit or down on command, while the other eight continued. This was alternated by one or the other circle jumping or both circles jumping in a clockwise or counterclockwise direction at the same time.

*Loading the show van. Note the doorway to the Karinda Hut in rear
with exotic-bird cages at each corner of the building.*

PHOTO COURTESY ANDREW MONTGOMERY

The show dogs and handlers I've already mentioned were driven by the chauffeur, Mr. Bird, in the maroon show van, accompanied by the dog ambulance painted in the same kennel colours.

The Send Danes were often used in films; dogs were regularly supplied to Pinewood and other studios by Bob Montgomery.

Phyllis Hill remembers, "One time studios needed several dogs on the same day at different shooting locations. So they asked me to take three dogs, and not only did they use the dogs but put me in that Gracie Fields film as an extra. In the film, Gracie had to come down a wide staircase in a hotel and look down on a milling crowd of dogs and their owners on the hotel foyer. That was a thrilling day for me as a young impressionable girl. I was in the movies!"

This chapter gives you some idea of the strict professionalism that Stewart demanded from his staff and his Danes. After all, the name of Gordon Stewart was at stake, and he had plans, I firmly believe, for that

Bob Montgomery supervised loading the show van. That's handler Audrey Field to the centre with Phui May just behind her.

PHOTO COURTESY ANDREW MONTGOMERY

The Crystal Palace. The mammoth exhibition complex was totally constructed of glass panels and windows. It had been re-erected from Hyde Park in London to Sydenham, south of London, in 1888. Many early dog shows and Send Kennel exhibitions were held there. It does not exist today.

name to one day be titled and well known throughout England's aristocracy.

In 1930 Stewart, ever the showman, made sure he'd always be remembered by dogdom. For the world-famous Crufts Dog Show he commissioned five elegant Send gold vases to be made by a goldsmith in London. They are solid nine-carat gold.

Each of the group winners at Crufts would receive a Send gold vase. Not to keep, of course, as they were too valuable. At that time there were five groups: (1) Sporting (other than Gundog or Terrier) (2) Gundog (3) Terrier (4) Non-Sporting (other than Toy) and (5) the Toy Group.

Champion Mavis of Send, the sister of Champion Midas and the same bitch Mavis I refer to at the end of the chapter on Augustus John, won the Send gold vase that year as best exhibit in the Non-Sporting Group.

Another identical vase was added by the Kennel Club in 1967 (as Stewart had died in 1952) when the Non-Sporting Group was split into the Utility and Working Groups. As I write this in 1998, the Kennel Club is splitting the Working Group into the Herding and the Working Groups, so the club will have to dig deeply to have another identical gold vase made.

Today, each Send gold vase is of tremendous value.

The Kennel Club has kindly provided me with a photo of one of these exquisite Send gold vases to include with this chapter. Whenever you're at Crufts, be sure to see the display of the wonderful Crufts cups in their protective glass cases. There you'll see the Send gold vases, another remarkable example of Stewart's generosity and thoughtfulness towards the world of pedigree dogs.

A Send gold vase. One of five presented by Gordon Stewart to the Kennel Club in 1930 for each group winner at Crufts Dog Show annually. The trophies are guarded and held at the Kennel Club as they are invaluable and are solid nine-carat gold. Gordon Stewart was a generous benefactor for dog shows and Great Dane clubs.

PHOTO COURTESY THE KENNEL CLUB

The cover of the September 1931 Tail-Wagger shows the
famous photo of one hundred Send Great Danes perfectly behaved.
Show dogs and field or obedience champions were encouraged to join
the Tail-Waggers Club for a small fee. The publication came out
each month with various doggy articles.

Training on the same field used for "The Tail-Waggers 100" photo. Note the outdoor dog race courses. 1931. PHOTO COURTESY NORA WEST

The actual "Tail-Waggers 100" photo taken from Bob Montgomery's office on stilts, overlooking the training field at the rear of the Send Kennel grounds. In front centre on his box is Champion Lancelot of Send. Handler Audrey Field is second row centre. Nora West is third row far right. An unbelievable picture of perfect obedience showing all five colours of Great Dane. 1931. PHOTO COURTESY WIN LEAKE

Training for the "Say Grace" article in the Tail-Wagger magazine in 1931. Chaos breaks out. As dogs mount the table Bob Montgomery rushes in to restore order. Champion Lancelot at far right calmly looks on in disgust at such bad behavior. That's Nora West hidden by Montgomery trying to restrain her dog. 1931. PHOTO COURTESY ANDREW MONTGOMERY

Order is restored. All give thanks. Champion Lancelot at right still sits calmly at his end. In the photo used in Tail-Wagger magazine Champion Ulana sat at the head of the table at the other end. 1931.

PHOTO COURTESY ANDREW MONTGOMERY

Audrey Field training Lancelot to distance jump while Ulana awaits her turn. PHOTO COURTESY GORDON V. STEWART

Audrey Field training Lancelot over the high obstacle.
PHOTO COURTESY ANDREW MONTGOMERY

Augustus John photographed by his friend Vandyk.

Sketch of a whippet by Augustus John. I couldn't find one of a Great Dane but expect he would have done some while working at Send on the Swiss-mountain scenes for the Karinda Hut.

CHAPTER THIRTEEN

Augustus John

But if in the know
You'll hasten to go
Where all the best people have gone
His portraits don't flatter
But that doesn't matter
So long as you're painted by John.

That little ditty just about says it all about one of England's best-known and most prolific artists of the first half of the twentieth century. Prolific indeed!

The philosophy of Augustus John seemed to be that sex was a joke and everyone loves a joke. He used to say that when he went out for a walk he patted every child on the head as he passed — in case it was one of his.

Once again Stewart went first class when building his Swiss village. He knew Augustus John as a friend. They'd hung out together as young men in the clubs and restaurants in London when John was a struggling artist. By the time Stewart was ready to decorate his Karinda Hut, John was a well-known Impressionist and in demand everywhere. But Stewart was able to convince him to lay aside his commissions for awhile and help him create his Swiss village.

I've generally told you about the Swiss design concept and briefly mentioned the Swiss Karinda Hut. As you can see from photos, it was a magnificent building and could hardly be called a hut or a barn.

"In fact," Phyllis Hill, a former kennel maid, recalls, "it was given the name 'Karinda Hut' by Stewart himself."

It was quite large, about the dimensions of a good-sized community hall. Beautifully designed outside in Swiss chalet style, with lovely hanging baskets of colourful flowers, it was landscaped

The interior of the Karinda Hut was a huge area. Large Swiss scenery paintings by Augustus John hung over the two end galleries. Gordon Stewart is watching the show from the gallery, to the left of the numbers spinning wheel. This shows the dog race where the dice or wheel gave the space numbers a dog would move. PHOTO COURTESY WIN LEAKE

professionally with cobblestone walkways, shade trees and beautiful gardens. There was really nothing like it in England.

Inside was a gallery around the hut, overlooking the floor below. The carved hand railings and wall plaques all carried through the Swiss decor. The floor had a tennis court, and Stewart brought a tennis pro up from London once a week to give the kennel maids free lessons. At other times, the net was taken down, and dog shows and demonstrations were presented for large crowds of Stewart's friends.

On the ceiling were magnificent paintings by Augustus John.

Kennel maids Phyllis Hill (nee Hudson) and Margaret Fife Failes (nee Tracy) described the paintings. It seems they were huge. One was located near Stewart's office, at one end of the hut, and the other at the opposite end, near Stewart's photographic and dark room where he had

Front of the Karinda Hut where two Augustus John paintings
showed magnificent scenes. Beautifully landscaped Swiss design.
PHOTO COURTESY ANDREW MONTGOMERY

his equipment. They went from the gallery and up to the roof —
wonderful Swiss-mountain scenery and pine forests with beautiful
effects of clouds and mountain breezes.

Margaret Tracy says they were really wonderful.

When you see photos here of the interior of the Karinda Hut, you
can visualize the size these paintings must have been. That wasn't
unusual for John, as he had painted large murals for other projects and
even stage scenery for the theatre. Hill can't remember if the paintings
were done in panels or canvas sections — she can't remember the
construction at all.

John was born in Wales on January 4, 1878. That's about seven
years before Gordon Stewart, so they were generally of the same
generation and experience. John's mother died when he was six, and
his father, a solicitor, was a hard, cold disciplinarian.

Perhaps because of his early childhood, John was antisocial and shy, but an exhibitionist at times. His sister Gwen equalled, and some say bettered, his artistic talent. Her works hang in many galleries of the world.

John was a big, imposing man, almost six feet at age eighteen, with a flamboyant red beard. All his life he had trouble making friends and then retaining any friendships, except with women. He loved the outdoors and would join the gypsy caravans and travel throughout Britain with hardly the shirt on his back.

With a legacy of forty pounds from his mother, he was able to go to the Slade School of Arts in London. It was an important, respected art school, founded on the traditions and styles of the old masters. He spent hours at the National Art Gallery at Trafalgar Square and at the British Museum; he could never get over their magnificent collections.

During this time, John lived in the London suburb of Acton, and that's where Stewart, as a young man of twenty-one, set up his first company shop. Like many good artists before him, he gained much inspiration from music-hall performers and constantly sketched them. His portrait of Arthur Roberts, the renowned English comic, is in the National Portrait Gallery in London.

The Canadians Opposite Lens. *A preparatory forty-foot*
mural sketch, charcoal on paper, by Augustus John.
He never finished the actual oil painting.

Walter Russell was a teacher at the Slade School and went on to be
one of England's greatest painters, was knighted, and would become a
trustee of both the Tate and the National Galleries.

The great developing artists of that day also painted each other.
The William Orpen portrait of Augustus John (which John disliked)
hangs in the National Portrait Gallery now. It is truly magnificent.

John was not a talker, he was a listener. His friends called him a
non conformist, and there was always a wildness in him. He loved
wine, women and song but still found time to practise his art. Today,
his paintings are owned by most of the worlds' famous galleries.

It was about the turn of the century when he began to exhibit, and
his reputation grew and grew. At that time, there was a circle of young
artists and writers you would recognize today — men and women who
painted and wrote about each other as good friends will do.

John hung out in Hampstead, in London, with his close friend and poet W. B. Yeats, whom he greatly admired. He was also closely associated with Wyndham Lewis, another great artist friend. His inner circle held Bernard Shaw, Dylan Thomas, Yeats, Virginia Woolf, and D. H. Lawrence, just to name a few.

In fact, he did three oil portraits of Bernard Shaw in one week. The most unusual and impressionistic of them all — of Shaw having fallen asleep while posing — was always Shaw's favourite. It's owned by the Queen Mother, Elizabeth, and hangs in Kensington Palace in London.

Over the years, just about everyone who was anyone at all lined up for an Augustus John portrait. Lloyd George, Field Marshall Montgomery and other lords and ladies of Britain sat for him. On August 4, 1928, John wrote, "I don't find it amusing to paint these stupid millionaires, when I might be painting for my own satisfaction."

By 1910 he became a well-known impressionist all over Europe and developed new talents after spending many months in France. His exhibition at the Chenil Gallery in London later showed much improved and accepted talent, and was entitled "Provencal Studies and Other Works."

The Americans were also discovering Augustus John, and during his frequent visits to that country in later years, prominent citizens clamoured for his portraits and attendance at their cocktail parties and galas.

He hated all that!

In April 1914, he and a couple of friends opened the Crab Tree Club in London, for artists, poets and musicians. This was the same year that a struggling young motor-car salesman was tramping the streets of London, so Stewart could well have met John there. These young, ambitious men of the day hung out at the Cavendish Hotel in Jermyn Street, Café-Verrey in Soho, Bertorellis, the Saint Bernard Restaurant on Charlotte Street near the Scala Theatre and the luxurious Eiffel Tower on Percy Street. These were the "in" places of that time in London.

In 1917 a group of his friends and students at the Slade School of Arts put on a "Monster Matinee" at the Chelsea Palace Theatre. They had little plays about Rosette Whistler and others, and it was there that

Augustus John painting Tallulah Bankhead, the actress.

Augustus John with James Joyce, the author, in Paris.

a group of the students performed the quaint little song quoted from at the beginning of the chapter. (At the end is the whole performance.)

By now John had painted his way through France, Italy and the United States, with great attention, turmoil and success. But before all you British, French, Italians and Americans claim him as your own, let me tell you about his Canadian caper.

He had bad knees, so could not enter military service at the start of the First World War in 1914. That suited him just fine, of course. He was not a killer — he was a lover. But he felt out of place without a uniform, as all his pals had joined up. So he wrote the British government to offer himself as a painter, to record the fighting men of Britain at the front. But the red tape bogged down his request, and John became exasperated and wouldn't wait any longer for his acceptance, although it did come eventually.

He meanwhile volunteered for the Canadian War Memorials Fund instead. Sir Max Aiken, who hailed from New Brunswick and was known as Lord Beaverbrook, the publishing baron, jumped at the chance to start a picture collection of the Canadian war effort. The Canadian War Records Office shows that John was given a full honorary commission in the Overseas Military Forces of Canada, with the rank of major. He got full pay, allowances and an extra three hundred pounds expenses to start his paintings.

He could now strut his stuff as a fully uniformed army officer, around the cafés and clubs of London, without going off to be killed at the front. He was indeed impressive as Major John.

His chief assignment was to paint a huge mural, forty feet long, of the valour of the Canadian men and women at war. Although Lord Beaverbrook said later, "Do you know what work I got out of John — not a damn thing!"

The drawing for that mural (only sketched on paper in charcoal), not yet painted, went on display in this unfinished state at Burlington House, London, in January 1919, at a Canadian War Memorial Exhibition. It was indeed magnificent. It now (the charcoal drawing on paper) rests with the National Art Gallery in Ottawa. They have kindly granted permission to show it to you here (see pages 150–151).

The mural was supposed to grace the entrance hall of a War Memorials Museum building to be built in Ottawa. But the building was never built, and the mural never painted by John. Here is that mural. The charcoal drawing is forty feet long, consisting of eight panels, five feet wide and ten feet tall. Just look at the detail of that drawing — what a shame it was never painted by John.

Many of his smaller war paintings and drawings went to the Canadian National Art Gallery in Ottawa, and Lord Beaverbrook got only two drawings and two paintings for his Art Gallery by the River, in Fredericton, New Brunswick.

The Art Gallery of Ontario owns the outstanding portrait, *The Marchesa Casati*. John painted it in Paris in April 1919. She poses in her negligee, with Mount Vesuvius as a background.

In 1917 John held the largest exhibition of his paintings ever assembled, at the Alpine Club in London. The *London Times* called him the most famous living English painter, and even Lord Beaverbrook conceded that "John is the greatest artist of our time!" Fashionable folk flocked to this show and clamoured for his work.

In 1919 John was invited to France to the Peace Conference in Paris, as one of two British painters. The other was his friend John Orpen. They were to memorialize the events of that historic meeting. He painted portraits of the prime ministers of Canada, New Zealand and Australia, kings and maharajas, dukes and generals, lords of finance and law, Lawrence of Arabia and many other celebrities. John gave the Imperial War Museum in Lambeth eight drawings of wartime subjects.

In the twenties he got his second wind and painted actresses, actors, airmen, matinee idols, bankers, businessmen, Wimbledon champions, writers, musicians and even the emperor of Japan — whom he polished off in a one-hour sitting!

It was at this time that Stewart was building and decorating the Swiss Karinda Hut at Send Manor, and Augustus John agreed to do the Swiss-mountain oil paintings for him.

John loved anything that broke him away from the dull portrait sittings that he loathed. But he had to do them to finance his homes, his wife, his mistresses and many children.

His portraits of Gerald du Maurier and Tallulah Bankhead, of the theatre, were marvellous. Tallulah's portrait, done in 1930, is owned by the Smithsonian National Portrait Gallery in Washington.

In her autobiography, Tallulah wrote, "My most valuable possession is my Augustus John portrait." Perhaps that was true, as Lord Duveen offered her one hundred thousand pounds for it.

On Tuesday, October 31, 1939, John began the first sitting to paint Queen Elizabeth (the Queen Mother now). She was, of course, married to Stewart's close friend King George VI. John delayed and delayed finishing the painting, and it was 1961 before Queen Elizabeth finally got it. She said, in a letter to John, "It looks so lovely in my drawing room and it has cheered it up no end! The sequins glitter, and the roses and red chair, give a fine glow and I am so happy to have it...."

Of his American trips, John exclaimed in disgust, "Offers for portraits are pouring in. There are millions to be made, but I'd rather paint vegetables!"

In the early twenties, there was another connection, by John, to Stewart's circle of friends. Augustus sold his Chelsea home in Mallard Street, London, to Gracie Fields, about whom you'll read later.

By 1931 John's alcohol problems were catching up with him. His friend D. H. Lawrence noted that "John is in ruins but still a giant of a man — at once exciting, honest, uncanny."

In 1936, ten years before Stewart bought the Strand Theatre, John was persuaded to enter the world of the theatre. He painted the scenery for J. M. Barrie's play, *The Boy David*. But when he attended opening night, John left after the first act and stayed at the bar. The scenery director massacred his work while redesigning the scenes, and without John's approval.

In 1961 Augustus John died at the age of eighty-three. He'll always be remembered in the art world as a truly great impressionist. Yet Stewart was able to talk him into painting those Swiss-mountain scenes for the Karinda Hut at Send Manor.

But where have those Augustus John paintings gone?

There is also something else to ponder. In 1928 Augustus John met a beautiful sex kitten named Mabel Wright, working at the Café Royal in London. She was gorgeous, tall and nineteen. Everyone called her Mavis. John got her pregnant and they had a son, although she was married to his friend Horace de Vere Cole at the time.

All through the later twenties and early thirties. Mavis was John's favourite "model." In that same year, 1928, a lovely fawn Great Dane bitch puppy was born, and Stewart registered her as Mavis of Send at the Kennel Club in 1929. She became an important Champion later. Her litter brother was Champion Midas of Send, to be owned by Prince George, the Duke of Kent.

Was this just a coincidence? Or was Mavis of Send named after that beautiful sex kitten, Mavis, of the famed Café Royal?

"AUGUSTUS JOHN"

Sung by Mrs. Grundy and the John Beauty Chorus
Music by H. Fraser-Simson
Words by Harry Graham
Performed in 1917 at the "Monster Matinee" at the Chelsea Palace Theatre

Some people will squandor
Their savings away
On paintings by Rankin or Steer;
For Brangwyn or Conder
Huge sums they will pay
And they buy all the Prydes that appear!

But if you'd be smart
As patrons of Art
It's almost a sine qua non
To prove your discretion
By giving possession
Of works by the wonderful John!

Augustus John!

REFRAIN:

John! John!
How he's got on
He owes it, he knows it, to me

Brass earrings I wear
And I don't do my hair
And my feet are as bare as can be;
When I walk down the street,
All the people I meet
They stare at the things I have on!
When Battersea — Parking
You'll hear folk remarking;
There goes an Augustus John!

CHORUS:

John! John!
If you'd get on
The quaintest clothes you must don!

When out for an airing,
You'll hear folks declaring:
There goes an Augustus John!
Good people acquainted
With Sargent or Strang
Will sit to them week after week!
It's nice being painted
By Nicholson's gang
And McEvoy's touch is unique!
But if in the know,
You'll hasten to go
Where all the best people have gone:
His portraits don't flatter
But that doesn't matter
So long as you're painted by John!

Augustus John!

REFRAIN:

John! John!
If you'd get on,
Just sit for a bit and you'll see!
Your curious shape
He will cunningly drape
With an Inverness Cape to the knee!
What a wealth of design!
And what colour and line!
He turns every goose to a swan!
And, though you're not handsome
You're worth a king's ransom
If you're an Augustus John!

CHORUS:

John! John!
How he's got on
He turns every goose to a swan!
You needn't be pretty
Or wealthy or witty
If you're an Augustus John!
Our ancestors freely

Expressed their dislike
Of all conventional styles
They raved about Lely
They worshipped Vandyke.
And Leighton they greeted with smiles!
Today if one owns
A Watts or Burne-Jones
Its subject seems bloodless and wan!
One misses the vigour,
The matronly figure,
That marks all the drawings of John!

Augustus John!

REFRAIN:

John! John!
How he's got on!
He's quite at the top of the tree!
From Cotman to Carot,
From Tonks to George Morrow
There's no one as famous as he!
On the scrap heap we'll cast
All those works of the past
By stars that once splendidly shone!
Send Hoppners and Knellers
To attics and cellars
And stick to Augustus John!

CHORUS:

John! John!
How he's got on
No light so brightly has shone!
The verdict of Chelsea's
That nobody else is
A patch on Augustus John!

This song and other details about Augustus John are with the permission of Michael Holroyd, from his wonderful biography entitled Augustus John, *published by Vintage/Random House.*

Posing at Send is Prince George, Duke of Kent, with his dog Champion Midas of Send. This is the most famous photo used by the press and by Hutchinson's Dog Encyclopaedia.

PHOTO COURTESY ANDREW MONTGOMERY

CHAPTER FOURTEEN

The Royal Connection

T here can be confusion about Prince George, Duke of Kent and King George VI.

Doggie people might tell you that His Royal Highness, Prince George, Duke of Kent, had been given a Great Dane by Gordon Stewart. Then they sometimes go on to talk about Prince George as the future king, George VI, with this dog Midas.

So before we go any further I'll tell you what the registrar of the Royal Archives told me, and I quote, "As for the dog, Midas, this belonged, as your copies show, not to the Duke of York (Prince Albert), but to his brother, Prince George, the Duke of Kent. I realize that this is rather confusing, as the Duke of York (Prince Albert) later became King George VI."

So there you have it. His Royal Highness Prince Albert decided in 1937, when he was crowned the King of England, that he would take the name George instead of staying Albert. His wife, Elizabeth, the Queen Mum, has just turned one hundred. King George VI died in 1952, and the present Queen Elizabeth, his daughter, took the throne.

His Royal Highness Prince George, Duke of Kent, was sadly killed in a mysterious plane accident in 1942.

Stewart and His Royal Highness Prince George, the Duke of Kent, met first when the prince was patron of the Great Dane Club in England. The Duke shared Stewart's love for Great Danes, but he almost didn't get the dog Midas.

Champion Midas of Send was born May 29, 1928. His sire was the Dutch import Champion Urlus of Send, and his dam, Fahne Ruhrtal of Send. He was a fawn puppy, registered by Stewart with the Kennel Club as number 778KK. His litter sister Mavis, mentioned in the chapter on Augustus John, became an important show bitch and a Champion as

*Left to right: Prince Henry and Mrs. Beddoes with backs to camera;
Gordon Stewart; Prince George, Duke of Kent, with his dog
Champion Midas of Send.* PHOTO COURTESY WIN LEAKE

well. She was Best Bitch in Show All Breeds at Crufts and again at the
Taunton Show.

Champion Midas was all set to be sold to a maharajah in India but
became ill and another dog was sold in his place. Perhaps Midas
recovered quickly when he found out he didn't have to go! Lucky
Midas, he got to stay home, join the Royal family and become a famous
film star to millions of British children.

Stewart presented Midas to the Duke of Kent on behalf of the Great
Dane Club. The dog never left Send Kennel, but the duke came often
to watch his dog perform at Send, as did his brothers Prince Albert,
Duke of York (later George VI), and his other brother, the Duke of
Gloucester. They came to watch the races, steeplechase and hurdles.
You'll see photos shortly of a Royal family outing, watching the fun. In
this group picture, besides Stewart and the Duke of Kent holding

Left to right: Gordon Stewart, Colonel Beddoes, Prince Henry,
Mrs. Beddoes, Mrs. Gordon Stewart and Prince George with Champion
Midas of Send, given to him by Gordon Stewart. At Send Kennel.

PHOTO COURTESY GORDON V. STEWART

Midas, are seen Colonel Beddoes and his wife. Beddoes helped Stewart plan out Send Kennel and the Swiss village. Also, there is Prince George's brother, the Duke of Gloucester, and Mrs. Stewart, not wearing a hat. In a later chapter entitled, "The Midas Touch," you'll see how well trained and intelligent Midas was, as he starred in the Safety First film, *Alert To-Day — Alive To-morrow.*

Again, Prince Albert, Duke of York, enters our story. He acts in the picture with Midas, his brother's dog. The prince was patron of the National Safety First Association, which Stewart had founded in 1916. It was a powerful group of industrial leaders and members of London's Safety First Councils.

The minutes of association meetings from 1931 to 1938 show Gordon Stewart as vice-patron. The ministers of transport and of health were also vice-presidents. The secretary of mines, Lord Mayor of

London, knights, lords and ladies, armed-services generals — all belonged.

Stewart and Prince Albert, of course, became quite good friends and close associates over the years through this association. In 1933 Stewart produced and paid for the remarkable Safety First film, *Alert To-Day — Alive To-Morrow*, and Midas played the star role as the dog "Alert."

So here we have the Duke of Kent's dog in a starring role for the association film. His brother, the Duke of York, not only was patron of the association but he also appeared in the film. The minutes also show that in 1935, Stewart was now president.

On May 24, 1937, Prince Albert was crowned King George VI. But he continued on as patron of the association, with Stewart as president. In late 1936, Stewart announced the formation of the Coronation Year Safety First Crusade. He resigned from the National Safety First Association to devote full time to the new crusade. The crusade was separately run and financed by Stewart, but there would still be close co-operation between the association and the crusade.

The 1937 minutes of the association show Stewart as past president, King George VI as patron and Lord McGowan K.B.E. as president in place of Stewart. Stewart had carefully nurtured his relationship with the Duke of Kent, the Duke of Gloucester and the Duke of York, who had now become the King of England. And his Champion Midas of Send was now a distinguished member of the Royal family.

In later years Gordon Stewart, left, accompanies his friend King George VI (Prince Albert, Duke of York) to an official function at Hendon Aerodrome. PHOTO COURTESY GORDON V. STEWART

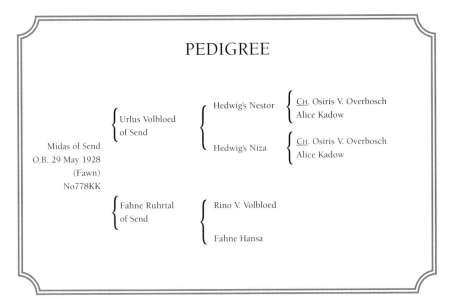

PEDIGREE

Midas of Send
O.B. 29 May 1928
(Fawn)
No778KK

- Urlus Volbloed of Send
  - Hedwig's Nestor
    - CH. Osiris V. Overbosch
    - Alice Kadow
  - Hedwig's Niza
    - CH. Osiris V. Overbosch
    - Alice Kadow
- Fahne Ruhrtal of Send
  - Rino V. Volbloed
  - Fahne Hansa

Watching the dumbbell races at Send Kennel. In background left to right: Prince George, Duke of Kent; Gordon Stewart; Prince Henry, Duke of Gloucester, with hands in pockets.

PHOTO COURTESY ANDREW MONTGOMERY

Prince George coaxes Colonel Beddoes' Alsatian over the hurdle. Left to right Prince Henry, Gordon Stewart, Colonel Beddoes, Mrs. Beddoes, Mrs. Stewart, Prince George. At Send Kennel.

PHOTO COURTESY GORDON V. STEWART

Joined by the ladies. Left to right: Colonel Beddoes, who helped Stewart plan the kennels; Gordon Stewart; Prince Henry, Duke of Gloucester; Mrs. Beddoes; Mrs. Stewart; Prince George, Duke of Kent. At Send Kennel. PHOTO COURTESY ANDREW MONTGOMERY

A hurdles race at Send for the Royal visitors. Champion Lancelot of Send leads the pack. PHOTO COURTESY ANDREW MONTGOMERY

The Duke of York hands Champion Midas a message for him to deliver to the theatre, to be read to the children. In the film, he runs along the office corridor, into the lift, along the road and waits to cross at a stoplight.

The Great Danes in Alert To-Day — Alive To-Morrow wait for a "go" signal to cross the road. Their kennel maid sits precariously over the stoplight on a scaffold.

CHAPTER FIFTEEN

The Midas Touch

Gordon Stewart and British Broadcasting Corporation's Uncle Peter (C. E. Hodges), both threw up their hands, and to the tune of "Pack Up Your Troubles in Your Old Kit Bag," belted out their Safety First campaign song:

> *Mind what you're doing*
> *When you cross the road*
> *Just stop — look — think*
> *Folks who are sensible*
> *And play the game*
> *From rash conduct shrink*
> *What's the use of scurrying*
> *To land on danger's brink*
> *So mind what you're doing*
> *When you cross the road*
> *And stop — look — think!*

Then they both roared with laughter at the astonished look on the face of the *News Review* reporter who'd come for an interview.

Hodges, very popular with England's children because of his *Uncle Peter* show on BBC radio, had helped Stewart produce a wonderful Safety First film for children called *Alert To-Day — Alive To-Morrow*.

Stewart explained to the reporter, "I was appalled to find that fourteen thousand children have been killed on our roads in the last ten years and four hundred thousand injured. As the largest distributor of motor cars in England, I have to personally do something about that. For two years now I've experimented in a certain district to educate our children to be road conscious. The experiments were based on a sound knowledge from experts on child psychology. Latest reports show,"

"Alert" (Champion Midas of Send) dives in to save "Foolish Freddie"
when the "not so bright" little boy gets into trouble in deep water.
(See film script this chapter). PHOTO COURTESY WALTER GUIVER

Stewart continued, "that road deaths in that district have been greatly reduced."

So, in 1932 he began production of the film, using his own funds and his own cinematography equipment and crew. Filmed partly on the back training areas at Send Manor and partly in London, it was a mammoth undertaking. Hours of takes were filmed to create this forty-minute-long, black-and-white talkie.

Margaret Fife Failes (nee Tracy) was there as a kennel maid. She recalls that it was filmed around Send and at Reigate and Frenshaw Ponds in Surrey. The "litterbins" scene was filmed at the Embankment in London, beside the Thames River. "We had to teach the dogs," she remembers, "to swim and rescue a drowning child. To call the fire department in Reigate and pick up banana skins."

On Friday morning, May 26, 1933, prominent dignitaries were shown the film in the Gaumont-British Picture Corporation's New Victoria Cinema, in London. The Duke of York as patron of the National Safety First Association would be there, and Stewart would present his film to the association for their use. The audience also included two thousand London schoolchildren, who were bussed to the theatre. The film was a huge success, and Stewart was delighted.

His friend, Sir Malcolm Campbell, couldn't attend, so Stewart read a message from him that he'd sent for the schoolchildren:

My dear Children:

I am very sorry that I cannot be with you today to greet you, but I have to leave for the Continent, on business, otherwise I would surely have been here.

I do so hope that you will pay very great attention to the film which you are here to see and also to the lesson which can be learned therefrom.

I do want to impress upon you the fact that to be a credit to yourselves and to the Nation, you must always regard your own personal fitness as of prime importance. Therefore, if you do happen to get injured, through lack of caution on your part, this will be a very great handicap indeed to you for the rest of your life.

I am sure that every child in this gathering will wish to achieve great things in his future life and it is only by looking after yourself that this ambition can ever be realized.

The children went wild! Sir Malcolm was their hero and at that time was probably the most famous man in Britain.

The Royal Archives at Windsor Castle were able to find the exact timetable prepared for the visit of The Duke of York to the theatre. It appears on the following pages.

SUGGESTED TIME-TABLE FOR VISIT OF
H.R.H. THE DUKE OF YORK to the New Victoria Cinema
Friday, May 26th, 1933

The occasion is the holding of a "Children's Hour" of the kind which has now been given to over 500,000 school children. About 2,000 L.C.C. school children will be present; a number of Mayors and councillors from London Boroughs; and a number of delegates to the Congress.

The "Hour" will be conducted by Mr. Meynell C. Bloomfield, the Association's area organizer, who was the pioneer of this particular form of lecture, and has already given hundreds of them all over the country.

The new sound film, which Mr. Gordon Stewart is presenting to the Association, will be shown. H.R.H. took part in some scenes in this film.

For the last few months, Mr. Gordon Stewart has devoted the majority of his time to the making of this film. A large part of his place at Send was used as a studio. Many of his Great Danes were specially trained to take part.

Sir Malcolm Campbell is amongst those who voluntarily gave their time to act in it.

The following is the suggested programme:

10.00 - 10.20 a.m.
Children arrive.

10.20
H.R.H. arrives at the WILTON ROAD entrance to the New Victoria Cinema.

He will be received by the officers:
Sir Herbert Blain - President
Mr. Gordon Stewart - Vice-Patron
Sir Gerald Bellhouse - Chairman Executive Committee
Mr. A. Hume Nicholl - Chairman London Safety First Council

10.20 - 10.28
In the alcove in the entrance hall - it is hoped that H.R.H. will have
a word with one or two persons including:
Mrs. Gordon Stewart
Mr. Isidore Ostrer - President of the Gaumont -
British Picture Corporation, Ltd.
Mr. Mark Ostrer - Chairman
(*who have lent us the Cinema for this Children's Hour, as they did last year too*)
Sir Malcolm Campbell.
The representatives from overseas safety organisations in Africa,
Australia, Holland, India and Switzerland – Names to follow.
Mr. Howard-Hodges, lately appointed Organizing Secretary of the
Association, which he has served for many years.
Mr. M.C. Bloomfield, the lecturer

10.28
H.R.H. proceeds to his seat in the theatre.

10.30
Start of Children's Hour
Mr. Bloomfield addresses the children

10.35 - 11.15
Film

11.15 – 11.20
The actors in the film go up on the stage, and are introduced by
Mr. Bloomfield

11.22
H.R.H. goes up on the stage and shakes hands or speaks to some of
the actors

11.25
Curtain lowered in front of actors. H.R.H. leaves by stage door,
whilst Mr. Bloomfield says a last few words to the children.

11.28
H.R.H. leaves

11.30
Children leave

Scenes from the film Alert To-Day — Alive To-Morrow.

PHOTO COURTESY GORDON V. STEWART

Bob Montgomery, training manager, and his assistant, Leslie Hill, worked for months selecting the right dogs and training and perfecting the routines of both the dogs and kennel-maid handlers according to the script. Some stills are reproduced here! The quality is not the best for these sixty-five-year-old shots, so please remember how old they are.

Bob Montgomery pulled out all the stops and used every trick he knew. Look at the photo of the dogs sitting on the sidewalk looking up at the stoplight (see page 168), and notice that the top of the stoplight is cut off. Cynthia Young, in an interview with my wife Shirley and me, years ago, laughed and said, "Montgomery built a kind of scaffold beside the stoplight with a platform over the light. A kennel maid crawled up on the platform over the light. The dogs, of course, knew her and were actually looking at her and not at the stoplight. The dogs are colour blind."

"Isn't that hilarious!" Young laughed and slapped her knee. Just remembering that day again was a tonic for her.

I have never been able to find a copy of that film or any others that Stewart produced. His heirs say they didn't have a copy. Neither did the association or the Royal Archives. The National Film Institute looked, and so did Gainsborough, Pinewood Studios and Gaumont-British. But what did I expect after sixty-five years?

However, the National Safety First Association did have this copy of the screen writers' script in an old file, so I'm reproducing it in its entirety for you.

Production Script Summary for the Talkie Film
"Alert To-day – Alive To-Morrow"

The opening scene shows Sir Herbert Blain, President of the National Safety First Association, seated amidst a group of children. One by one he introduces them to Sir Malcolm Campbell, "Miss Aviator," "Mr. Robot," "P.C. Robert," and "Mr. and Mrs. Red Triangle." They each deliver their special message to the children, and make their exit. Sir Herbert Blain then introduces a group of children known as the "Bright Lot who know what to do." Another group of rather sullen children appear termed "The Not-so-Bright Lot." Mr. Gordon Stewart, Vice-Patron of the Association and donor of the Film, then enters with his Champion Great Dane, "Alert," which "stars" in the Film. He tells the children that even a dog can be made to understand the meaning of "Safety First" and as an illustration the scene changes to a lonely house in the country. A baby is asleep in its pram, guarded by "Alert." A tramp approaches the house, but, directly he lays hand on the gate, the dog gives the alarm – he promptly decides that discretion is the better course. The scene now shows a blackboard and "Alert" with chalk. Close-up of paw drawing. Then follows a series of familiar sketches of people and things to whom "Safety First" is the greatest importance. A ship, with look-out man in mist; then follows Lifeboat drill. The paw draws a train; scene shows the watch kept by look-out man for workers on permanent way. Then an aeroplane takes shape; followed by scene at aerodrome – ground staff at work on 'plane – passengers boarding and 'plane taking off. Map of Miss Amy Johnson's route to Australia appears on screen, and mention is made of the immense attention paid to Safety details before the flight.

The next object drawn by the paw is a car. Scene changes to Brooklands track where Mr. Gordon Stewart is talking to Sir Malcolm Campbell, the famous motorist. Then a race and at the conclusion Sir Malcolm gives his message for all children. Once more the picture flashes back to the original group of children and Mr. Gordon Stewart invites them to go for a ride in his car, with the object of putting into practice the principles of "Safety First." As the car proceeds along the road various incidents occur – "Thoughtless Thelma" runs across the road. The "Bright Lot" give an illustration of the correct way to cross. A boy runs from behind a lorry and the "Bright Lot" again show how to look right and left before coming from behind a stationary vehicle. A boy falls from a lorry but picks himself up and runs off. It might have been serious – "stealing rides" is very dangerous. A cross-road sign comes in view, and Mr. Stewart explains to the children the need for caution. Ah! Someone has not heeded the sign – an ambulance is drawn up and St. John Ambulance men are seen giving first-aid to a careless cyclist. The next sign to be seen is a Red Triangle and here again it is explained to the children. Then a robot is inspected by the children, and the meaning of the signal lights demonstrated. A traffic pointsman regulates the traffic at another point and the "Bright Lot" cross the road in accordance with his signals. Farther on a little boy wishes to cross and is taken by a man. A schoolgirl appears and takes two smaller children across, after a careful glance each way. Mr. Stewart says that he will show them how his Great Danes carry out "Safety First" principles.

They proceed to cross the road after a careful scrutiny of the traffic lights; at the pointsman's signal; then one dog is seen with several puppies on the kerb and when the road is clear, takes them across. "Alert" the hero of the film barks his message of "Stop-Look-Think." Thoughtlessness for others is next demonstrated. Boys are seen playing football on the kerb – a blind man appears led by his dog and Mr. Stewart warns the children of the hazard of throwing things at passing motorists. Some children walk by, dropping banana-skins on the pavement. The Great Danes, with almost human intelligence, pick up the skins and carry them to the refuse bin. Next the scene shows a boy in a boat, he stands up and immediately goes overboard, but "Alert" is there and rescues the boy. Next scene shows the boy learning that very useful accomplishment – swimming. The car with its occupants, Mr. Stewart and children, proceeds along the country road and draws up opposite a couple of cyclists. One of them is questioning the other regarding the correct position of rear reflector and this is shown in a

*"Alert," at the end of the movie, carries a message from
His Royal Highness, the Duke of York (later King George VI),
and waits to safely cross the road. Alert rushes into the theatre and
Gordon Stewart reads it to the children.* PHOTO COURTESY GORDON V. STEWART

close-up. Mr. Stewart interrogates the boys regarding correct hand-signalling for cyclists and they demonstrate. The car goes on and a hospital is reached where the children go inside. General view of ward occupied by members of the "Not-so-Bright Lot" who are now suffering from the results of their disregard of "Safety First" rules. "Carless Carrie" lies in bed, swathed in bandages. Left at home one day to bath the baby, she filled the bath with boiling water, dashed out to get some cold water and on her return started playing with the dog, and in doing so fell backwards into the boiling water. The next patient is "Clumsy Clara" who fell over the scooter, which she had carelessly left across the hall floor. "Meddlesome Mike" is another small patient as a result of serious burns. His story is also told by the film. The next scene shows how "Meddlesome Mike" received his injuries through playing with matches. He drops them about and the house is set on fire. A man runs out of the house and sounds the fire-alarm. The Great Danes, however, race madly along the streets to the Fire Station and give the alarm. The fire engine turns out and there follows a good demonstration of fire-fighting. "Meddlesome Mike" is rescued by the firemen. Then Mr. Stewart talks to the children.

The next portion of the film deals with the visit of H.R.H. The Duke of York to the Association's new offices at Terminal House. H.R.H. is seen signing a message to the children which he hands to "Alert." The dog runs along the corridor and into the lift. He emerges from the lift and runs along the street. At the corner he awaits the pointsman's signal before crossing, then is seen entering cinema, runs through the tea-room and gives up his message. A close-up of the message follows which reads:

Dear Children,

Always keep a good look out. If you are going to succeed in life, you must keep your eyes open and your wits awake.

So I ask you to remember the rules that you have learnt here. Obey those rules yourselves, and help other people to do the same.

(signed) ALBERT.

The final scene shows a lighthouse which slowly dissolves into that well known symbol of the the red triangle.

National Safety First Association

The outstanding tricks and performance of Midas of Send throughout this long film production were remarkable, to say the least, and these stills will show you some of that.

I know of no other canine performance anywhere in the world to equal that "Midas touch," and the professionalism of this film in 1932–33 (the early days of making talking movies in England) showed once again that Stewart only went first class.

*The model of "Alert" (Champion Midas of Send) presented by the
Safety First Association on May 24, 1933. It is silver on bronze.
Sculpted by Ernst von Otto, and now owned by the author.*

PHOTO BY RON DICKENSON

In 1986 I was asked to attend Crufts Dog Show to autograph my
book, *He Whacked the Bloody Lot*, about my pal Bill Siggers. The
publisher (*Dogs Monthly* and Andrew Brace) had a booth for this
purpose at the show at Earls Court in London.

My wife, Shirley, came up to me and said, "You'd better come with
me. There's a Dane model for sale that you'd better see."

I followed her to an antique dealer's trade stand, and featured there
was the most beautiful Dane statue I'd ever seen. Finished in gilt (silver on
bronze) and so finely sculpted, after casting, that the fine hairs on the coat
were visible all over. Most good models are just smooth bronze castings.

On the black wooden plinth was a small silver shield that just said:

"Alert"

May, 1933

Presented To

Gordon Stewart, Esq.

By His Grateful Colleagues Of

The National "Safety First" Association

I asked the antique dealer what the model was and he said he didn't know, some lady had asked him to try to sell it at Crufts. Through some hard checking, I found out later that the lady was Betty Moodie (nee Turner) who'd been a kennel maid at Send and featured in Stewart's will when he died in 1952. More about that later.

Well, I knew what the model was and who the dog was, from my research on Stewart, even way back then. I was probably lucky that no one else at Crufts knew. I asked the price and almost cried!

Shirley and I had brought money for the trip, of course, and when we totalled all that up and threw in all our credit card balances, I was still one thousand pounds short. I went back and told Andrew Brace about the model, and he quickly said, "I owe you more than a thousand pounds in commissions on the book right now!"

Andrew came with me, and he knew the dealer. He promised to pay him the funds, and I took "Alert" home to Canada. I'm looking at that wonderful model as I write this. It was sculpted by the German, Ernst von Otto, and is one of a kind, commissioned especially by the Safety First Association for a presentation of gratitude to Stewart. It's about twelve inches long and stands about twelve inches high on its black plinth. Very heavy. I've had a photo taken of it for you to see.

On Wednesday, May 24, 1933, there was a private showing of the film before its debut on Friday, May 26, at the theatre. At that meeting, Sir Herbert Blain, the president, presented Gordon Stewart with this silver replica of "Alert," the dog that stars in the film. It's the one I found at Crufts.

He went on to say that the association "owes so much to Gordon Stewart, for in December 1916, Stewart organized and called the first small meeting, out of which grew the National Safety First Association.

"The people of Great Britain always thought," said Sir Herbert, "that the money for such associations came from the Carnegie Trust or some other invisible force.

"But in fact," he continued, "Gordon Stewart provided the force, the service and the financing for the association to go ahead."

In answer, Stewart replied, "I've always felt that my friend Sir

Gordon Stewart, left, welcomes His Royal Highness Prince Albert,
Duke of York (later King George VI), to the New Victoria Cinema
to view the premiere of Alert To-Day — Alive To-Morrow.

Herbert Blain was the father of the National Safety First Association
and feel like a virtuous son who has just received his father's blessing."

Laughter and applause followed.

Most pleasing to Stewart was the sight of his long-time friend, Sir
Malcolm Campbell, with Lady Campbell and their little daughter
sitting in the front row of the meeting that day, paying homage to
Stewart and throwing their weight behind this wonderful crusade for
children's safety.

RECEPTION BY MR. GORDON STEWART

One of the most unique functions during the Congress was the visit to Send Manor on the evening of Wednesday, 24th May, when the Association's Vice-Patron, Mr. Gordon Stewart, very kindly entertained the delegates.

During the evening there was a private showing of the new Safety First "Talkie" Film which Mr. Gordon Stewart has generously made and presented to the Association; and a most attractive performance by some of Mr. Stewart's specially trained Great Danes, several of which figure prominently in the new film.

On behalf of the Association Sir Herbert Blain, the President, presented Mr. Gordon Stewart with a silver replica of "Alert," the dog which takes the leading rôle in the film. Sir Herbert Blain expressed the thanks of the company to Mr. Stewart for the unique entertainment they had witnessed. There was, he went on, no one more entitled to say what the Association owes to Mr. Gordon Stewart than himself, for in December, 1916, he called the first meeting, out of which had arisen the National Safety First Association with its undoubted usefulness to the whole country. The people of Great Britain were curious folk, in that they always thought that such movements were subsidised by the Carnegie Trust or that the money came from some other invisible source! The only thing they complained about was that more work was not done! (Laughter.) Someone found Mr. Gordon Stewart to help the National Safety First Association, and from the day he was introduced to the work, he had not only given service of a personal character, but had been generous to a degree. He was sure that with Mr. Stewart it was a

Sir Herbert Blain presenting Mr. Gordon Stewart with a replica of "Alert."

labour of love, but he wanted him to know how deeply grateful the Association was for what he had done and for what he was doing. There was too little expression of the gratitude due to public-spirited men.

Not the least important and certainly the most successful work the Association had been able to do was the education of children in "Safety First" principles. That was clearly proved by the investigation into fatal accidents. Fewer children of school age were implicated in those accidents than in any other age of human life. The "Children's Hours" were a most important feature of the Association's educational work, and Mr. Gordon Stewart had been good enough to present the Association with a new film. He was inclined to think that paying for the film was the least part of what Mr. Stewart had put into it, and that the name "Patience" should be added to those he already possessed.

It was really very difficult to express what they thought of Mr. Stewart in his presence. He hoped Mr. Stewart would realise that there was no one connected with the movement who did not honour him for his generosity and love him for his personality.

Replying, Mr. Gordon Stewart described Sir Herbert Blain as the "Father of the National Safety First Association," and said he felt like a virtuous son who had just received his father's blessing. (Laughter and applause.)

Among those present, in addition to the Officers and Executive Committee of the National Safety First Association, were Sir Malcolm and Lady Campbell and their little daughter.

The presentation of the model "Alert" to Gordon Stewart, right, by Sir Herbert Blain on May 24, 1933.

Gordon Stewart hands the Duke of York the Safety First Association's
charter at their new offices at Terminal House, London. "Alert,"
Champion Midas of Send awaits his instructions.

PHOTO COURTESY GORDON V. STEWART

CHAPTER SIXTEEN

The Duke of Kent

P rince George couldn't make it to the film premiere of his Great Dane, Midas. He'd gone to ground, to stay out of the public eye.

It was in that year, 1932, that the diplomat Sir Robert Bruce Lockhart wrote in his diary about the duke's scandal with a young man in Paris. A princely sum was paid to get back letters the duke had written to him.

Queen Elizabeth's problems today with her sons Prince Charles and Prince Andrew are tame stuff compared to what the Royal family endured with Prince George throughout the twenties and thirties.

He was about twenty in 1922, when he met Noel Coward. Coward later proclaimed he'd taken the duke's virginity in his dressing room. The world-famous actor was performing the play, *London Calling*, by coincidence, at the Duke of York's Theatre in London's St. Martin's Lane.

Coward was quoted as saying, "We had a little dalliance. He was absolutely enchanting, and I never stopped loving him." The affair didn't last long.

But the frivolous duke chose a dissolute bisexual lifestyle and throughout the twenties ran through a string of well-known ladies and gents with gay abandon. His worst scare was the police raid on a low-life night club called the Nut House, a hangout for gays. Prince George was scooped up in the raid in the company of a homosexual friend, but his identity wasn't discovered until after he'd spent the night in the cells.

Homosexuality was against the law in Britain then, and the palace had to pull out all the stops to prevent the duke's ruin.

Women formed a part of his life too. An early mistress, Freda Dudley Ward, called him "shallow and frivolous." But mistresses cast aside have a tendency to say such nasty things. His night-life affairs also included a debutante — Lois Sturt. Then on to Poppy Baring, who was the banking heiress. Baring Bank was caught up in the Asian financial scandal a few years back, which virtually sealed its fate; at that time it was revealed that Barings held large accounts for the Royal family.

Prince George then met a grandson of the Kaiser, and they became an item. Prince Louis Ferdinand of Prussia described his new partner as "artistic and effeminate and I loved his use of strong perfume."

Then along came Jorge Ferara, whom everyone, except the duke, knew to be a corrupt Argentine. They were joined by the flamboyant heiress from the United States, Kiki Whitney Preston. Kiki was truly kinky, and the ménage à trois was on. But Kiki was mega trouble indeed, as she was also known as "the girl with the silver syringe." Sadly, she started the prince on a downhill slide with cocaine and morphine.

George's big brother came to the rescue. The Prince of Wales, later to abdicate the throne for Wallis Simpson, had Ferara brought to him at St. James Palace.

"You will leave England at once," the prince roared at Ferara. "Where do we send your bags?"

Ferara tossed his head and replied disdainfully, "To Paris. To the Prince of Wales Hotel."

The Prince of Wales then rented a house in Berkshire, quite near Sunningdale. A group of private nurses were brought in, and the house sealed off from anyone else by tight security. We cannot imagine the horror of those torturous few weeks, when Prince George endured his withdrawal from drugs — cold turkey.

When King George V was made aware of his son's problems, he was devastated. He thought marriage and a family would be the answer for the prince. So Prince George became engaged in August 1934, to his cousin Princess Marina of Greece.

But Noel Coward couldn't keep his mouth shut. He was heard to comment, bitterly, "Poor darling. She knew what she was in for."

Then the unimaginable happened. George V died, and the next in line, the elder brother the Prince of Wales, was to become king. But before he was crowned, he announced that he would marry the divorcee Wallis Simpson and give up the throne.

All hell broke loose for the Royal family and for the British government. The next in line, Stewart's friend Prince Albert, Duke of York, wasn't sure he wanted the job. He only wanted a quiet private life with his family. The British Parliament thought he might be too withdrawn to be an effective king, and it certainly appeared that war with Germany could be possible in the very near future. England needed someone strong.

The next in line was the problematic Prince George. The Secret Service files on his escapades were crammed full of all his instabilities.

So there was a great sigh of relief all around when Prince Albert, Duke of York, was finally crowned King George VI in May 1937.

Stewart had never imagined in all his wildest dreams that his close friend "Bertie" would one day be the King of England. Sadly enough, Prince George's unhappy life would end tragically on August 25, 1942. Thirty-two minutes after flying out of Invergordon, on the far north coast of Scotland in a Sunderland flying boat, the prince and fourteen other passengers were instantly killed. The plane crashed into the cliffs at Eagle's Rock in Caithness.

The captain, Flight Lieutenant Frank Goyen, was blamed. The report read out in the House Of Commons simply stated that the captain "took the wrong flight plan."

But is that what really happened? There was one survivor, who lived until 1978 and said nothing. But when he died, his widow, Elspeth Jack, claimed her husband had told her quite another story. He said the Prince and the crew had been boozing it up heavily before the flight, and he claimed that Prince George was flying the plane and not Flight Lieutenant Goyen.

However, the palace shut the door on all investigative reports — everything to do with Queen Elizabeth's uncle is still sealed up. None of Prince George's papers in the Royal Archives are available to the public to this day.

What makes it worse is that the crash reports and investigation documents that should have been in the files of the public records office are not there. They've all just mysteriously disappeared.

The palace does not allow biographers to write about the Duke of Kent. He is, without doubt, still the greatest embarrassment to the Royal family.

The secretive mystery, of course, started all kinds of vicious rumours. Did the prince commit suicide to end his unhappy life? Was it just a drunken accident? Then came the most vicious one of all — was the prince the victim of a planned assassination? The victim of his amorous, dissolute way of life over the past twenty years?

It is inconceivable that Stewart knew nothing of the problems surrounding Prince George in the 1920s and 1930s. He was too well connected. He did not need George as an introduction to the Royal family. Stewart had been working with his brother, Prince Albert, for a long time. Albert was patron of the National Safety First Association founded by Stewart in 1916, and Stewart was president. So they saw each other quite frequently, as good friends will do.

Stewart was often seen at 145 Piccadilly Street, where Albert lived with his wife, Elizabeth. The prince had a problem with stammering, and Stewart said he'd often met with Bertie to try to train him to speak around the problem. He and Albert had become close friends long before Stewart met George.

Stewart met Prince George through the Great Dane Club. George was its patron, and on behalf of that club, Stewart had presented him with his prized Champion Great Dane, Midas of Send. Prince George was not an habitual visitor to Send Manor — certainly not on public show or race days. Whenever Royal family members came to Send to see the dogs, the visits were private affairs.

In all the research I've done, and with all the people I've spoken to who knew Gordon Stewart, I've never heard an unkind word. Indeed, he was always portrayed as sincerely kind and considerate. Helpful, in any way he could be, to everyone.

So perhaps Stewart, the thoughtful man that he was, just extended a helping hand to a man who really needed sincere friends. He thought of Prince George as a friend in need, and left it at that.

Sir Malcolm Campbell's aeroplane that he designed, built and crashed in 1909. PHOTO COURTESY THE BROOKLANDS MUSEUM

Sir Malcolm Campbell in his 1928 Bluebird. He set the land speed record of 206.96 miles per hour in Daytona Beach, Florida.
PHOTO COURTESY THE BROOKLANDS MUSEUM

CHAPTER SEVENTEEN

Sir Malcolm Campbell

I n life there are ordinary men who do extraordinary things. Men and women who strive unknowingly to throw off the harness of convention, who break the bonds of what the world expects young people to do. There are men and women who must go where no one else has gone, whom mothers never understand, and fathers beg to "just go out and get a regular job."

Such a young man was Malcolm Campbell.

Born in 1885, the very same year as Stewart, at Chislehurst, Kent, Campbell was educated at a prep school near Guildford, Surrey, and went on to Uppingham Public School in Rutland, Leicester. He was the son of William Campbell, a wealthy Scottish jeweller and diamond merchant at Cheapside in London.

At fifteen Malcolm Campbell was sent to Germany to work in an engineering works and, it was hoped, learn German and a bit about business. The following year was spent in France to do the same. In his seventeenth year, his father set him up in business with a friend at the insurance company Lloyds, while he was still living at his parents' home in Kent.

He took an interest in motorcycles, and after racing those, at age twenty-three entered his first motor-car race in a 1903 Renault.

Campbell saw the birth of a new idea — that men could learn to fly — and on a trip to Selfridge's Department Store, he was able to examine Bleriots's 1909 cross-channel monoplane that was on display. Later that year, he went to the first European Aviation Meeting held in Rheims, France, and was hooked.

Malcolm Campbell vowed he was going to fly.

He rented a farm building near Orpington, Kent, and began building his own plane from his own design. But when he tried to fly it, down he went. He modified his design, but crashed again. In frustration, and with the realization that perhaps this wasn't quite his thing, the plane was sold for scrap for twenty-two pounds.

In 1913 he married his first wife and soon found himself in the Royal West Regiment as a second lieutenant. But by 1915 he was able to transfer to the Royal Flying Corps. He finally learned to fly at RFC Gosport, in Hampshire, and ferried new planes to France, then flew back slightly damaged ones for repair.

By 1916–17 he was a flying instructor at Coventry, and even published five thousand copies of a booklet, *Hints to Beginners on Flying*, telling his students to stay away from building their own planes. Campbell was promoted to captain and awarded the Medal of the British Empire before leaving the service in 1919.

In 1920, at age thirty-five, Malcolm Campbell inherited two hundred and fifty thousand pounds at his father's death and promptly bought his own private aeroplane. It was while struggling with his own design and crashes that Stewart met Campbell. Stewart had his Mulliner 1 Monoplane designed, built and showing at the first Aero Show at Olympia in 1910.

They met again at Brooklands Race Track in 1913–14. Campbell now had a keen interest in the motor-car trade, and Stewart was promoting his Morris Oxford to gain recognition and publicity for his new Morris agency in London.

Campbell first raced cars as early as 1910 at the Brooklands track. He called those early cars the "Flapper," after a favourite race horse.

But by 1912 he became really serious about his career in racing. After seeing Maeterlinck's play, *The Bluebird of Happiness*, he went home and repainted his old 1906 Darracq the colour blue, because he thought it would be lucky for him. That was an idle wish, I guess, because in his first attempt with his newly painted blue racer, both right wheels fell off, and he finished the race precariously balancing on the two left ones.

But fate pushed Campbell on. He became better and better, driving Peugeot, Renault, Charron and Gregoire racing cars. By now the smell

The 1935 Bluebird. Sir Malcolm Campbell in the cockpit,
while his son Donald looks on.

of oil, the track dust and the booming noise of the motors were in his blood. His offices at Lloyds and his father's legacy in 1920 gave Campbell the backing he needed to finance good cars. He campaigned with Talbots, a GP Peugeot, a Fiat, a Ballot and a Chrysler.

All very serious, fast stuff indeed.

In 1913 he bought Louis Coatalen's old 350-horsepower, V-12 Sunbeam that Kenelm Lee Guiness had been racing. Malcolm Campbell finally reached for his star at Pendine Sands in Wales. On that day in March 1925, he averaged 146.16 miles per hour and knew he would one day break the world record.

In 1930 he clocked five miles faster, but his car was now too old, so he finally began work in earnest on his record-breaking "Bluebirds." When he felt he was ready, he took his new Bluebird to Daytona Beach, Florida, to try to break the world's record. In 1928 he did it, with an amazing speed of 206.96 miles per hour.

Soon Ray Keech, later knighted Sir Henry Segrave, would better that speed.

In 1931 Malcolm Campbell received his knighthood from George V, the Duke of York and Duke of Kent's father. That same year, Campbell, with his new Rolls-Royce-powered and engineered Bluebird, set a two-way average speed of 246.09 miles per hour and by 1930 drove over 300 miles per hour on the salt flats in Utah.

In 1932, soon after Campbell was knighted, Stewart called him to work on the children's Safety First film, *Alert To-Day — Alive To-Morrow*. Campbell gladly agreed to help his old friend.

You have already read that Prince Albert, Duke of York, appeared in the film with Sir Malcolm, as did Stewart. The star was Champion Midas of Send who played "Alert."

Although a hero to most in England, to others Sir Malcolm was seen as a bit of a cad.

One of these people was the writer Wentworth Day. He'd written a book called *The Boys Life of Sir Henry Segrave*. You'll remember Segrave beat Campbell's speed record set in 1928.

The publisher reasoned that the book would sell more if Sir Malcolm Campbell was shown as the author, as his name was revered by every school boy in Britain. So Wentworth Day had to agree to let Campbell's name go on the book for a deal to split half the royalties. A good deal for Day, really, as he earned far more in commissions than he would have done as the listed author. The book was a tremendous hit.

Campbell went around England taking all the credit. Even at those events attended by Day, the real author.

Sir Malcolm had guts. Two years later, he asked Wentworth to come to his house. He wanted him to ghost-write another book, entitled *My Greatest Adventure*, but with Campbell listed as the author. These two men knew their limitations. Campbell couldn't write books and Day couldn't race cars. So they made a deal again, and both made good money.

Campbell's chief mechanic, Leo Villa, himself a race-car legend and a loyal servant, was the real genius behind Campbell's great racing success. But even he was heard to remark, "He's so mean he wouldn't give you the time of day, even though it's free."

Wentworth Day later became the personal representative to Lady Lucy Houston, DBE, undoubtedly the richest woman in Britain at the time, with a wealth of about six million pounds — a great fortune in those days. Wentworth's job was to run interference between Lady Lucy and all those trying to strip her of her cash. One morning, Day recalls, he was summoned to her room to review the day's appointments and mail. Lady Lucy was elegantly propped up in her massive bed with a Union Jack draped around her. She glared at Day, her blonde wig sitting lopsided on her head. For some reason she was hot about Sir Malcolm Campbell. "If your friend Campbell wants someone to pay for his funeral, he must go someplace else," Lady Lucy snarled. "His father left him plenty of money. Why doesn't he use some of that?

"He talks about doing something for the country," she hollered. "That's a lot of rubbish. What he really wants is someone who will do something for Campbell, the publicity seeker."

Lady Lucy had just received a note from Sir Malcolm, soliciting funds for Stewart's children's safety drive.

Was that why Sir Malcolm gladly appeared in Stewart's film? To be seen again and worshipped by six million school children? Who knows. But Stewart knew how to capitalize on using people. And if Sir Malcolm Campbell could benefit as well, then it was a good deal for both men and a better deal for the children of England, who greatly benefitted from these safety campaigns.

After turning his efforts to seeking the World Water Speed Record, Sir Malcolm's eyesight worsened. In his later years, he was mostly ill and remained at home.

On New Year's Eve in 1949, Sir Malcolm Campbell died at the age of sixty-four, just three years before Stewart's death on January 21, 1952. These two ordinary men, who were born in 1885 and whose extraordinary lives crossed many times, both left the world in their sixties. But in those six decades the two of them led the most interesting, daring, storybook lives imaginable.

Sir Malcolm Campbell's fame lives on, but whatever happened to Gordon Stewart?

CHAPTER EIGHTEEN

The Hound of the Baskervilles

I n 1932, sound in motion pictures was in its very early years in Britain and around the world. Because it was new, Stewart learned all he could about cinematography. He saw the potential for this not only as entertainment, but as a new dimension for commercial promotion. It would be a wonderful tool for publicity campaigns on his Morris cars, because now a vocal message could be delivered by prominent personalities to generate new sales. Now you could appeal to the extra sense of sound as well as sight.

At the opposite end of the Karinda Hut, from his office on the gallery, Stewart built a production room for his movie cameras and other cinematography equipment. Beside it was his darkroom.

He was an idea man with great vision, so he could develop scripts and envisage scenes for his productions. His wealth enabled him to be producer as well as director, so he could control all aspects of the films as he wished.

Alert To-Day — Alive To-Morrow was scripted, directed, produced and filmed by Stewart and was a huge success. Obviously it not only got the message across, delivered by famous celebrities, but it showed for the first time that well-trained animals, as actors, held enormous appeal.

AT LEFT: *An actual still photo from the Gainsborough 1932 movie,* The Hound of the Baskervilles. *Champion Egmund of Send, who played the star role in the film as the hound, has just been shot by Sherlock Holmes. Here he plays out his death scene. Note the bloody bullet wounds to his neck and heart. Filmed on the moors of Dartmoor in Devonshire, England. 1932.*

Stewart and his Great Danes caught the attention of all the major studios in Britain. Gainsborough, Pinewood, British-Gaumont, and J. Arthur Rank all realized that now they could make movies with animals to faithfully portray popular books that they had had to reject before. They contacted Send for the Great Danes.

Indeed, the chairman and the president of British Gaumont Studio had both attended Stewart's premiere of the Alert film in the New Victoria Cinema.

A young man named Michael Balcon, who had established Gainsborough Studios in 1928, took particular notice. Balcon in later years would head up British-Gaumont, Ealing and MGM British Studios. He also discovered a young British director named Alfred Hitchcock, and liked what he saw. Together they produced many outstanding, successful movies, including the masterpiece *The Thirty Nine Steps*.

One evening Stewart received a call at Send Manor, and Balcon introduced himself. He told Stewart he'd bought the movie rights to the classic Arthur Conan Doyle mystery *The Hound of the Baskervilles*. Stewart had read the Sherlock Holmes book and knew that the story centred around a legendary ferocious beast on the moors that attacked the heirs of the Baskerville family.

Balcon wanted one of Stewart's Great Danes to play the hound, and when Stewart agreed to work with him he sent a copy of the screen play to Stewart's office in London.

Stewart brought the script home and sat down with his trainer Bob Montgomery to go over every scene. Bob did not agree that Midas should be used again — he felt that another male trained specifically to do these scenes would be a better and safer idea.

Bob selected his assistant Leslie Hill and handler Nora West to work with him on this. Weeks of intense training were planned and carried out at Send Manor. Word got out about the planned production of the Gainsborough film, and a newspaper reporter wrote an item that the new movie would star the Great Dane Hans of Send.

That reporter hadn't done his homework, because the dog trained and used in the production was, in fact, the huge fawn Dane, Champion

At rehearsal. Champion Egmund of Send teaches John Stuart
(playing Sir Henry Baskerville) how to act out a scene on
the Dartmoor moors. From the 1932 Gainsborough
production of The Hound of the Baskervilles.

Egmund of Send. Balcon and his director, V. Gareth Gundrey, came to Send as the training progressed, and screen tests for Egmund's acting, growls, barks and snarls turned out perfectly for the part.

It was a feature film in black and white and the first talkie of any Sherlock Holmes adventure.

Nora West, now Mrs. Napoliello of Colorado, still remembers travelling to Pinewood Studios with Leslie Hill and Egmund for days and days of shooting. Some scenes were shot on the back lot at Send Manor. The eerie misty "Scottish" exteriors were actually filmed on the moors of Dartmoor, in Devonshire.

A review of the film obtained from the National Film Institute's archives shows the stars as:

Robert Rendel — Sherlock Holmes

Frederick Lloyd — Dr. Watson

John Stuart — Sir Henry Baskerville

Reginald Bach — Stapleton

Heather Engel — Beryl

Wilfred Shure — Dr. Mortimer

Sam Livesey — Sir Hugo

Elizabeth Vaughn — Mrs. Laura Lyons

Sybil Jane — Mrs. Barrymore

Leonard Hayes — Cartwright

Henry Hallett — Barrymore

Champion Egmund of Send — The Hound of the Baskervilles

It was given a two-and-one-half star rating.

The director of this 1932 classic was V. Gareth Gundrey; the screenwriter, Edgar Wallace; the cinematographer, Bernard Knowles and film editor Ian Dalrymple. You probably remember Basil Rathbone, Wendy Barrie, Nigel Bruce and John Carradine in the picture, but that was a much later version produced by Fox Studios in 1939.

Critics of the Gainsborough film said it "was flawed and suffered from questionable casting decisions." But Egmund's performance was rated first class.

The 1932 Gainsborough film is thought to be lost, as only a few short sequences remain, and the sound track has completely disappeared. It is probable that a few prints do still remain in private collections, but Stewart's copy, which he often showed to house guests on his projection equipment, simply vanished at his death.

Here you will see the only existing still photo of Egmund acting out his death scene on the moor. The scene begins with Sherlock Holmes and Dr. Watson hiding by the rocks along the path on the moor. It's a strange, eerie night of heavy, swirling fog. Sir Henry Baskerville passes them, hurrying along the stony path. Then out of the dense fog charges a huge, ferocious, snarling beast after Sir Henry, glowing in the dark — a frightening ghost of the moors.

Sherlock and Watson each fire a shot. The beast screams horribly, but rushes on. Sherlock chases after it, and just before it attacks Sir Henry, he empties five shots from his revolver into the side of the lunging animal. It dies, writhing, moaning and frothing on the moor.

Sherlock finds it's a huge dog, covered in phosphorus to give it that hideous glow in the dark. Here, in this rare still, you see Champion Egmund of Send dying on the moor with bleeding bullet wounds to his neck and heart.

A wonderful, gripping performance by Egmund and Send trainer Bob Montgomery.

Gordon Stewart, left, and William Morris (Lord Nuffield)
sign the charter for the Children's Safety Crusade in 1936.

PHOTO COURTESY HARRY EDWARDS

Some of the Morris Children's Safety Crusade vans lined up outside
Send Manor, on Ripley Green in Surrey, 1937.

PHOTO COURTESY GORDON V. STEWART

CHAPTER NINETEEN

The Pied Piper of Hamelin

Jack Townsend lived in the village of Ripley, south of London, in Surrey. And he was sure Gordon Stewart had gone mad.

Stewart had sent for Jack to come to see him at Send Manor. He pedalled his bike from the village and was directed to a beautiful building that looked like a Swiss chalet. Townsend climbed the staircase to Stewart's office and looked around him in awe. He had never been to Switzerland, but he'd seen pictures of chalets like this one in magazines and books.

Townsend was the one everyone called to get the pests and vermin out of their homes and shops. He'd seen lots of buildings, but nothing like this one.

Stewart opened his office door and greeted him.

"Good-day to you Townsend," he said. "Thanks for coming out. Sit down. I've a proposition to put to you."

Stewart walked behind his desk and sat looking at Townsend. He smiled warmly and said, "I want you to catch a few hundred rats and bring them over here to Send Manor."

His grin widened as he watched Townsend's expression.

That's when Townsend knew that Stewart was a madman. People got him to drive rats away — not catch 'em.

"But I need them alive," Stewart continued, "and as big as you can find them." Townsend almost fell off his chair. "You see, Townsend," said the Lord of Send Manor, "I'm going to make a moving picture that will require a lot of rats. You'll be working with Albert Hepburn, who's going to train them for me. I'll pay you well. What do you say?"

"I'll be damned," was all Townsend could say.

"Well, Mr. Stewart," he finally offered slowly, while he rubbed his rough, gnarled fingers over his forehead. "Catching rats that are still alive is not quite my line. I usually just kill 'em. But if you say you want 'em alive, then you'll get 'em alive."

Townsend hesitated a bit and warily watched Stewart's eyes. "It'll cost ya a bit more you see."

"Agreed," shot back Stewart. "When can you get started?"

"I guess first thing at dawn," answered Townsend. "But where will we put 'em when I catch 'em?"

"Leave that to me," said Stewart. "I'll see to it. You just contact Reg Giles here when you're ready."

Reg Giles, the foreman/carpenter at Send Manor, was given instructions by Albert Hepburn, the proposed rat trainer, on how to build the cages they'd need to hold the captured rats. Giles was also given the plans to build a whole authentic European village street at the back of the Send Manor property. That would be the village of Hamelin set for the film. Stewart planned and personally directed the construction, as well as funded it. This movie would be his modern version of *The Pied Piper of Hamelin*.

Now you can just imagine the stories that went around the villages of Ripley and Send. Reg Giles, Albert Hepburn and old Jack Townsend couldn't wait to hit the pub each night, and as their stories grew so did the eyes of the villagers. But Stewart hadn't gone mad. He would produce a film that all England would talk about in a few months.

Stewart could no longer control the National Safety First Association that he'd founded — it had gotten too big and successful. Too many stiff old codgers running it with no imagination at all. Too much bureaucracy now.

"A man can't do a job and get attention that way," he mused. So he resigned from the National Safety First Association to devote his time to this new venture.

His idea all began in 1936. The next May his friend Prince Albert, the Duke of York, would be crowned George VI, King of England. Stewart had developed a plan to further help the children of England, and he'd throw all his finances and marketing skills behind his Children's Safety Crusade, to commemorate Albert's coronation year.

The inaugural luncheon for the launching of the Children's Safety Crusade held at the Savoy Hotel, London, on December 2, 1936. Left to right: Minister of Transport, Lord Leslie Hore-Belisha; Gordon Stewart; and Bill Morris (Lord Nuffield).

* * * * * * *

Stewart's Daimler pulled up at the entrance to the Savoy Hotel in London. His chauffeur jumped out to open his door, and he stepped onto the pavement and looked up at this grand old building. It was just before noon on December 2, 1936, and the holiday spirit had taken over the hotel.

The entrance was covered with the twinkling lights and crystal angels of Christmas. The huge, ornate lobby was aglow with decorations, and a massive fir tree stood in the centre, beautifully dressed for the holiday season.

"Right this way, Mr. Stewart," the Savoy manager said, as he swept his distinguished guest along. "Many of your guests are here already, in the salon outside your private dining room. I thought we'd receive your friends there with refreshments and then proceed to the tables in the great hall. The menu is just as you directed, sir!"

The people who had assembled and others still arriving read like a who's who of Britain — the titled gentry, ministers of state, and barons of business. Anyone who was anybody was invited by Stewart, and they all came.

Guests included the Duke of Richmond, his old friend Lord Nuffield (William Morris), Lord Iliffe, Lord De La Warr, Lord Greenway, Lord Elton, Sir Arthur Griffith-Boscawem, Sir Lynden Macassey, Sir George Sutton, his pal Sir Malcolm Campbell, Sir Cyril Hurcomb, Sir Henry Pelham, Sir George Mitcheson MP, Sir Patrick Hannon MP, Sir Robert Evans, Captain Austin Hudson MP, Sir Gerald Bellhouse, Sir Charles Igglesden, Sir Ernest Renn, Sir Frederick Hobday, Sir Stenson Cooke, Mr. J. Henderson Stewart JP, Lieutenant-Colonel J. A. A. Pickard and the Minister of Transport, Mr. Hore-Belisha.

The luncheon menu and vintage wines were superb and impeccably served.

As they began their coffee and cigars, Stewart rose and welcomed them. He thanked them for coming and launched right into his plan for his new Children's Safety Crusade.

"The crusade will use every device to appeal to eye and ear. We'll cover every city, town, village and hamlet in England," Stewart began. "We'll contact and work closely with every youth organization we can find. We'll make use of films, gramophone records, stories, verse, puzzles, painting books and children's games. Anything children like will become a marketing tool for the campaign."

He held up a printed card. "Children will be asked to take this pledge and sign this card. 'I promise to do my best to obey the rules of safety when I am on the roads, when I am at home, when I am at work and when I am at play and to try to help others do the same.'"

Stewart was at his best! The flamboyant car salesman burst forth as he excited and worked up his audience. This was what Stewart did best, and what he was born to do. He was a promoter, and promote the Children's Safety Crusade he did. He explained why the Pied Piper symbol was chosen to appeal to the children, then unveiled the crusade's symbol — the traditional Pied Piper, changed a bit to fit

CORONATION YEAR CHILDREN'S SAFETY CRUSADE

INAUGURAL LUNCHEON
AT THE SAVOY HOTEL, DECEMBER 2nd, 1936

MENU

Huîtres de Whitstable
Hors d'œuvres de Choix
Saumon Fumé

—

Turbotin Gallieni

—

Faisan Doré Smitane
Croquettes Washington
Céleri au Gratin
Salade de Saison

—

Soufflé Paquita
Petits Fours

The actual luncheon menu planned by Gordon Stewart for the launching of the crusade.
SAVOY HOTEL ARCHIVES
FROM DECEMBER 2, 1936.

modern times and carrying the green torch of safety. This was the appeal for the children.

"This symbol," continued Stewart, "will be known to everyone in England in just a few months. The film we'll produce will be a modern version of *The Pied Piper of Hamelin*, and seen by every child in the country," he explained. "Within months, the children will be singing our campaign songs that we'll introduce with the help of our famous film and stage-star friends who are helping with the campaign."

"Why am I proposing this campaign?" Stewart asked his audience. "Because every half hour people are being killed by road accidents and are injured every thirty seconds. A large number of these are our children."

An excerpt from the luncheon program launching the Children's Safety Crusade, December 2, 1936. Signed by Bill Morris (Nuffield), Lord Hore-Belisha and Gordon Stewart.

The minister of transport hung on every word Stewart said. This was the worrisome political problem his government was facing every day.

As Stewart finished his talk, the crowd roared their approval of his plan. The Minister of Transport, Mr. Hore-Belisha, rose to his feet, and the guests grew silent.

"My government entirely endorses Mr. Stewart's plan to protect the children of Britain," he said grandly, "and the prime minister has instructed me to pledge the first contribution of five thousand pounds for this Children's Safety Crusade campaign."

Then Lord Nuffield stood. He thanked his long-time friend Gordon Stewart for his wonderful contribution and devotion over the years to the safety of children. He pledged that the Morris Foundation would

Gordon Stewart broadcasts the news of the Coronation Year Children's Safety Crusade, 1937. Note his lapel badge showing the torch symbol of the crusade. PHOTO COURTESY GORDON V. STEWART

double any individual contribution made the first week of the campaign.

He smiled and dryly noted that obviously he would already be contributing ten thousand pounds just to match his government's timely gift.

Stewart profusely thanked his old friend. He knew that's what he needed to put his financial campaign over the top. He'd hoped to raise one hundred thousand pounds for the campaign, but more than that was pledged that very first day by his distinguished guests at the Savoy luncheon.

"All pledges can be sent to the Children's Safety Crusade, care of Send Manor, Ripley, Surrey," Stewart announced.

Meanwhile, back at the manor, things were going great guns. The set production and stage preparations for the modern-day version of *The Pied Piper of Hamelin* were moving right along.

Our modern Pied Piper leads the children to safety.

In this film, the piper offers his magical powers to the local safety council in the village. They'd been plunged into total despair by increasing casualties of children on the village streets. With the aid of his green torch and new perky outfit, Albert Hepburn, the magnificent trainer of the rats, was a handsome sight to see in the village of Ripley, as he trudged off each morning to work at "Hamelin" on the back lot at Send Manor.

His rapport with the three hundred rats he'd trained was astonishing to see. On the set during filming, they obediently hung out of his pockets, his collar, his sleeves and his wonderful boots with the jingling bells.

Albert fed them, as a reward, after each trick they did for him in the performance.

Somehow, he trained scores of them to follow him as he trailed off down the street blowing on his little pipe. The special-effects people, even in those early days of film production, made those scores of rats look like hundreds — even thousands!

The film was a masterpiece of children's entertainment, and Stewart paid for it all himself.

Of course, the Hamelin set had to be well away from the kennels. Those hundreds of Great Danes would make short work of Albert Hepburn's bread and butter. Stewart was having great fun as he directed the film carefully every day. This was the important main cog in the marketing campaign — everything depended on the excellence of this film.

But just think how very busy and committed he had to be, with a huge motor-car empire to run, his British Poultry Development operation, and the Send Grist Mills to manage. Not to mention a huge Great Dane kennel and his demanding social responsibilities. And by then, in 1936, the winds of war were blowing across Europe.

"Adolph Hitler," thought Stewart, "looks like big trouble."

But ever the optimist and showman, he plunged ahead, setting up recording studios for the production of gramophone records. Celebrities, stage and film stars were recruited to lend their talents to the musical productions, and Lupino Lane, Laddie Cliff, and Leslie Henson from the London stage, Transport Minister Hore-Belisha and Sir Malcolm Campbell all recorded messages to the children.

Gracie Fields was often at Send Manor, playing with the Danes, and was only too willing to help.

There was her
Safety First song:

And another tune to the melody of
"There's a Long, Long Trail a Winding . . . ."

When you cross the road
By day or night
Beware of the dangers
That loom in sight
Look right and left
And again to the right
And you'll
Never
Never
Get run over!

There are big bright pairs of beacons
Along the roads I must tread
And I never cross just anywhere
But there instead
There are lanes that give protection
Inside a white warning line
Let the crazy people jaywalk

A line-up of some of the forty Morris vans
ready to go to the Children's Safety Crusade, 1937.

PHOTO COURTESY GORDON V. STEWART

Besides the Morris loudspeaker vans, they had a number of mobile units
equipped with all the film gear needed to show the film to six million
schoolchildren. Here's a shot of one of these Morris cars. 1937.

Close-up of the Children's Safety Crusade Morris van. Note the Pied Piper carrying the green torch symbol of the crusade. The painting of the forty vans was donated by Cunard. That's a huge loudspeaker mounted on the roof. 1937. PHOTO COURTESY GORDON V. STEWART

When he had all his sight and sound promotion material ready, Stewart pulled off his greatest public relations stunt. He designed and outfitted forty Morris vans and painted them with the Pied Piper scene on the sides and rear. There was a huge loudspeaker installed on the roof, and each van had a sound reproduction studio inside and was outfitted with a desk, microphone and broadcasting equipment for the operator or lecturer to use. The Pied Piper scenes on the vans were painted, as a donation, by the Cunard Motor and Carriage Company.

These vans hit every city, town, village and hamlet in England, just as Stewart had predicted in his speech at the Savoy Hotel luncheon, for the opening meeting of the Children's Safety Crusade.

But there was a downside to all this that no one had anticipated.

Rats escaped while training and filming, and they found the food and grain stores at Send a real bonanza. They urinated in the dogs' food and water, and it wasn't long before the kennel had a horrendous outbreak of the dreaded disease leptospirosis, and it killed many dogs.

While Stewart was saving the children of England, he was losing his Great Danes at Send Manor.

CHAPTER TWENTY

Family Portrait

Men of power have a problem. They feed on power — and power feeds on them. Without power, recognition and adulation, a kind of empty starvation sets in.

Stewart began breaking down his kennels in 1937. He sensed an aching void in his life as he walked down the avenues of the Swiss village with their silent, empty buildings. His days, and certainly weekends, weren't the same. Gone were the glamour and excitement of the Karinda Hut, the laughing, flirtatious women of stage and screen, the fawning affection of the actors and celebrities milling around aimlessly, and the barking, boisterous Great Danes straining to start the races, while the voices of the onlookers urged on the wagers from the happy, noisy crowds.

The fear of war was taking its toll. Stewart knew he wouldn't be able to feed all these dogs. Men would be enlisting so he'd lose his managers and staff. His German trainers had left for home. Even his kennel maids would go into the war effort. So he'd set about to sell and give away his dogs and reduce his breeding to a minimum.

He hated the silence and felt very alone. There were only echoes of the past. A big part of his life was gone. The rich and famous, the powerful men of British business no longer had an excuse for driving their Bentleys and Rolls out of London and south to Send Manor.

The thundering silence gnawed at him. He had loved the attention, but the sometimes shallow friendship of the theatre crowd only lasted until his parties ended, then they moved on.

In 1937 all of England knew Stewart when he produced and directed the mammoth publicity campaign for the Children's Safety Crusade — his personal tribute to his friend Bertie, now King of England.

But that was all gone.

So he decided to turn to the theatre itself. Producers had power. A producer controlled the careers and destinies of many people. Samuel Goldwyn and Louis B. Mayer had found that out quickly enough in Hollywood with their motion picture stable of stars. Actors and actresses would adore him again. His name would appear on the marquee — in lights. Newspapers once more would write his name.

Stewart contacted old friends on Broadway and bought the rights to an American production called *Family Portrait*. It was the story of the life of Christ. He rewrote the play himself, adapting it to English taste. Then he negotiated a contract with the Strand Theatre, Aldwych, in London's main theatre district, for what he hoped would be a long, successful run. But the very night *Family Portrait* opened in 1939, France fell to the advancing hordes of Adolf Hitler's war machine.

There was no newspaper space next day for the opening-night reviews. The people of Britain were on edge and afraid. Theatre ticket sales dwindled. Wartime jitters drastically cut down any chance of his new play's success.

The day after the opening, Stewart came to his office at Stewart and Ardern late, glanced sadly at his secretary, Karen Meadows, and they exchanged the normal "good mornings."

He silently closed his office door, took off his coat and hat and flung them on a leather chair in the corner. Karen winced and started a bit as he thumped his fist on his mammoth oak desk.

That day, Stewart vowed he'd have that son of a bitch Adolf Hitler. The little twit had cost him a fortune and dealt a real blow to his reputation. That was even worse.

"By the time we're through with you," Stewart murmured, "you'll be wearing that ridiculous little moustache as window dressing for your arse!"

And have him he would. Stewart plunged into the battle for Britain with every resource he could muster. The night life of the theatre would just have to wait. He promised himself he'd be back, as he rubbed Edwin's dime at the end of his watch chain. And back he would come in 1946.

The year he bought the Strand Theatre.

Send Manor overgrown during the Second World War.
There were no gardeners to care for the grounds.

PHOTO COURTESY GORDON V. STEWART

CHAPTER TWENTY-ONE

The War Years

B y 1935, Adolf Hitler and his Nazi party had been given dictatorial powers in Germany, and the winds of war were blowing. There was still a lot of resentment amongst some of the German population over having lost in 1918.

The British politicians tried to pretend it was not going to happen, but astute businessmen such as Stewart knew that things didn't look good. He saw the problems coming. How to feed tons of meat to his five hundred Great Danes? It just wouldn't be available. Nor would the other feed from his grist mill or poultry farm. That would all be needed to feed the people of Britain and the men and women who'd go overseas to fight.

By 1936 he'd begun giving away and selling as many dogs as he could.

Mrs. Cynthia Young worked at Send Kennel, and remembered, "He gave me fifteen to twenty Danes before the war, and I looked after them somehow during those bad years."

Stewart's kennel manager, Mr. Huber, and the German trainer Herr Eickenbaur, had returned to their homes in Europe by 1934. Bob Montgomery, his show and training manager, had left Send with his new wife Audrey (Field) Montgomery, who had been in charge of the dog-training section. Leslie Hill, Bob's assistant manager over the years, left and went over to Montgomery's kennel and took with him his new bride, Phyllis Hudson, who had worked in the hospital section at Send.

Stewart knew that if war came, he'd have a terrible time finding men and women to staff that huge Send operation. They'd all be in the war effort. So, without the managers to train the dogs and staff to look after them, Stewart made his plans to dissolve the Send Kennel operation.

In 1938 Hitler occupied Austria. Two days later, he took over Poland. Britain and France declared war on Germany and all hell broke loose at Stewart and Ardern. By the end of 1939, a new motor car was rare. Morris production was re-geared for wartime.

At Stewart and Ardern (S&A), service and repair was all-important, to keep both commercial vehicles and private cars on the road. Of course, petrol would be rationed and virtually unattainable for private vehicle use anyway.

Acton and many S&A workshops started planning and converting to rebuild vehicles. Thousands of damaged army trucks were completely re-manufactured and returned to the army from those workshops. Then came the RAF and Civil Defence equipment and vehicles. S&A did large-scale work all through the war on reconditioning engines, axles and gearboxes.

In 1940 the German Luftwaffe flattened the police headquarters garage at Lambeth, and S&A were called in to pick up the pieces. They rescued six coaches and enough parts and scrap for three new chassis, and mounted new bodies on them.

By September 1940, huge numbers of machine tools from bombed-out factories urgently had to be rebuilt to keep the munitions and equipment going to the troops. Most arrived from the Woolwich Army Arsenal, bent, twisted and half melted from the fires, and S&A were given a four-year contract to rebuild them.

The car showrooms at the depots were used to assemble American lorries. They came over in boxes, off the Merchant Marine ships that crossed the Atlantic. They also reconditioned searchlight generator sets and overhauled artillery limbers, compressors and pontoons.

At the Wembley Works, S&A manufactured metal artillery boxes and the Royal Engineers bridging equipment, both wooden and metal components. They also built the bodies for the "Commander Cars." The chassis and cabs came from the United States.

S&A had to design and manufacture their own tools and equipment for these wartime jobs, as there were none to buy and there was nowhere to buy them.

They made nine thousand of the new overload petrol tanks for the Allied Air Forces, and five thousand coolant header tanks for the Rolls Royce Merlin and Griffon engines were turned out. Repairs had to be done, later, on many of these.

Three-inch anti-aircraft rocket components were ordered, rush, rush! But these required special lathes from the United States, which would take three months to arrive, even if they got through on the convoys. So S&A built the machines themselves for this contract and got the job done on time.

According to War Department and S&A records, no fewer than 2,719,973 machining operations of the most complex nature were done by Stewart's company, for the completion of a variety of parts desperately needed for the Lancaster, Sunderland, Mosquito, Seafire and Typhoon aircraft.

There was a horrendous shortage of labour, so they found women very good indeed on these jobs. They used refugees — Germans, Austrians, Czechs, Belgians and French — and anybody else they could find with two hands that they could train. Early in the war, S&A established a school to train second-class vehicle fitters for the army. They trained two thousand, five hundred men by the end of the war.

In 1943 their huge Acton works was requisitioned by the Ministry of Aircraft Production. They also lost their Southend, Catford, Croydon, Golders Green and Staines premises. They only had six weeks to leave Acton, and found space at Earl's Court, in London, that had been an old, abandoned railway shed. They moved office, canteen, all stores and equipment and took it in their stride. Soon, armed services vehicles were being overhauled there.

During the prolonged air raids, Acton suffered direct hits, but their other locations fared pretty well. S&A personnel lost their homes, and family members were killed and injured. In 1940–41 they had to evacuate premises many times during the heavy bombing. By 1943 the raids were sporadic, but then came the dreaded flying bombs and rockets that were so demoralizing to the British people. By March 1945, some five thousand rockets carrying one-ton warheads had reached Britain.

Gracie Fields, centre, helping two women workers stamp a shell case at an ordnance factory. She was there to give a "Munitions Concert" to boost morale.

PHOTO COURTESY
IMPERIAL WAR MUSEUM

When they weren't at work, all S&A managers and employees had to share fire-watching duties, and did so gladly.

When I re-read all this that I've written, I marvel at the tenacity and unbelievable spirit of the people of Britain. As explained in other chapters, Prince Albert, Duke of York, had been Stewart's friend and associate for many years in their charity programs. He became King George VI in 1937, and was already married to Elizabeth.

Although a shy and reserved young man because of his stuttering impediment, he proved a solid leader during the Second World War. Adolph Hitler called Elizabeth, the queen consort, "the most dangerous woman in Europe," because she could so successfully boost the morale of the British people during the terrible Blitz. These two friends of Stewart's proved to be the strongest monarchs to come along in a long time.

As I write this chapter, I wonder if George VI and Elizabeth, as they viewed the rubble of London, ever passed by the devastation of Stewart and Ardern buildings and thought of Gordon Stewart. The business acumen, organizational ability and supernatural energy of Stewart, over those war years, cannot be believed.

No wonder, indeed, that Hitler lost the war, with men like this on the home front.

Throughout the war, Stewart also served in the reserves of the Royal Flying Corps. That went back to the days of 1909–1910 when he was designing aeroplanes and working on the first Hendon Aerodrome.

By 1945, all looked forward to returning to their old premises at S&A. The returning men and women brought home new skills and training learned during the war years and new ideas galore. Stewart, always positive in his thinking, said, "Those war years did us a lot of good. We were badly bombed and did a lot of work. But it gave us, at the end, a breather to tool up again. We had a great opportunity to expand, and we took it. Without the war," Stewart reflected, "we could have stayed in the same old rut getting lazy in our ways. A good company needs change!"

Now don't forget Stewart's other duties and problems at Send Manor during the war. The Grist Mill and Poultry Company had both expanded to pump out food products at a tremendous volume for the population and troops. During the war years, Stewart also ran experiments at Send, on Jersey heifer calves. In controlled studies, swabs were taken by the government, and it was found that a vaccine (which was produced by Stewart's science staff), when injected into the udder of a young heifer, made it more elastic. This resulted in a much greater milk production at an earlier age. Stewart built a laboratory building at Send for these experiments and studies. He called it Swab House.

Molly Brown managed the operations of the British Poultry Development and this heifer project during those years. Her sister, Diana Edmonds, was a guest at Send during the war, and you'll hear more about her later.

All the kennel ranges were used for food storage. The once-beautiful Swiss Karinda Hut was stripped, and this too was used by the ministry for wartime storage. Stewart had to organize and direct all this, plus look after Stewart and Ardern and handle his reserve duties in the Royal Flying Corps.

From 1939 to 1945 Gordon Stewart was a very busy man!

A long-range Avro Lancaster BMK III bomber, fitted with Rolls Royce Merlin 38 engines and a saddle tank as produced by Stewart and Ardern.

PHOTO COURTESY IMPERIAL WAR MUSEUM

A De Havilland Mosquito of No. 487 Squadron in February 1944 with a five-hundred-pound bomb beneath each wing. One of its most important roles in Bomber Command was to deliver incendiary markers onto the night targets for the main force of heavy bombers.

PHOTO COURTESY IMPERIAL WAR MUSEUM

The London Fire Brigade during the Blitz. By the end of 1940 nearly twenty thousand incendiary bombs had been dropped on London alone. PHOTO COURTESY IMPERIAL WAR MUSEUM

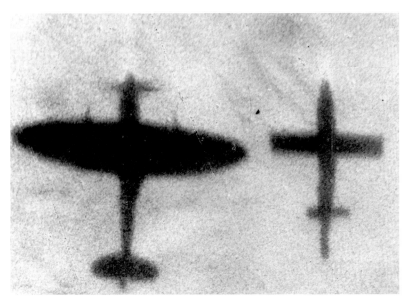

An RAF Spitfire draws closer to a V-1 flying bomb. The heroic pilot uses his wing to tip it off course to miss its target in Britain.
PHOTO COURTESY IMPERIAL WAR MUSEUM

CHAPTER TWENTY-TWO

After the War

T he aftermath of the war lasted long past 1945. The government had to start de-commissioning all the properties they had taken over. But these arrangements for reparation couldn't be done overnight, as government equipment, parts and machinery had to be disassembled, destroyed, sold or stored somewhere else.

Then Stewart and Ardern had to redesign and plan the new décor for the showrooms, service depots, shops and factory areas that had been taken over, at the same time trying to sell any new Morris cars and trucks they could find, and rebuild or repair private vehicles that hadn't been able to get proper service during the war.

As Stewart had said, this whole reorganization and rebuilding of their premises was a good thing really, because there was tremendous advancement in equipment and technology developed for wartime that could now be put to use for the public good. Returning men and women from the services were rehired and retrained to do things the new Stewart and Ardern way.

It wasn't until 1949 that they had all eleven regional showrooms and service departments humming at full tilt again. Their prestigious building at Berkeley Square in the centre of London, with forty thousand square feet of space, had been requisitioned by the Auxiliary Fire Service in 1939. Then in 1940 the shipping section of the Ministry of War Transport had taken over from them.

Naturally, wartime agencies couldn't be expected to be careful and caring tenants, particularly when at any time the building could be flattened by the Luftwaffe anyway. The Berkeley Square facilities were not returned to Stewart and Ardern until 1949, and then the planning, remodelling and rebuilding was begun for that wonderful site.

On October 10, 1951, Lord Nuffield headlined the program for the official reopening.

In his speech, he pointed out the tremendous volume of business that had been developed since he and Stewart had first met in 1913, from the first moment of mutual trust, when he had sold Stewart on a plan for his new motor car, the Morris Oxford, with only a mock-up model of the car and dummy wooden engine. And now today, the two companies had done a massive trade with each other of twenty-one million pounds. And that's wholesale!

But which of them had had more gall? Stewart placed his order for the first four hundred Morris Oxfords to come off production and he didn't have a motor-car showroom or sales force, let alone a car that could run.

Coincidentally, that same day of the ceremony was Lord Nuffield's seventy-fourth birthday, and the Morris Company rolled its two-millionth vehicle off the assembly line in his honour.

Each man wondered, as they sat in that room remembering old times, what might have happened if they hadn't met at that Manchester Motor Show in 1913. It is absolutely astonishing to know that Stewart's company, Stewart and Ardern, owned and occupied premises worth one million pounds in 1951. A lot of assets for those days. All from that little beginning in a garage in Acton. All planned and developed by a remarkable man, who apprenticed at a sheep-shearing equipment company as a young man after running away from home.

In 1959, seven years after Stewart died, the huge Morris Commercial House was opened, adding once again to the empire. It was convenient to the North Circular Road, London, and was built to sell and service the rapidly expanding commercial vehicles business. It was open twenty-four hours a day, seven days a week. They also built a body-building division there for specialized commercial vehicle production. Stewart had become the largest motor vehicle distributor in all of Great Britain, through his company Stewart and Ardern.

After the war, Send Kennel was no more, of course. The Danes were long gone.

Those beautiful buildings of the Swiss village and lovely tree-lined avenues throughout the kennel grounds were a mess, as were the kennel ranges. All had been a huge food stores operation for the ministry during the war. The Send Grist Mill and British Poultry operations had flourished, and these two had grown rapidly during the war.

Stewart had hired Mollie Brown to run the poultry operation, and because of the shortage of premises, she and her sister, Diana Edmonds, had moved into Send Manor house while Mollie ran the poultry company and helped with the general management of the Send Manor property.

Diana Edmonds was an aspiring young actress. Stewart thought she had great promise for the London stage, and we'll learn more about her later, with Stewart's purchase of the Strand Theatre, in London's exciting West End.

Bustling traffic in 1987 outside the Strand Theatre, Aldwych, London.

PHOTO COURTESY GORDON V. STEWART

CHAPTER TWENTY-THREE

✦

The Strand Theatre

Remember Reg Giles? He was the carpenter who built all the cages to hold the rats for *The Pied Piper of Hamelin* movie. As years went on, he became foreman at Send Manor.

Well, old Giles became something of a historian, and before he died, he wrote an article on Send Manor. It was included in the Send & Ripley Historical Society's "Twentieth Anniversary Bulletin" of May/June 1995. And here's what Giles said. "Stewart wanted to put a kennel maid amateur actress in a musical, but he fell out with Jack Sylvester, who was running the show (at the Strand Theatre). Stewart bought the Strand and fired Sylvester, and took on Joe Loss and his band and put the girl, whose name was Diana Yardley, in the show, and she was a huge success. The theatre is still owned by Send Manor Trust, according to the programmes."

He also said Stewart bought the Strand in 1935–36. Well, that little quotation caused me months of disappointment and rejection, as it contained some misleading leads. Then I found, tucked away near the end of Russell Street, facing Covent Garden, in the theatre district of London, the marvellous Theatre Museum.

If you're in London and have an interest in the theatre, I strongly recommend a few hours there. They have the most wonderful, huge collection of old and new costumes, with theatre memorabilia that goes back a long way. And the exhibits are wonderfully displayed. The scope of this museum includes all the performing arts, such as circus, magic, opera, ballet, music hall, rock and pop. In their archives they have reconstructions of early theatres, including the 1614 Globe, and memorabilia of the great actors and actresses.

In 1924 Mrs. Gabrielle Enthoven gave her outstanding collection of theatre memorabilia to the Victoria and Albert Museum. To this were added collections of the British Theatre Museum, and the Friends of the Museum of Theatre Arts, plus many more trusts over the years.

By 1974 the Theatre Museum (as you see it today) had become a separate department of the Victoria and Albert Museum. But it has its own building on Russell Street. On June 10, 1998, my wife, Shirley, and I were allowed access to the study room of their research collection.

Although "closed access," you may request an appointment behind the scenes in this study room if you call four to five weeks in advance. The research collection is out of bounds, but you can browse through the index cabinets and ask experienced staff to help you find files. The facility is used by all kinds of research people, and there are tens of thousands of photographs, articles, books, programmes and anything else imaginable pertaining to the performing arts and going back centuries.

There were a lot of inconsistencies in Reg Giles's statement.

First about the Strand Theatre supposedly being bought by Stewart. Well you don't just buy a theatre easily, and I'll clarify that later. Then, the statement that Stewart bought it in 1935–36. There was no record of that in those years because those dates were way off.

And who was Diana Yardley? Do you remember in the chapter "After the War," there was mention of Mollie Brown and her sister Diana Edmonds, who was an aspiring young actress? Well, I found later that Diana Yardley was indeed Diana Edmonds's stage name.

Then what was the Send Manor Trust? Here's the scoop on that. The answer was with the Theatres Trust. This trust was established by act of Parliament to "promote the better protection of theatres for the benefit of the nation." David Cheshire, their research and information officer, helped set me on the right track. Their files show that the Strand Theatre, Aldwych, London, in the West-End theatre district, goes back to May 22, 1905, when it opened as the Waldorf. The Waldorf Theatre was located at the corner of Catherine Street, in a block of buildings that had the Waldorf Hotel in the middle and, at the other end at the Drury Lane corner, the Aldwych Theatre.

It remained the Waldorf until 1909, when it became the Strand. Then the name was changed in 1911 to the Whitney and back again to the Strand in 1913, which it remains today. It has a capacity of one thousand, two hundred and two seats, and was redecorated in 1930, when the boxes round the back of the dress circle were removed. The decor remains basically the same today, although there has been further refurbishing done in recent years.

During the Blitz of the Second World War, Donald Wolfit, the manager, kept the Strand going; he held lunch-time Shakespeare. In 1942 there was a production of Offenbach's *Tales of Hoffman*. Then in December 1942, *Arsenic and Old Lace* began, and lasted for one thousand, three hundred and thirty-seven performances.

Stewart's Send Manor Trust bought over the Strand lease in 1946, not 1936 as Giles had said. Lionel Falck was made director; he'd been connected with the Strand since 1936. There was no record of a Jack Sylvester as reported by Reg Giles.

After *Arsenic and Old Lace* came *Cage Me a Peacock* (1948), then *Queen Elizabeth Slept Here*, which ran into 1950. In 1950 *Will Any Gentleman* was produced, with *And So to Bed* in 1951 and *The River Line* in 1952.

Feffie Somerfield of *Dog World* newspaper had an interesting article that was written February 1, 1952, by columnist Phyllis Robson. In it she says that Stewart produced and ran *The Wizard of Oz* for two years. That was in the time just after he bought the Strand in 1946. *Arsenic and Old Lace* began in 1942 and ran about three years, then the *Wizard*. Stewart could hardly expect Dorothy to cavort along the yellow brick road holding a hulking big Great Dane as Toto, so he had to seek out something a bit smaller.

Phyllis Robson said she was able to get Mrs. Charters to lend him her Sealyham terrier for the first year, and the second year Mrs. Coventon loaned him a poodle to star.

Stewart was an important owner in theatre circles, because the Strand was active, profitable and healthy during his tenure. Ownership of a theatre in London is a very complex subject, but I'll try to walk you through what I discovered. For information on this, I researched a document entitled "Theatre Ownership in Britain," which is a report that was prepared in London in 1953 for the Federation of Theatre Unions.

Prior to this report, ownership records were sketchy. Many theatres in London sit on land owned by the big estates of the titled gentry of England, going back centuries. Many are on Crown land. So the land area on which a theatre sits (or other buildings as well) may be leased only, or sometimes sold freehold.

It gets more complicated, as some theatres seem to sit partly on freehold and partly on leasehold land.

Building leases, particularly in London, are usually granted for ninety-nine years. But there were some leases of nine hundred and ninety-nine years (or with a right of perpetual renewal), so the 1873 commission on leases treated these as virtually equivalent to freehold. If that isn't complicated enough, you have instances where people sublease remaining years of the ninety-nine-year lease that had been granted for a theatre site.

On freehold land there could be a ground lease paid. Then if a theatre had been built on this ground, there could be a building lease to pay for on top of the ground lease. The Strand Theatre ground lease balance of fifty-seven years was taken over by Stewart in 1946, at an annual rental of four thousand, six hundred and fifty pounds. He paid a sum of one hundred and fifty thousand pounds for the lease balance.

As the corporate vehicle for this purchase, Stewart formed the Send Manor Trust. Here is the exact registration record for that company:

Exempt Private Company NO: 418031

Date of Registration: 26.8.46

Capital:

       In ordinary shares of 1 pound

       Authorized 10,000 pounds.

       Issued 1,400 pounds

       Loan Capital:

       65,000 pounds mortgages and 83,000 pounds debentures.

Directors:	No. of Shares held
Gordon Stewart	
(Stewart and Ardern etc.)	1,200
Diana Edmonds	100
Lionel Louis Falck	100

[Author's note: I have two spellings for Lionel — Falk and Falck, springing up here and there. He was appointed director of the Strand by Stewart in 1946. The correct spelling is Falck.

Diana Edmonds lived at Send Manor during the war years and used the stage name Diana Yardley.]

Now let's look at Gordon Stewart, the businessman. Here's what happened. The mortgages and debentures at incorporation time totalled one hundred and forty-eight thousand pounds. Send Manor Trust paid one hundred and fifty thousand pounds for the outstanding fifty-seven-year lease. Stewart leveraged the Strand deal — he agreed to pay one hundred and fifty thousand pounds, but borrowed one hundred and forty-eight thousand to do it. So, in fact, Stewart put up only two thousand pounds cash.

However, there are no records to say that Stewart didn't hold these mortgages and debentures himself or through one of his own companies, because, according to investment records existing then, an astute businessman could double his return on the ground lease amount of four thousand, six hundred and fifty pounds per annum that Stewart had agreed to pay in his original deal.

Here's what the Theatre Unions 1953 report on theatre ownership in Britain said: "The orthodox financial method for dealing with interest and amortization (i.e. spreading interest and repayment equally over the years so that interest goes down and repayment goes up) and, assuming an average borrowing rate of four percent at that time, we reach an annual "financial" overhead charge, including the ground rent (of 4,650 pounds annually) of roughly 11,300 pounds a year, for the Strand Theatre."

What Stewart probably did was fund the mortgages and debentures himself, then each year pocketed eleven thousand, three hundred pounds and paid out four thousand, six hundred and fifty. Not a bad annual return on investment!

David Cheshire, the research and information officer for the Theatres Trust, brought me up to date. He told me that the Send Manor Trust held the Strand Theatre until 1980, even though Stewart died in 1952. The trust ceased operations then, and seems to have wound up. The Strand is now run by Louis I. Michaels, which set up the company Strand Theatre to buy out the Send Manor Trust lease in that year of 1980.

Records mention that in 1950 the freehold of the Strand was owned by the Strand Theatre Trust, one of the Guinness (beer) family trusts.

Evidently, Stewart's Send Manor Trust would have paid rent to the Guinness family.

Trust Stewart to once again be as involved with the excitement, complications and almost bizarre business of the theatre as he was when he used his Send Danes in the thirties for the show business acts at the Karinda Hut and midnight hotel cabarets. That's the kind of man he was.

*These six Send fawns had no idea that their lovely handler,
Gracie Fields, would become Britain's highest-paid film star
and world famous.* PHOTO COURTESY ANDREW MONTGOMERY

*Famed stage actress Diana Wynyard was often at Send Manor as a
guest of Gordon Stewart. Here she stands with a Send harlequin
at one of the hotel cabarets in London's posh West End.*

CHAPTER TWENTY-FOUR

Curtain Time at the Strand

"D iana, I've bought you the theatre. Now, let's make you a star!" exclaimed Stewart.

He was always kind, thoughtful and extravagant with his ladies, and when my wife, Shirley, and I arrived at the Theatre Museum archives, we found out just how far he would go!

On June 11, 1998, we travelled by train into London from Ashtead, Surrey. At Waterloo Station, we jumped into a London cab for the short ride to the end of Russell Street, near Covent Garden, went down a long ramp at the rear of the theatre and through a white stage door. The security guard admitted us into the outer room of the study room, hidden underneath the museum building itself.

The lady attendant was expecting us, as two months before I'd made a firm appointment to make use of their archives. We outlined what we wanted. The subjects I needed to cover in this book — the Strand Theatre, Gracie Fields, Diana Wynyard, Gordon Stewart, and Joe Loss and his orchestra were just a few of the things to check out.

The files on Gracie Fields contained hundreds of photos, clippings, and newspaper reviews on Dame Gracie's career in song and film over the years. Shirley took the files for some of the years and I took others. We wanted to find confirmation of her appearance as a young girl in the 1920s. And there she was in other pictures, just as she appears in the photos in this book as a young girl at Send Manor with the dogs. We'd finally confirmed that it was indeed "our Gracie" in our photos.

The pictures of Gracie in this book date about 1927–1929. She was performing at that time at the Lyceum Theatre in London in *The Show's the Thing*. You'll find the program with this chapter.

For those who know little about Dame Gracie Fields, here's a brief trip through her life. Born Gracie Stansfield in 1898, this bubbling

The young Gracie Fields was a familiar sight at Send Manor.
Here she poses with a team of Send show harlequins in the garden.
Circa 1930–31. PHOTO COURTESY WIN LEAKE

Lancashire lass would win the hearts of the world. Her comedy routines and romantic ballads made her the top recording star of the day. Gracie didn't start films until her thirties, but became the highest-paid film star of that time. She was made a dame by Queen Elizabeth in 1979, the same year she died of a heart attack.

Her wartime shows for the troops and home front will long be cherished and remembered by the people of Britain.

Some of her most memorable films were *Sally in Our Alley* in 1932; *Looking on the Bright Side*, 1933; *This Week of Grace*, 1934; *Love, Life and Laughter* and *Sing as You Go* in 1935; *Look Up and Laugh*, 1936; *Queen of Hearts*, 1937; *The Show Goes On*, 1938; *We're Going To Be Rich* and *Keep Smiling*, 1939; *Shipyard Sally*, 1943; *Stage Door Canteen* and *Holy Matrimony* in 1944; *Molly and Me* in 1945 and *Paris Underground*.

Her films were produced both in Britain and the United States, and in between she did scores of stage shows. Here is the actual program of Gracie's 1929 stage hit, *The Show's the Thing*, at the Lyceum Theatre in London.

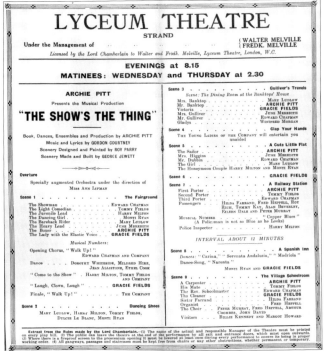

Program for The Show's the Thing *at the Lyceum Theatre, London.*
Gracie Fields starred with Archie Pitt. The back cover sponsor is Gordon
Stewart, promoting his Morris cars.

A program cost three pence. The front cover and inside showbill will interest you, but look at the back cover. Gracie's old pal Gordon Stewart supports her performance with a full-page, back-cover ad for his company, Stewart and Ardern, on all the programs. You'll also see the front cover of the program for Stewart's production, *And So to Bed*, starring the famous stage actor Leslie Henson. This was playing in 1952 at the Strand when Stewart died.

See what's printed, very faintly, at the bottom. The theatre pit orchestra was conducted by a young orchestra leader named Mantovani. Stewart sure knew how to pick future stars. There were a few clippings about the Joe Loss Band that Stewart hired in 1946 for programs at the Strand Theatre. Joe Loss and his band were hired by Stewart in 1946, when he bought the theatre, because they were the leading band of the day. He played his signature tune, "In the Mood," long before Glenn Miller popularized it. He introduced the boomps-a-daisy to Britain and the twist. One of his early band singers was Vera Lynn.

There were lots of file clippings and information on the beautiful Diana Wynyard, whose picture was taken at a London hotel with the Danes. She had attended one of Stewart's cabaret shows with the dogs. Diana was gorgeous and made her first stage appearance in London, in 1925, before making her New York debut in 1932. It was back to London to star in *Wild Decembers* in 1933, and in 1939 she played Gilda in Noel Coward's *Design for Living*. Her appearance in *Watch on the Rhine* in 1942 was followed by leading Shakespearean roles in 1948 and 1949. Then it was on to star with John Gielgud in *The Winter's Tale*, in 1951. She was awarded the order of Commander of the British Empire in the Queen's Honours List at New Years 1953.

That same year, at her wedding reception at Hyde Park Hotel, the three-hundred-guest list read like a Who's Who of the theatre: Mary Martin, Dame Sybil Thorndyke, Flora Robson, Sir Laurence Olivier, Vivien Leigh, John Gielgud, Joyce Grenfell, Emlyn Williams, Moira Shearer and a host of others.

Diana Wynyard in her early twenties was a friend of Stewart's.

But what of Reg Giles's statement about Stewart buying the Strand

Here is the actual playbill from the Strand Theatre for the production of Gordon Stewart's Wizard of Oz. He'd just bought the Strand Theatre in 1946. Note that the star, Dorothy, is Diana Yardley. She stayed at Send Manor during the war. Her maiden name was Diana Edmonds. Shown here are the outside front cover and an inside page of the folded program.

to put his girlfriend Diana Edmonds in a starring role? Her stage name, according to my research, was Diana Yardley. But the Theatre Museum had nothing on Diana's career. No one had ever heard of her, and I was just about to think that Giles made all that up, when Shirley turned to me from one of her files and said, "You'd better look at this."

The major productions listed for the Strand by the theatre revues during Stewart's time showed *Arsenic and Old Lace* playing since 1942 (for one thousand, three hundred and thirty-seven performances), followed by *The Wizard of Oz* for two years after that. Then came *Cage Me a Peacock*, 1949; *Queen Elizabeth Slept Here* (it ran until 1950); *And So to Bed*, 1951-52; and *The River Line* which began in 1952.

Shirley handed me an actual program of the *Wizard of Oz*, presented by Gordon Stewart and directed by Edward Beaumont under the supervision of Stewart. See the playbill above. Note that the Strand

Theatre director shown on the front cover is Lionel Falck, to whom Stewart gave ten shares in the Send Manor Trust, along with the ten he gave Diana Edmonds when he bought the Strand lease. Now Shirley opened up the program and held it out to me.

The lead part of Dorothy in Stewart's production of the *Wizard of Oz* and the first show he produced was played by none other than the elusive Diana Yardley. Old Reg Giles had it right all along! The unknown girl, Diana Edmonds, who lived at Send Manor during the war years, was suddenly shot to stardom.

I haven't found a thing about her since.

Diana Yardley must really have been pretty good, because Dorothy is not just another pretty face. She had to sing, act and dance in that role. Remember when Judy Garland played the part in the film? It ran for two years, twice daily according to the program, at 2:30 P.M. and at 7:00 P.M. Not an easy job. What a guy was Stewart — a man true to his word. It was payback time at curtain time at the Strand for Diana Yardley/Edmonds.

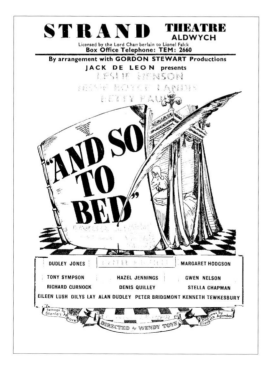

The production And So to Bed *was running at the Strand Theatre when Gordon Stewart died in January 1952. Leslie Henson was the star. Note at the bottom of this cover for the playbill program that the leader of the pit band was a young man named*

Joe Loss at the Hammersmith Palais. He was famous for his rendition of "In the Mood" long before Glenn Miller played it.

BRIEF ENCOUNTERS

In The Mood

DAVID TAYLOR beats time with the maestro of romantic rhythm, **JOE LOSS**

Joe Loss and his orchestra were hired by Gordon Stewart just after Stewart bought the Strand Theatre in 1946. It was the hottest band of the day.

St. Martins in the Fields Church, Trafalgar Square, London.
In April 1952, a memorial service was held here for Gordon Stewart.

PHOTO BY THE AUTHOR

♦

CHAPTER TWENTY-FIVE

The Final Hours

I t was a blustery winter night that Monday, January 21, 1952. Gordon Stewart pulled his long, wool scarf higher around his neck and put on his heavy, tweed overcoat. He trudged across the green in front of Send Manor to have dinner with Betty Moodie and friends in Send Dale Cottage, a short distance away. It was a cold and frosty night.

Later, he invited the men and women back to the manor house and had his staff build up the fires in the huge old fireplaces until they were blazing brightly in the oak-beamed rooms of his magnificent home. Shadows danced gaily around the walls.

Bottles of his finest cognac and sherry were opened. While his guests happily chatted amongst themselves, Stewart set up his projection equipment to entertain them with one of England's latest movies. He'd felt tired and restless all evening.

The lights were lowered, and as they all watched the screen the Lord of Send Manor felt a sudden excruciating pain across his chest and down his arm. He slumped down in his chair, gasped, whimpered softly and reached out, appealing for help.

Gordon Stewart's life had ended.

Even the doctor, who was one of the guests, couldn't save him from that massive heart attack. During those sixty-six years of life, from 1885 to January 1952, the world watched one of the most innovative and motivated men England would see this century.

An entrepreneur and aviator, trusting and bold. A pioneer in the motor-car industry and flamboyant race-car driver. A man who loved life and lived it to the fullest. He was always shoulder to shoulder with other great men, royalty and the titled gentry of the land, and was one of the greatest breeders of Great Danes the world will ever know. A man who saw a chance, took it, then excelled in what he did.

Stewart had the Midas touch.

In all these years of research that I've spent on Gordon Stewart, I never once heard an unkind word about him. Tough and demanding of people, yes, but always kind, generous and thoughtful of others. The people who worked with him and for him seemed to have loved him. The women he had loved were all well looked after.

Detractors might say he had a darker side. Kennel maids and others confirm he had an appreciative eye for lovely young ladies, actresses in the theatre and girls on the staff at Send Manor. I do know that he had affairs and mistresses. But so what! He evidently had a distant and unhappy life with the lady he married, but he never abandoned her. Whatever Stewart did, his accomplishments improved the lot of many men and women, not only in England, but throughout the world.

Stewart was buried in the little churchyard of St. Mary the Virgin, in Send, Surrey — his ashes placed in his mother's grave. In April 1952, a memorial service was held at historic St. Martins in the Fields Church in London. A huge crowd attended.

His will shows once again that he didn't forget those who had stuck with him over the years — he always repaid loyalty with kindness. Here are the benefactors as set out in his will:

His grandfather Edwin Smith had left him an ongoing trust, bequeathed to "Willie Gordon Stewart." The income from this trust was left to his wife, Constance Ethel Irene Stewart. When Irene died on August 8, 1979, at age eighty-six, there was still one hundred and eighty-eight thousand, nine hundred and ninety-nine pounds in this trust, and she gave it all away to friends in her will.

One thousand pounds to his sister Madeline Stewart of 5 Gordon House, London. (Note the name of that apartment, which Stewart still owned at his death)

One hundred pounds to Dorothy Stewart, sister, care of Coutts Bank, Strand, London.

Gordon House, at 37 Wellbeck Street, in London. Gordon Stewart owned this building. Both his sister Madeleine and his wife had flats there. 1986.

PHOTO COURTESY GORDON V. STEWART

The front door to 37 Wellbeck Street, London. Gordon Stewart's building was left in trust when he died. Photo 1986.

PHOTO COURTESY
GORDON V. STEWART

One thousand pounds to his friend, George Frederick Baker, a director of Stewart and Ardern.

One thousand pounds to his friend Paul Charles Pendock Stanley, a director of Stewart and Ardern.

One thousand pounds to his friend George Arthur Royston, a director of Stewart and Ardern.

One hundred pounds to Samuel Francis Michael Carrington, of Manor Cottage, Ripley, Surrey.

One hundred and fifty pounds to Reginald Frederick French of 1 Manor Cottage, Ripley, Surrey. (The baker for the kennels.)

One hundred and fifty pounds to Leonard Curtis, Dane End, Send Road, Ripley, Surrey.

Two hundred and fifty pounds to Winifred Tapp, 181 Boundary Road, Woking, Surrey. (A former kennel maid.)

Two hundred and fifty pounds to Isobel Winifred Leake, Rosslyn Edwin Road, West Horsley. (A former kennel maid.)

To his wife Constance Ethel Irene Stewart, all clothes, personal jewellery and personal effects.

To Diana Margaret Edmonds, Shelmerdene, 27 Ashley Drive, Walton-on-Thames, Surrey, all his numerous cinematography and photographic equipment. (Her stage name was Diana Yardley and she lived at Send Manor during the war.)

To Elizabeth Frances Moodie, Send Dale, Send Green, Ripley, Surrey, or if she should predecease him, then to her children and if more than one, in equal shares, all his furniture, fittings and effects of household use or ornament (but not motor cars, carriages, animals, consumable stores, money, securities for money, deeds, contracts or other legal instruments). (She had started at Send as a young kennel maid named Betty Turner.)

To James Strachan, Devoncroft, West Clandon, Surrey, manager of Send Grist Mills Limited, all his shares in Send Grist Mills, together with the freehold of such land and buildings forming part of Send Manor Estate as the trustees determine. But he had to secure the release of the estate of any guarantees or liabilities which were undertaken by Gordon Stewart on behalf of Send Grist Mills Limited, and had rights of way to this land and other reasonable access to the roads surrounding the Send Manor Estate.

To Harold Giles, foreman of Ederslie Cottage, Pynford Lane, Send, Surrey, the freehold of Ederslie Cottage. (Carpenter and foreman.)

To Elizabeth Frances Moodie, or if she was dead, to her child or children, and if more than one, to all of them jointly, the option of purchasing the Send Manor House and parts of the garden and pleasure grounds as the trustees determined, at a price equivalent to the final evaluation for the purposes of obtaining the probate of the will and otherwise on the terms and conditions in the sole discretion of the trustees. (A former kennel maid, she or her children had one month to accept this option.)

After probate, to Gordon Rogers, of the Corner Cottage, Send Green, Ripley, Surrey, the option to purchase the cottage property at the market value. (He had one month to accept.) Gordon Rogers had to still be living in the cottage at Stewart's death or this clause was void.

All the residue of his real and personal estate of whatever nature, into a trust to be directed by his trustees to sell, call in, convert into money and hold the proceeds for the following trusts:

To pay all debts and funeral expenses.

Invest the remainder in such investments as hereinafter authorized by his will.

To hold 30 percent of this remainder in trust for his wife, Constance Ethel Irene Stewart, and the remaining 70 percent in trust in equal shares to Elizabeth Moodie, Diana Margaret Edmonds and Mollie Patricia Brown of Tudor Cottage, Drakes Close, Esher, Surrey. If Irene, his wife, did not survive him by more than one month, her 30 percent of the trust would go to the other three equally. (She did live many years longer.)

The trustees were to have full powers to invest this estate remainder as they saw fit conclusively.

The will was dated April 5, 1951, not long before Stewart's death in January 1952.

A codicil was executed on November 21, 1951, expressing his wish that the trustees endeavour to consult with and obtain approval of the directors of Stewart and Ardern and of Morris Motors before selling or disposing of any stock shares in Stewart and Ardern which he owned at the time of his death.

The will was signed by Gordon Stewart and witnessed by Jocelyn Nenk, private secretary, and S. A. N. Plant. The trustees were Reginald Laird Wells, Kenneth Mines (a chartered accountant) and Thomas William Hayes.

There are things in this will that are curious. For example, in only Betty Moodie's case was Stewart concerned that her offspring of one or more be looked after if she predeceased him. Why would he be concerned? Betty Moodie had the option to buy the manor house, got all the furniture, fittings and household effects and shared in at least 23 1/3 percent of a very large trust set up by the will.

This trust would have contained the value of his shares in Stewart and Ardern. In the chapter "After the War," you see the tremendous volume of business they did as the biggest motor-car distributor in

Britain. They owned and occupied, in 1951, premises worth over one million pounds. That was a valuable asset to this trust. There would also be the shares in the Send Manor Trust that owned the Strand Theatre lease and the British Poultry Development Company, which had grown tremendously during the war.

His cars, cash, bank accounts, securities and real estate not divided up in his will would be included. Personal properties he owned, such as the Gordon House apartments at Wellbeck Street, London, would be substantial. This trust must have been very sizeable indeed.

Yet, whenever I contacted Betty Moodie, as the obvious main beneficiary, to seek out Stewart's kennel records, cups, photos and trophies and all the other things that would have helped give us the story of this great man's life, she would always refuse to see me or discuss my requests. She adamantly maintained that she had nothing of Stewart's left and couldn't really remember anything, as it was so long ago.

Betty Moodie started out in the early thirties as a kennel maid at Send, when her name was Betty Turner. And although she said she didn't have anything of Stewart's left, in 1986 she did! She put up the silver model of Midas, the Duke of Kent's dog, for sale at Crufts, and I bought it. The will clearly states that Mrs. Moodie was to have (among a lot of other things) his "effects of household use or ornament."

That, to me, would include all his cups, trophies, photos and I'd assume records, because surely they were kept in the house and not in a small kennel office where there would be no security at all.

The story from other kennel maids is that as a young girl she left Send for awhile and went to live in London to look after her sick mother and that Stewart brought the two of them back. He built a cottage for them on the lane across from Send Manor estate and they lived there for years.

Later on, Betty Turner married Dr. Moodie, the local medical doctor, and it is obvious from Stewart's will that she still lived in either that same cottage or another like it called Send Dale at Send Green, Ripley, Surrey, close to Send Manor.

In 1998 this was all that was left of the pigeon loft that
Gracie Fields stood before. Note upper left where a belching steam
shovel chews up the Send Manor land for a housing development.

Betty Moodie is the only eyewitness alive, that I know of, who would know about Stewart from the early thirties right up to his death. Other kennel maids and employees only worked there parts of those years. Mrs. Gordon Stewart is deceased, as are all the directors of Stewart and Ardern, Sir Malcolm Campbell, the Duke of York, and the Duke of Kent. Managers Bob Montgomery and Leslie Hill are both gone.

It is inconceivable to me that all of Stewart's possessions and records just vanished at his death. Where did they go?

Where are the huge paintings for the Swiss Karinda Hut, by the world-renowned Augustus John? Stewart wouldn't have left these hanging there to be beat up and soiled while the hut was used for food storage during the war. Those paintings are worth a king's ransom today, but where are they?

It is also obvious from the codicil added to Stewart's will that it had dawned on him that his death required a smooth transition into the future for Stewart and Ardern. I had heard that one of the deceased directors of Stewart and Ardern had a wife still alive. But when I wrote to Mrs. Eustace Watkins, I was too late. However, her son kindly wrote to me and explained that in the late 1950s, after Stewart's death, the family firm Eustace Watkins did a partial merger with Stewart and Ardern, whereby each company bought some of the other's ordinary shares and two directors went on each other's board of directors.

"When George Royston, a beneficiary in Stewart's will and the chairman of Stewart and Ardern Limited, retired," he went on to explain, "Mr. Eustace Watkins became chairman and managing director of both companies. At his retirement, Mr. Watkins sold out to the Henly Group, and they absorbed Stewart and Ardern Ltd. under their name."

Stewart and Ardern still thrives under the umbrella of the Henly Group.

Audiences still stand and uproariously yell out "encore," at the Strand Theatre.

Offspring of those magnificent Send Great Danes still carry the bloodlines all over the world.

Children live on today because their grandmothers and grandfathers paid heed to the Children's Safety Crusade and children escaped death on the roads of England.

But there was no encore for the Stewart family. He and his wife Irene had no children to continue the family line. On that cold night of January 21, 1952, it all just ended, and any trace of Gordon Stewart's life seemed to dry up and blow away.

In March 1998, after judging the Great Danes at Crufts, I went to Send Manor, on the green in Ripley, with Andrew Montgomery, Send Kennel Show Manager Bob Montgomery's son. Les Bowerman, who bought the property in 1977, kindly showed us through that marvellous old home — showed us the rooms, magnificent fireplaces, oak beams and winding staircases of the great house.

As we walked through the gardens and looked over where the kennel ranges had once been, I'm sure Andrew could feel the presence of his father, Bob Montgomery, who spent so many years standing where we stood, training those lovely Great Danes and teaching the young, exuberant kennel maids the science of caring for the magnificent dogs.

I found the whole experience eerie and humbling. The ghosts of the past were all around us. The ghosts of all those who had come alive for me, during the many years of research.

To be right there...
where kennel maids
had laughed and cried,
where the puppies
had played
then grown up and died...

And I remembered the Gordon Stewart I'd come to know so well, even though I'd never met him, that dapper, kindly man. Always in his fashionably tailored suit and waistcoat, wearing his little pince nez glasses and always carrying the American dime on the end of his watch chain — the dime his Grandfather Edwin had bet him so long ago.

CHAPTER TWENTY-SIX

To Rest in Peace

O n my way to judge the Great Danes in Johannesburg in June 1998, my wife, Shirley, and I stopped off in England a few days.

We took the train to visit a friend of many decades, Jean Lanning, at her new home in King's Somborne, Hampshire. Jean was driving us back to where we were staying in Ashtead, Surrey, with Elizabeth Osborne, when I suggested we drive by the church in Send where Stewart was buried. I wanted to take pictures of the church and of his grave.

About a mile out of Send, Surrey, we found the parish church of St. Mary the Virgin. I wasn't prepared for the peace and serenity of that wonderful churchyard. The church itself was old and magnificent. Small, yet gracious and stately. It is mentioned in the Domesday Survey of 1086. The oldest surviving part still there is the chancel, built around 1220. The chancel is the eastern end of a church, containing the high altar.

As we stood in the old churchyard, I could see and hear the river Wey trickling lazily by the tombstones. Black and white magpies were flitting about from tree to tree. The tombstones were centuries old, their carved messages now worn and blurred by time, a wide variety of styles and carvings to commemorate loved ones over those nine hundred years, some elaborate, others very plain. Some were toppled over and forgotten — memories of the past.

The entire churchyard was overgrown with long grass, and it took us a while to find the Stewart grave.

There were two other people wandering through the cemetery as the sun was slowly setting that evening. I approached and asked if they knew the layout of the churchyard. Could they point out the Stewart grave? With their help we found Stewart's mother's grave, with his small marker, towards the rear of the cemetery.

Looking at St. Mary's Church from Gordon Stewart's grave site.
Monuments go back nine hundred years. 1998.

PHOTO BY LES BOWERMAN

St. Mary the Virgin Church in Send Village, Surrey. Note at front bottom right Shirley Heal waving at left, and at far right is Jean Lanning. 1998.

His mother's gravestone was not an elaborate memorial, but classic and adequate. He had buried his mother there in 1933. The carved inscription reads:

Eleanor C. S. Stewart

Passed Along April 30th, 1933.

There Is A Link That Death Can Never Sever

Love And Remembrance Last For Ever

At the foot of her grave was another small, insignificant stone, not carved. Its inscription was simply letters of lead affixed to the stone. The letters were peeling and missing, so it was difficult to see or read the message, which simply said:

In Loving Memory

of

Gordon Stewart

May 13, 1885

January 21st 1952

Gordon Stewart's ashes were buried at the feet of his mother. The grave site was badly kept in tall grass. His mother's stone is standing at the rear, and Stewart's small stone has toppled over. 1998.

PHOTO BY LES BOWERMAN

The two markers were almost lost in the tall grass, alone, forlorn and forgotten. Stewart's was toppled over.

The peacefulness of that church and its churchyard is hard for me to describe, so calm and comforting. The air was very still on that rainy June night, the only sound the chirping of the birds and our feet pushing through the tall, wet grass.

I cannot imagine a better place.

When I commented on the tranquillity of that spot, the wandering couple told us that they had found the church fifteen years earlier. They had visited these grounds every day since then, good weather or bad, winter or summer. They said they felt cheated and restless if they didn't come. Yet their home was some miles away.

But as much as the churchyard was at peace, I felt restless and angry. My thoughts were far from peaceful. I thought of all those ungrateful, selfish people who had benefitted from his life and his death. I remembered the millions left in his will to those who survived him — and have forgotten him.

There his ashes lie at his mother's feet, forgotten by everyone in the tall, coarse grass. A pitiful small stone, not even properly engraved. A memorial that at best, in 1952, might have cost fifty pounds.

I was disgusted with them all!

Was this a deliberate indignity? A pointed insult from his wife, Irene, who survived him many years. And what of all the others, still alive, whom Stewart looked after handsomely and never forgot? They were willing to be indiscrete years before, but surely those indiscretions needn't keep them at a distance now.

That's all that's left of Gordon Stewart — his pitiful little stone. They lost and destroyed his records, his personal belongings . . . his memories.

As I walked out of the quiet churchyard that lovely evening with Shirley and Jean, I felt the humbling sensation of finality wash over me from that centuries-old place. Here indeed was the final chapter in his life.

May Gordon Stewart forever rest in peace.

CHAPTER TWENTY-SEVEN

The Big Question

Gordon Stewart knew royalty personally. His close associate for many years in the National Safety First Association that Stewart had founded in 1916 was Prince Albert, Duke of York, who was crowned King George VI in May 1937.

Prince George, the Duke of Kent and his brother the Duke of Gloucester visited Stewart at his home at Send Manor many times. Stewart even gave his prized Great Dane, Champion Midas of Send, to Prince George.

You've read how he went out of his way to cultivate friendships with the titled families of England. He was generous without question.

Not only did he establish and organize the Children's Safety First Drives, but he funded them himself. He gave his time to many worthwhile charities, and his Danes entertained at fund-raising events for good causes throughout Britain. His war effort was outstanding.

The Stewart companies provided essential manufacturing and maintenance services for vehicles and aircraft parts, and machine tooling for secret components for armament. All these things surely made him personally known to the prime minister, cabinet ministers and members of Parliament. His other companies, British Poultry Development and Send Grist Mills, provided tons and tons of food for the embattled nation throughout the war. All his beautiful buildings at Send Manor were voluntarily turned over to the British government for food storage.

Stewart's associates and lifelong friends, Bill Morris and Malcolm Campbell, were knighted. Many others close to him received titles and state honours.

So what happened with Gordon Stewart?

One of his kennel maids thought she had the answer. She

wondered if Stewart's affairs with certain young ladies had hurt him. "He often had pretty actresses staying over at Send Manor," she said. "And there were things that went on with some of the female staff as well. Maybe he'd just been too close to the eventual King of England. Maybe Prince Albert, the Duke of York, knew too much," she reasoned.

Or was Stewart being slighted for his friendship with Prince George, Duke of Kent? Because of their common love and appreciation of Great Danes, they were naturally seen together quite often with the dogs. Certain members of the press, even in those days, gave little quarter to the Royal family. The *Daily Mail* alleged that Prince George was addicted to cocaine and morphine. It said he had affairs with the well-known homosexual Noel Coward and female impersonator Douglas Byng.

"In those days," the kennel maid continued, "things were very proper. No matter how discrete the duke was, perhaps word got around and that's why Stewart was passed over."

There is no doubt that this self-made man was searching for personal recognition. Not the recognition of his great success in business — lots of men achieve that. He had another plan — a hidden agenda. He'd worked hard for a title.

He always remained in the public eye with his good deeds and great ideas, with films and children's crusades. His committees for these charities were always loaded with the Who's Who of Britain. Stewart's chauffeur was instructed to stay in line directly behind celebrities whenever he attended social functions so he would appear "connected."

His last big hurrah in the 1937 Coronation Year of his close friend, the Duke of York, was blasted all over England. Bertie was to become King George VI that year. For the Children's Safety Crusade, he produced *The Pied Piper of Hamelin* film and paid for it himself. It was shown with much fanfare to six million schoolchildren and their parents. Forty Morris vans, painted with the Pied Piper scenes and fitted with roof-top loudspeakers, touted his crusade throughout the land. And it certainly was known as Stewart's Crusade.

How could he not be noticed! This was surely a man crying out, "Look at me. I'm Gordon Stewart!"

When Gordon Stewart died in January 1952, virtually everything about this great man became nothing, as if he'd never been on Earth.

The winds of time just blew him away. As if he were nothing.

But this book will prove otherwise. There was, indeed, a Gordon Stewart and he was a big story in England the first half of the twentieth century. But the big question is — whatever happened?

Why was he never honoured or even recognized?

Well, there was a little secret that was kept very quiet all those years. His friend of many decades, Prince Albert, Duke of York, didn't forget him at all. King George VI, just before the Second World War, offered Stewart a knighthood.

But he turned it down!

* * * * * * *

Nearing the end of my research I again contacted all of my sources who had known Stewart and I posed my big question to them.

Several told me what finally happened. How he was offered a knighthood — why he decided to turn it down and what he said to King George.

Stewart had asked them not to reveal all this but that makes no sense at all. He would leave people to feel that there must be something sinister about him. A black side that prevented him from receiving his country's honours. That would have done him an unjust disservice.

Here's what was said to have happened!

CHAPTER TWENTY-EIGHT

You Needn't Call Me Sir

Gordon Stewart had returned to Send Manor early that day in 1939. Things were depressing at his office in London. Everyone was on edge as they watched Hitler's forces drive across Europe. Stewart and Ardern was laying plans to retool for wartime production.

As he walked to his study to pour himself a much-needed whisky and water he automatically picked up the day's mail on the hall table. It lay on a lovely silver salver that one of his Champion Great Danes had won. The housekeeper placed it there to catch his attention whenever he returned home.

It all looked pretty boring, but as he settled down in his favourite wingback leather chair, with the drink in his hand, he noticed a small white envelope with the deep blue crest of the Royal family.

It was from the secretary of the committee that awarded the nation's honours for the King's list at Christmas time, and simply said that he'd been chosen for a knighthood that year and would he please advise the committee if he'd accept the honour.

Stewart stiffened in his chair. There it was. Finally. The recognition he'd wanted all his life. He'd worked and planned so hard to be remembered by his country, yet something was wrong.

He knew himself better than anyone. There wasn't the exhilaration he'd expected. The excitement wasn't there. Stewart stood up and refilled his glass, then walked through the great house and out the massive oak door to the lovely garden. The fresh, clear, Surrey air brushed his face.

He walked slowly past the rose garden and pond and through the big iron gates onto the avenue that led to the Swiss village he'd spent so many years building. The canteen was silent now — all the kennel girls and boys were gone. At the puppy ranges the runs stood strangely empty. He sadly remembered the joyful yapping and whining that greeted him years before.

Stewart wandered over to the Karinda Hut and through the carved doors into that great Swiss hall. Up on the balcony he could see the huge wooden wheel and the large numbers, 1 to 6, that had sent his Great Danes down the lanes for the dog races. The wheel stood silent and alone.

The joy, laughter and howls of delight from the crowd of celebrities came hauntingly back to him as if it were yesterday.

He walked up the stairs to his balcony office, entering slowly, and looking around at all his familiar things. Then he sat down at his desk and put down his glass. The old memories were all there.

As he continued his walk through the past, he found himself on the training grounds, and looked up at Bob Montgomery's office on stilts above the long range of silent kennels. No one looked down at him.

A soft, cool breeze seemed to come out of nowhere and caressed the back of his hand.

He remembered Champions Midas, Lancelot, Ulana, Mavis and so many other great old friends. They would lovingly nuzzle his hand as he stood in that very spot. But now there was only the cool breeze. Had they come back to touch him one more time?

There was a deep sadness in him. But Stewart felt a kind of contentment as well, as he thought and remembered it all, those wonderful echoes of his past.

When he reached into his waistcoat pocket for a cigar, his hand touched the small American dime attached to his watch chain — the dime Grandfather Edwin had bet him almost forty years before.

And then suddenly he knew. It hadn't been a bet at all. It was a memento to him from the grand old man. His grandfather knew then how he would turn out, knew just what he was made of, that some day his grandson would realize that this tiny, almost worthless gift had challenged him to accomplish great things. He'd known how stubborn, ambitious and brilliant the young lad was.

Stewart, for the first time, saw clearly that he had accomplished many things that other men would never do. He realized that he was different from other men and stood proudly above most of them with what he had done.

Thousands of men and women had received knighthoods from their kings and queens throughout history. Did he want to become another one of that crowd? Not one of them carried Grandfather Edwin's little American dime. He already had his award and hadn't known it. It made him very different from all the rest.

Stewart now knew that he had been jousting at windmills all his life. The things he'd thought were important had never been important at all. The thrill was in the doing. The reward, that he'd done things other men could not do.

For the first time in his life he was calm and at peace with himself.

The next morning, when he arrived in London at his office, he picked up his phone and dialled the private line to the palace and asked for the King's personal secretary, who came on the line and, knowing of their close friendship, put Stewart through to King George in his study.

Bertie was delighted to hear from him. It would be a bright spot in an otherwise troubled day.

Stewart asked for Elizabeth and the children. They chatted for a few minutes, then Stewart decided to come right to the point. He told the King about receiving the letter and thanked him profusely for remembering him with such a great honour. Then he told him what his answer would be that morning.

"I'm going to turn down the honour, Your Majesty," he told him.

There was a stunned silence. Bertie asked, "But Gordon, whatever for? You, above all, have done so much for England and for me."

"I suddenly realized," continued Stewart, "that I'd like to remain the way I am. Just receiving your offer has been honour enough.

"I do not need the touch of your sword on my shoulder, Your Highness, or a 'Sir' before my name to always remain your faithful friend."

King George paused, then quietly answered, "I can well appreciate how you feel, Gordon. Elizabeth and I have often wished that things could stay the same as they were for us before I took the throne. But you have a choice and I didn't. I quite agree with you. I also like you just the way you are."

Gordon Stewart had made the biggest decision of his eventful life. And that is the measure of a truly great man.

*Gordon Stewart handles
Champion Lancelot at right and
Champion Ulana in the middle
with one of her pups at the left.
Stewart was always perfectly dressed,
even while working with his dogs.*

PHOTO COURTESY ANDREW MONTGOMERY

Andrew Montgomery's mother, Audrey Field, with the blue Champion Lancelot of Send. PHOTO COURTESY ANDREW MONTGOMERY

Note the choke chains on these fawns from 1932 are the same as we use today, sixty-six years later. PHOTO COURTESY ANDREW MONTGOMERY

Obedience training for a fawn team.
PHOTO COURTESY ANDREW MONTGOMERY

Left to right are Sybil Church with Midas, Miss Ryde, Vic Allfrey with the harlequin Donna, Phui May, Margaret Tracy with Mona and Audrey Field with Lancelot. On the training field at Send.
PHOTO COURTESY ANDREW MONTGOMERY

The import Arco Romerturm of Send.

December 11, 1929, at the Birmingham National Dog Show, Bingley Hall, Birmingham, Warwick. Left to right are Fay of Send (catalogue No. 141), handler Miss Ecob, Champion Midas of Send (No. 140), Audrey Field, and Champion Ulana of Send (No. 142).
PHOTO COURTESY ANDREW MONTGOMERY

The blue Champion Lancelot of Send.
PHOTO COURTESY ANDREW MONTGOMERY

Left to right: Champion Lancelot of Send, a blue Great Dane and on the right is the black Winifried of Send.

A successful day. Audrey Field holds the cup. At left is Champion Ulana of Send and at the right is Champion Lancelot of Send. Kind of pooped after a hard day's work.

Head study of the blue Dane Champion Lancelot of Send.

PHOTO COURTESY ANDREW MONTGOMERY

Left to right: Winifried, Wotan and Lancelot of Send.
Winifried is Wotan's litter sister.

PHOTO COURTESY ANDREW MONTGOMERY

Champion Rahie of Send (Black)

*Alick of Send by Champion Lancelot
Ex Rimini of Send (Blue)*

Draga of Send, trained by Margaret Tracy, clears a six-foot obstacle. Training for the Associated Police and Army Dog Society Trials at Crystal Palace, October 16, 1932.

PHOTO COURTESY MARGARET TRACY

Send Danes
You Might Know

I 'd have liked to have known the genius at Send Kennel who had to dream up the names for the thousands of Stewart's dogs. What a job that must have been!

In this chapter, I've given you the first-line pedigree information on nine hundred and eighty-seven Great Danes that I know belonged to or were registered by him. The registrations began in 1925 and ended in August 1939, when Stewart went out of breeding, gave away or sold his dogs and went on to other things during the war years.

The cross-checking and research on this chapter alone took as much time as writing the rest of the book, but I felt it was important for those of you who are interested in the history of Send Kennel pedigrees.

There were probably more Send Danes, because he did not necessarily register some imports or puppies sold to those who wanted to use their own kennel names, or bitches who couldn't conceive and dogs who wouldn't breed.

I suspect this, because I ran across some who were registered as many as ten or eleven years after whelping. Why, I don't know.

Stewart used the names Send, Sendale and even Distin for registrations. Again, I know not why.

The *Kennel Gazette* listings also did not give colours, so I can't help you much there.

I cannot begin to thank Philip Robinson of the Kennel Club Library for all the photostats he pulled out and organized from stud books, breed record supplements and *Kennel Gazette* monthly issues over those many years. A mammoth job!

I then had to index and cross-check all this and cannot guarantee this is a complete list.

Where did all of Stewart's pedigree records go? There must have been masses of indexed files on hand at Send Manor.

If you require additional information or extended pedigrees on an individual dog, just write to this address below and for a small fee, they'll print out what you need from their wonderful computer bank.

Write to:
The Kennel Club
1 - 5 Clarges Street
Piccadilly, London
England, W1Y 8AB

Some Pedigrees
of Send Great Danes

Name	Sex	Born	Sire	Dam	Year Registered at Kennel Club
A					
Adda of Send (IMP)	F	1924 Jan. 28	Arno v. d. Arendsburg	Flora v. Heidof	1926
Ador Viktoria of Send (IMP)	M	1922 Jul. 16	Ador Tipp Topp	Aga v.d. Ruhr	1926
Annaliese Rott of Send (IMP)	F	1925 Feb. 6	Bodo v. Federsee	Toska v. Bohmer Wald	1926
Ajax Lindenstadt of Send (IMP)	M	1925 Jul. 2	Ceasar	Ria v. Alt Nurnberg	1926
Arco Romerturm of Send (IMP)	M	1925 Jul. 16	Tell v. Illertal	Asta v. Romerturm	1926
Aspe Amalienburg of Send (IMP)	F	1923 Mar. 19	Roland v. Riesenfield	Petrea Sauer	1926
Asta Galster of Send (IMP)	F	1925 Aug. 5	Rex v. Brandholz	Ada v. Reichswald	1926
Aida Volbloed of Send (IMP)	F	1923 June 12	Hedwigs Nestor	Hedwigs Niza	1927
Affra v. Schonbuch of Send (IMP)	F	1923 Apr. 8	Fels v. Schonboch	Amanda v. d. Rheinschanze	1928
Ayesha of Send	F	1927 Mar. 3	Arco Romerturm of Send	Alani of Sendale	1927
Alani of Sendale	F	1925 Feb. 25	Dion of Dicksonia	Lally of Axwell	1925
Achilles of Send	M	1927 Mar. 3	Arco Romerturm of Send	Alani of Sendale	1927
Adonis of Send	M	1927 Mar. 3	Arco Romerturm of Send	Alani of Sendale	1927
Alick of Send	M	1931 May 20	Ch. Lancelot of Send	Rimini of Send	1932
Anita of Send	F	1925 Feb. 25	Dion of Dicksonia	Lally of Axwell	1926
Amami of Send	F	1927 Mar. 3	Arco Romerturm of Send	Alani of Sendale	1927
Anchusa of Send	F	1927 Mar. 3	Arco Romerturm of Send	Alani of Sendale	1927
Anette of Send	F	1927 Mar. 3	Arco Romerturm of Send	Alani of Sendale	1927
Angela of Send	F	1927 Mar. 3	Arco Romerturm of Send	Alani of Sendale	1927
Atilla of Send	M	1927 Mar. 3	Arco Romerturm of Send	Alani of Sendale	1927
Annebel of Send	F	1927 Oct. 31	Baldur Daheim of Send	Asta Galster of Send	1929

Name	Sex	Date	Sire	Dam	Year
Alaric of Send	M	1928 Jul. 21	Urlus Volbloed of Send	Anchusa of Send	1929
Akbar of Send	M	1928 Jul 21	Urlus Volbloed of Send	Anchusa of Send	1929
Aprille of Send	F	1928 Jul. 21	Urlus Volbloed of Send	Anchusa of Send	1930
Armide of Send	F	1928 Jul. 21	Urlus Volbloed of Send	Anchusa of Send	1930
Asra of Send	F	1928 Jul. 21	Urlus Volbloed of Send	Anchusa of Send	1930
Audrey of Send	F	1928 Jul. 21	Urlus Volbloed of Send	Anchusa of Send	1930
Alan of Send	M	1929 Mar. 20	Casar Koger Bella Forsten	Riederquelle of Send	1930
Andron of Send	M	1931 Feb.18	Ch. Midas of Send	Londa of Send	1932
Andolf of Send	M	1931 May 20	Ch. Lancelot of Send	Rimini of Send	1932
Aymar of Send	M	1931 May 20	Ch. Lancelot of Send	Rimini of Send	1932
Adrian of Send	M	1931 May 20	Ch. Lancelot of Send	Rimini of Send	1932
Alexander of Send	M	1931 May 20	Ch. Lancelot of Send	Rimini of Send	1932
Aphrodite of Send	F	1931 May 20	Ch. Lancelot of Send	Rimini of Send	1932
Adela of Send	F	1932 Sept. 16	Ch. Lancelot of Send	Colleen of Send	1932
Althea of Send	F	1931 May 20	Ch. Lancelot of Send	Rimini of Send	1932
Alwin of Send	M	1932 Sept. 16	Ch. Lancelot of Send	Colleen of Send	1933
Agricola of Send	F	1932 Sept. 16	Ch. Lancelot of Send	Colleen of Send	1933
Alison of Send	M	1932 Sept. 16	Ch. Lancelot of Send	Colleen of Send	1933
Alisa of Send	F	1932 Sept. 16	Cleon of Send	Rosita of Send	1933
Amabel of Send	F	1932 Sept. 16	Ch. Lancelot of Send	Colleen of Send	1933
Amber of Send	F	1931 Feb. 18	Ch. Midas of Send	Londa of Send	1933
Avina of Send	F	1931 Feb. 18	Ch. Midas of Send	Londa of Send	1933
Abess of Send	F	1931 May 20	Ch. Lancelot of Send	Rimini of Send	1933
Anthea of Send	F	1933 June 9	Bernard of Send	Little Sister of Send	1933
Alix of Send	M	1933 June 9	Bernard of Send	Little Sister of Send	1934

Code: (IMP-Imported) (M-Male) (F-Female) (V-Von) (Ch.-Champion)

Name	Sex	Born	Sire	Dam	Year Registered at Kennel Club
Arpad of Send	M	1933 June 9	Bernard of Send	Little Sister of Send	1934
Argos of Send	M	1931 Feb. 18	Ch. Midas of Send	Londa of Send	1934
Alexia of Send	F	1933 June 9	Bernard of Send	Little Sister of Send	1934
Antonia of Send	F	1933 June 9	Bernard of Send	Little Sister of Send	1934
Andrew of Send	M	1933 June 9	Bernard of Send	Little Sister of Send	1934
Avril of Send	F	1933 June 9	Bernard of Send	Little Sister of Send	1934
Andrea of Send	M	1933 June 9	Bernard of Send	Little Sister of Send	1935
Adam of Send	M	1936 Apr. 1	Ean of Send	Genita of Send	1937
Anona of Send	F	1936 Apr. 1	Ean of Send	Genita of Send	1937
Annora of Send	F	1936 Apr. 1	Ean of Send	Genita of Send	1938
B					
Baldur Daheim of Send (IMP)	M	1925 Mar. 5	Ador v. Amalienberg	Edda v. Alt Potsdam	1926
Blanca Osterholz of Send (IMP)	F	1925 May 7	Hans v.d. Klasserburg	Maus v. Kernenturm	1926
Burggraf v. Falkenhorst of Send (IMP)	M	1924 May 9	Nero v. Schiff	Munster Afra Mikoda	1926
Bella Forstenruderquelle of Send (IMP)	F	1925 Mar. 10	Prinz Hofmann	Olga II v. Riesenfeld	1930
Bruno Rotenberg of Send (IMP)	M	1923 Jan. 16	Fels v. Osterholz	Tekla v. Schonbuch	1926
Brenda of Send	F	1925 Jul. 5	Professor of Falklands	Rufflyn Rouvia	1925
Beryl of Send	F	1925 Jul. 5	Professor of Falklands	Rufflyn Rouvia	1925
Boris of Send	M	1925 Jul. 5	Professor of Falklands	Rufflyn Rouvia	1925
Bernard of Send	M	1924 Oct. 15	Glinger of Axwell	Nada of Send	
Babette of Send	F	1927 Mar. 3	Jorg Osterholtz of Send	Springmere Sally	1927
Brenda of Distin	F	1932 Sept. 22	Bernard of Send	Rhanva of Send	

Name	Sex	Date	Sire	Dam	Year
Berthli of Send			Glinger of Axwell	Nada of Send	
Bacchante of Send	F	1925 Jul. 5	Professor of Falklands	Rufflyn Rouvia	1925
Barbara of Send	F	1925 Jul. 5	Professor of Falklands	Rufflyn Rouvia	1925
Bonita of Send	F	1925 Jul. 5	Professor of Falklands	Rufflyn Rouvia	1925
Bridgit of Send	F	1925 Jul. 5	Professor of Falklands	Rufflyn Rouvia	1925
Brunhilde of Send	F	1925 Jul. 5	Professor of Falklands	Rufflyn Rouvia	1925
Buccaneer of Send	M	1925 Jul. 5	Professor of Falklands	Rufflyn Rouvia	1925
Blanka of Send (IMP)	F	1923 Mar. 22	Floppa Moguntia	Ella v. Wendenburg	1926
Banquo of Send	M	1927 Mar. 3	Jorg Osterholtz of Send	Spring Mere Sally	1927
Baucis of Send	F	1927 Mar. 3	Jorg Osterholtz of Send	Spring Mere Sally	1927
Beatrice of Send	F	1927 Mar. 3	Jorg Osterholtz of Send	Spring Mere Sally	1927
Borgia of Send	M	1927 Mar. 3	Jorg Osterholtz of Send	Spring Mere Sally	1927
Beppo of Send	M	1927 Dec. 29	Urlus Volbloed of Send	Blanka of Send	1928
Bryda of Send	F	1927 Dec. 29	Urlus Volbloed of Send	Blanka of Send	1928
Bernice of Send	F	1927 Dec. 29	Urlus Volbloed of Send	Blanka of Send	1928
Babema of Send	M	1927 Dec. 29	Urlus Volbloed of Send	Blanka of Send	1929
Benoni of Send	M	1927 Dec. 29	Urlus Volbloed of Send	Blanka of Send	1929
Balaka of Send	F	1928 Jul. 28	Adonis of Send	Chloe of Send	1930
Bettina of Send	F	1930 Feb. 20	Eglon of Send	Belinda of Blendon	1930
Brutus of Send	M	1930 Feb. 20	Eglon of Send	Belinda of Blendon	1930
Basco of Send	M	1929 Mar. 26	Ch. Fedor of Send	Edna of Send	1930
Bacchus of Send	M	1929 Mar. 26	Ch. Fedor of Send	Edna of Send	1930
Bellona of Send	F	1929 Mar. 26	Ch. Fedor of Send	Edna of Send	1930
Bendigo of Send	M	1929 Mar. 26	Ch. Fedor of Send	Edna of Send	1930
Benhur of Send	M	1930 Feb. 20	Eglon of Send	Belinda of Blendon	1930

Code: (IMP–Imported) (M–Male) (F–Female) (V–Von) (Ch.–Champion)

Name	Sex	Born	Sire	Dam	Year Registered at Kennel Club
Brian of Send	M	1929 Mar. 26	Ch. Fedor of Send	Edna of Send	1930
Britta of Send	F	1929 Mar. 26	Ch. Fedor of Send	Edna of Send	1930
Brent of Send	M	1930 Feb. 20	Eglon of Send	Belinda of Blendon	1930
Bison of Send	M	1930 Feb. 20	Eglon of Send	Belinda of Blendon	1931
Ben of Send	M	1930 Feb. 20	Eglon of Send	Belinda of Blendon	1931
Bella of Send	F	1928 May 1	Baron Excelsior	Bella Forstenriederquelle of Send	1931
Bryanhilde of Send	M	1930 Feb. 20	Eglon of Send	Belinda of Blendon	1931
Belle of Send	F	1931 May 25	Ch. Lancelot of Send	Velma of Send	1931
Bodo of Send	M	1928 Jul. 28	Adonis of Send	Chloe of Send	1931
Botolf of Send	M	1931 May 25	Ch. Lancelot of Send	Velma of Send	1932
Blanche of Send	F	1931 Oct. 19	Yule of Send	Ysabel of Send	1932
Blaise of Send	M	1932 Sept. 19	Thor of Send	Megan of Send	1932
Basil of Send	M	1932 Sept. 19	Thor of Send	Megan of Send	1933
Beta of Send	F	1932 Sept. 19	Thor of Send	Megan of Send	1933
Beth of Send	F	1931 Oct. 19	Yule of Send	Ysabel of Send	1933
Brynhild of Send	F	1932 Sept. 19	Thor of Send	Megan of Send	1933
Brigita of Send	F	1931 Oct. 19	Yule of Send	Ysabel of Send	1933
Barri of Send	M	1932 Sept. 19	Thor of Send	Megan of Send	1933
Beorn of Send	M	1933 Jun. 13	Godric of Send	Paulette of Send	1933
Boda of Send	F	1931 Oct. 19	Yule of Send	Ysabel of Send	1933
Baldric of Send	M	1932 Sept. 19	Thor of Send	Megan of Send	1933
Berta of Send	F	1933 June 13	Godric of Send	Paulette of Send	1934

Name	Sex	Date	Sire	Dam	Year
Beatrix of Send	F	1933 June 13	Godric of Send	Paulette of Send	1934
Bea of Send	F	1933 June 13	Godric of Send	Paulette of Send	1934
Bianca of Send	F	1933 June 13	Godric of Send	Paulette of Send	1934
Bey of Send	M	1934 Dec. 18	Akbar of Send	Rispah of Send	1935
Biddy of Send	F	1934 Dec. 18	Akbar of Send	Rispah of Send	1935
Bertram of Send	M	1934 Dec. 18	Akbar of Send	Rispah of Send	1935
Bruin of Send	M	1934 Dec. 18	Akbar of Send	Rispah of Send	1935
Blue Manon of Send	F	1935 Nov. 20	Ch. Lancelot of Send	Blue deRoi of Blendon	1937
Blue Mischa of Send	M	1935 Nov. 20	Ch. Lancelot of Send	Blue deRoi of Blendon	1937

C

Name	Sex	Date	Sire	Dam	Year
Caesar Hegerburg of Send (IMP)	M	1926 Apr. 19	Adonis	Blanka of Send	1927
Caspar of Send (IMP)	M	1928 Jan. 18	Dolf v.d. Saalburg	Cella v. Ottoberg	1929
Cortes of Send (IMP)	M	1928 Jan. 18	Dolf v.d. Saalburg	Cella v. Ottoberg	1931
Carla Otterberg of Send	F	1926 Feb. 10	Emir v. Wendenburg	Festa Freya v.d. Rhon	1930
Cyclops of Sendale	M	1923 Apr. 24	Magpie of Etive	Varuna	1925
Cato of Send	M	1925 May 24	Cyclops of Sendale	Judy of Cuddington	1925
Chloe of Send	F	1924 May 24	Cyclops of Sendale	Judy of Cuddington	1925
Claude of Send	M	1925 May 24	Cyclops of Sendale	Judy of Cuddington	1925
Croesus of Send	M	1925 May 24	Cyclops of Sendale	Judy of Cuddington	1925
Cilli Illertal of Send (IMP)	F	1924 Feb. 2	Tell v. Illertal	Senta v. Durrfelden	1926
Cyrano of Send	M	1927 Feb. 26	Ajax Lindenstadt of Send	Chloe of Send	1927
Claudette of Send	F	1928 Jan. 10	Kastor Klasserburg of Send	Toska Bohnerwald of Send	1928
Chica of Send	F	1928 Jan. 10	Kastor Klasserburg of Send	Taska Bohnerwald of Send	1929
Carlos of Send	M	1928 Jan. 10	Kastor Klasserburg of Send	Toska Bohnerwald of Send	1929
Caprice of Send	F	1928 Jan. 10	Kastor Klasserburg of Send	Toska Bohnerwald of Send	1930

Code: (IMP-Imported) (M-Male) (F-Female) (V-Von) (Ch.-Champion)

Name	Sex	Born	Sire	Dam	Year Registered at Kennel Club
Cedric of Send	M	1928 Jan. 10	Kastor Klasserburg of Send	Toska Bohnerwald of Send	1930
Cleon of Send	M	1929 Mar. 24	Egbert of Send	Alani of Sendale	1930
Cluna of Send	F	1929 Mar. 24	Egbert of Send	Alani of Sendale	1930
Colleen of Send	F	1929 Mar. 24	Egbert of Send	Alani of Sendale	1930
Carol of Send	M	1928 Jan. 10	Kastor Klasserberg of Send	Toska-Bohmerwald of Send	1931
Cyrus of Send	M	1929 Jan. 27	Baldur Daheim of Send	Danne of Elverland	1931
Corinne of Send	F	1928 Jan. 18	Ch. Dolf v.d. Saalburg	Cella v. Ottoberg	1931
Clotilde of Send	F	1928 Jan. 10	Kastor Klasserberg of Send	Toska Bohmerwald of Send	1931
Caius of Send	M	1930 Feb. 26	Woden of Send	Imogen of Send	1931
Casilda of Send	F	1928 Jan. 10	Kastor Klasserberg of Send	Toska Bohmerwald of Send	1931
Cynthia of Send	F	1931 Oct. 24	Akbar of Send	Marya of Send	1932
Colin of Send	M	1931 Mar. 4	Sultan Chartreuse of Send	Norga of Send	1932
Conrad of Send	M	1931 Mar. 4	Sultan Chartreuse of Send	Norga of Send	1932
Cheetah of Send	M	1932 Sept. 22	Bernard of Send	Rhanva of Send	1933
Ciro of Send	M	1932 Sept. 22	Bernard of Send	Rhanva of Send	1933
Comet of Send	M	1932 Sept. 22	Bernard of Send	Rhanva of Send	1933
Cara of Send	F	1931 May 24	Thor of Send	Topsy of Cuddington	1933
Cyprian of Send	M	1932 Sept. 22	Bernard of Send	Rhanva of Send	1933
Canute of Send	M	1933 June 24	Zorro of Send	Josette of Send	1933
Cicero of Send	M	1933 June 24	Zorro of Send	Josette of Send	1933
Caleb of Send	M	1933 June 24	Zorro of Send	Josette of Send	1933
Clarice of Send	F	1933 June 24	Zorro of Send	Josette of Send	1933

Name	Code	Date	Sire	Dam	Year
Celia of Send	F	1932 Sept. 22	Bernard of Send	Rhanva of Send	1934
Centaur of Send	M	1932 Sept. 22	Bernard of Send	Rhanva of Send	1934
Carmen of Send	F	1933 June 24	Zorro of Send	Josette of Send	1934
Charon of Send	M	1932 Sept. 22	Bernard of Send	Rhanva of Send	1934
Clement of Send	M	1932 Sept. 22	Bernard of Send	Rhanva of Send	1934
Collette of Send	F	1933 June 24	Zorro of Send	Josette of Send	1934
Clare of Send	F	1931 May 24	Thor of Send	Topsy of Cuddington	1935
Cicely of Send	F	1936 Apr. 24	Laddie of Send	Meta of Send	1937
Chieftain of Send	M	1936 Apr. 24	Laddie of Send	Meta of Send	1937
Christopher of Send	M	1936 Apr. 24	Laddie of Send	Meta of Send	1937

D

Name	Code	Date	Sire	Dam	Year
Donar v. Falkenhorst of Send (IMP)	M	1924 May 9	Nero v. Schiff Munster	Afra Mikoda	1926
Diana Niederaichbach of Send (IMP)	F	1927 May 28	Alex v. Hohenthau	Frieda v. Niederaichbach	1931
Ch. Danilo of Send	M	1932 Apr. 29	Thor of Send	Erna of Send	1933
Donna of Send	F	1928 July 25	Baldur Daheim of Send	Freckles of Cuddington	1929
Dinah of Sendale	F	1925 May 13	Alexis of Lockerbie	Aprille of Ouborough	
Dolores of Send	F	1927 May 5	Bruno Rotenburg of Send	Bridget of Send	1927
Dakota of Send	M	1928 Aug. 19	Adonis of Send	Gaby of Send	1929
Desha of Send	M	1928 Aug. 19	Adonis of Send	Gaby of Send	1929
Duke of Send	M	1929 Mar. 29	Marcus of Send	Dinah of Sendale	1930
Dora of Send	F	1928 Aug. 19	Adonis of Send	Gaby of Send	1930
Dirk of Send	M	1929 Mar. 29	Marcus of Send	Dinah of Sendale	1930
Dea of Send	F	1929 Mar. 29	Marcus of Send	Dinah of Sendale	1930
Drummer of Send	M	1930 Feb. 27	Ch. Lancelot of Send	Wendy of Send	1931
Danella of Send	F	1928 June 27	Baldur Daheim of Send	Danner of Elverland	1931

Code: (IMP-Imported) (M-Male) (F-Female) (V-Von) (Ch.-Champion)

Name	Sex	Born	Sire	Dam	Year Registered at Kennel Club
Dira of Send	F	1931 Feb. 21	Eglon of Send	Diana Niederaichbach of Send	1932
Dan of Send	M	1931 May 23	Wolfram of Sendale	Janet of Send	1932
Draga of Send	F	1930 Feb. 27	Ch. Lancelot of Send	Wendy of Send	1932
Denis of Send	M	1930 Feb. 27	Ch. Lancelot of Send	Wendy of Send	1932
Dante of Send	M	1931 Feb. 28	Eglon of Send	Diana Niederaichbach of Send	1932
Dawn of Send	F	1930 Feb. 27	Ch. Lancelot of Send	Wendy of Send	1932
Dorenda of Send	F	1930 Feb. 27	Ch. Lancelot of Send	Wendy of Send	1932
Donald of Send	M	1933 June 24	Eglon of Send	Berthli of Send	1933
Dion of Send	M	1933 June 24	Eglon of Send	Berthli of Send	1934
Don of Send	M	1933 June 24	Eglon of Send	Berthli of Send	1934
Donys of Send	M	1933 June 24	Eglon of Send	Berthli of Send	1934
Delia of Send	F	1932 Apr. 29	Thor of Send	Erna of Send	1934
Daniel of Send	M	1933 June 24	Eglon of Send	Berthli of Send	1934
Dugald of Send	M	1933 June 24	Eglon of Send	Berthli of Send	1934
Duro of Send	M	1933 June 24	Eglon of Send	Berthli of Send	1934
Dermot of Send	M	1932 Sept. 28	Rafe of Send	Ufa of Send	1934
Dorine of Send	F	1930 Feb. 27	Ch. Lancelot of Send	Wendy of Send	1934
Dando of Send	M	1933 June 24	Eglon of Send	Berthli of Send	1935

E

Name	Sex	Born	Sire	Dam	Year Registered at Kennel Club
Ella v. Wendenburg of Send (IMP)					
Egon v. Falkenhorst of Send (IMP)	M	1924 Dec. 16	Bruno v. Federsee	Afra Mikoda	1926
Ch. Egmund of Send	M	1928 Jan. 29	Urlus Volbloed of Send	Beryl of Send	1929

Name	Code	Birth date	Sire	Dam	Year
Eglon of Send	M	1927 Mar. 16	Egon Falkenhorst of Send	Hedwigs Sonia of Send	1927
Eunice of Send	F	1927 Mar. 16	Egon Falkenhorst of Send	Hedwigs Sonia of Send	1927
Egbert of Send	M	1928 Jan. 29	Urlus Volbloed of Send	Beryl of Send	1929
Electra of Send	F	1927 Mar. 16	Egon Falkenhorst of Send	Hedwigs Sonia of Send	1927
Elmer of Send	M	1928 Jan. 29	Urlus Volbloed of Send	Beryl of Send	1929
Erna of Send	F	1930 Feb. 28	Ch. Lancelot of Send	Donna of Send	1931
Estelle of Send	F	1932 May 9	Bernard of Send	Carla Otterberg of Send	1933
Earl of Send	M	1925 Sept. 9	Cyclops of Sendale	Springmere Sally	1926
Elaine of Send	F	1925 Sept. 9	Cyclops of Sendale	Springmere Sally	1926
Ena of Send	F	1925 Sept. 9	Cyclops of Sendale	Springmere Sally	1926
Enid of Send	F	1925 Sept. 9	Cyclops of Sendale	Springmere Sally	1926
Ermine of Send	M	1925 Sept. 9	Cyclops of Sendale	Springmere Sally	1926
Eros of Send	F	1925 Sept. 9	Cyclops of Sendale	Springmere Sally	1926
Echo of Send	M	1926 Mar. 16	Egon Falkenhorst of Send	Hedwigs Sonia of Send	1927
Edna of Send	F	1927 Mar. 16	Egon Falkenhorst of Send	Hedwigs Sonia of Send	1927
Effendi of Send	M	1927 Mar. 16	Egon Falkenhorst of Send	Hedwigs Sonia of Send	1927
Endymion of Send	M	1927 Mar. 16	Egon Falkenhorst of Send	Hedwigs Sonia of Send	1927
Emir of Send	M	1928 Jan. 29	Urlus Volbloed of Send	Beryl of Send	1928
Euan of Send	M	1928 Jan. 29	Urlus Volbloed of Send	Beryl of Send	1931
Erwin of Send	F	1931 Mar. 2	Bernard of Send	Corinne of Send	1931
Elsa of Send	F	1931 Mar. 2	Bruno Rotenberg of Send	Sybil of Send	1932
Eryx of Send	M	1931 May 30	Tarquin of Send	Josette of Send	1932
Edmond of Send	M	1931 May 30	Tarquin of Send	Josette of Send	1932
Erika of Send	F	1931 Mar. 2	Bruno Rotenberg of Send	Sybil of Send	1932
Ewan of Send	M	1932 May 9	Bernard of Send	Carla Ottoberg of Send	1932

Code: (IMP–Imported) (M–Male) (F–Female) (V–Von) (Ch.–Champion)

Name	Sex	Born	Sire	Dam	Year Registered at Kennel Club
Edgar of Send	M	1931 Mar. 2	Bruno Rotenberg of Send	Sybil of Send	1933
Elissa of Send	F	1930 Feb. 28	Ch. Lancelot of Send	Donna of Send	1933
Elga of Send	F	1932 May 9	Bernard of Send	Carla Ottoberg of Send	1933
Eve of Send	F	1928 Jan. 29	Urlus Volbloed of Send	Beryl of Send	1933
Elise of Send	F	1932 May 9	Bernard of Send	Carla Ottoberg of Send	1933
Erlan of Send	M	1933 June 25	Thor of Send	Melissa of Send	1933
Eroff of Send	M	1933 June 25	Thor of Send	Melissa of Send	1933
Etzel of Send	M	1933 June 25	Thor of Send	Melissa of Send	1933
Eldred of Send	M	1931 May 30	Tarquin of Send	Josette of Send	1933
Eadgar of Send	M	1932 May 9	Bernard of Send	Carla Ottoberg of Send	1934
Emyrs of Send	M	1933 June 25	Thor of Send	Melissa of Send	1934
Eugen of Send	M	1932 May 9	Bernard of Send	Carla Ottoberg of Send	1934
Eveleen of Send	F	1933 Mar. 6	Rafe of Send	Serina of Send	1934
Eric of Send	M	1930 Feb. 28	Ch. Lancelot of Send	Donna of Send	1934
Errol of Send	M	1932 May 9	Bernard of Send	Carla Ottoberg of Send	1934
Ean of Send	M	1933 Mar. 6	Rafe of Send	Serena of Send	1934
Etta of Send	F	1931 May 30	Tarquin of Send	Josette of Send	1934
Edler of Send	M	1932 May 9	Bernard of Send	Carla Ottoberg of Send	1935
Elinor of Send	F	1936 May 11	Ean of Send	Roquette of Send	1936
Evan of Send	M	1936 May 11	Ean of Send	Roquette of Send	1937
Edana of Send	F	1936 May 11	Ean of Send	Roquette of Send	1938

F

Flora v. Heidof of Send (IMP)
Fulda Hansa of Send (IMP)

Name	Sex	Date	Sire	Dam	Year
Furst of Send (IMP)	M	1926 Dec. 13	Bosko v.d. Saalburg	Fulda Hansa of Ouborough	1931
Ch. Fedor of Send	M	1927 Mar. 16	Kastor Klasserburg of Send	Hedwigs Sonia of Send	1927
Falstaff of Send	M	1928 Mar. 16	Urlus Volbloed of Send	Affra Schonbuch of Send	1929
Fay of Send	F	1928 Mar. 16	Urlus Volbloed of Send	Affra Schonbuch of Send	1929
Freda of Send	F	1927 Mar. 16	Kastor Klasserburg of Send	Norga of Send	1927
Freya of Send	F	1927 Mar. 16	Kastor Klasserburg of Send	Norga of Send	1927
Fahne Ruhrtal of Send	F	1925 May 22	Rino v. Volbloed	Fahne Hansa	1926
Fiona of Send	F	1928 Mar. 16	Urlus Volbloed of Send	Affra Schonbuch of Send	1929
Fortuna of Send	F	1929 Apr. 25	Baldur Daheim of Send	Lola of Sendale	1930
Falcon of Send	M	1925 Sept. 8	Alexis of Lockerbie	Topsy of Cuddington	1926
Fenella of Send	F	1925 Sept. 8	Alexis of Lockerbie	Topsy of Cuddington	1926
Figaro of Send	M	1925 Sept. 8	Alexis of Lockerbie	Topsy of Cuddington	1926
Fakir of Send	M	1927 Mar. 16	Kastor Klasserburg of Send	Norga of Send	1927
Felicite of Send	F	1927 Mar. 16	Kastor Klasserburg of Send	Norga of Send	1927
Fernando of Send	M	1927 Mar. 16	Kastor Klasserburg of Send	Norga of Send	1927
Feodora of Send	F	1927 Mar. 16	Kastor Klasserburg of Send	Norga of Send	1927
Fra of Send	M	1927 Mar. 16	Kastor Klasserburg of Send	Norga of Send	1927
Fee v.d. Saalburg of Send	F	1927 July 2	Dolf v.d. Saalburg	Fulda Hansa	1928
Fabian of Send	M	1928 Mar. 16	Urlus Volbloed of Send	Affra Schonbuch of Send	1930
Faust of Send	M	1928 Mar. 16	Urlus Volbloed of Send	Affra Schonbuch of Send	1930
Fedra of Send	F	1928 Sep. 11	Adonis of Send	Niobe of Send	1930
Fergus of Send	M	1930 Mar.	Eglon of Send	Rosamund of Send	1931

Code: (IMP-Imported) (M-Male) (F-Female) (V-Von) (Ch.-Champion)

Name	Sex	Born	Sire	Dam	Year Registered at Kennel Club
Falk of Send	M	1930 Mar. 3	Eglon of Send	Rosamund of Send	1932
Fiola of Send	F	1930 Mar. 3	Eglon of Send	Rosamund of Send	1932
Flavia of Send	F	1931 Mar. 5	Eglon of Send	Clotilde of Send	1932
Florenta of Send	F	1930 Mar. 3	Eglon of Send	Rosamund of Send	1932
Friar of Send	M	1932 May 15	Bernard of Send	Little Sister of Send	1932
Fido of Send	F	1931 Mar. 5	Eglin of Send	Clotilde of Send	1932
Frieda of Send	F	1931 June 27	Sascha of Send	Rowena of Send	1932
Florian of Send	M	1932 May 15	Bernard of Send	Little Sister of Send	1933
Fex of Send	M	1932 May 15	Bernard of Send	Little Sister of Send	1933
Flavian of Send	M	1933 Mar. 7	Ch. Egmund of Send	Arina of Send	1933
Fax of Send	M	1933 Mar. 7	Ch. Egmund of Send	Arina of Send	1933
Fels of Send	M	1933 Mar. 7	Ch. Egmund of Send	Arina of Send	1933
Feodor of Send	M	1933 June 28	Godric of Send	Fay of Send	1933
Fingal of Send	M	1932 May 15	Bernard of Send	Little Sister of Send	1933
Fredina of Send	F	1932 May 15	Bernard of Send	Little Sister of Send	1934
Friday of Send	M	1933 Mar. 7	Ch. Edmund of Send	Arina of Send	1934
Fayson of Send	M	1934 Oct. 28	Sohrab of Send	Fay of Send	1935
Felix of Send	M	1935 Jan. 10	Ch. Lancelot of Send	June of Send	1935
Faume of Send	F	1933 Mar. 7	Ch. Egmund of Send	Arina of Send	1935
Fortune of Send	M	1935 Jan. 10	Ch. Lancelot of Send	June of Send	1935
Fame of Send	M	1935 Jan. 10	Ch. Lancelot of Send	June of Send	1936
Flash of Send	M	1935 Jan. 10	Ch. Lancelot of Send	June of Send	1936

Name	Sex	Date	Sire	Dam	Year
Faruk of Send	M	1936 May 23	Ean of Send	Delia of Send	1936
Frank of Send	M	1936 May 23	Ean of Send	Delia of Send	1936
Frey of Send	M	1936 May 23	Ean of Send	Delia of Send	1936

G

Gilli Illerthal of Send (IMP)

Name	Sex	Date	Sire	Dam	Year
Galahad of Send	M	1925 Oct. 10	Cyclops of Sendale	Pauline of Ouborough	1926
Gerda of Send	F	1928 Mar. 27	Ch. Dolf v.d. Saalburg	Carla Otterberg of Send	1930
Godric of Send	M	1931 June 18	Ch. Ramon of Send	Berthli of Send	1932
Garcia of Send	M	1925 Oct. 10	Cyclops of Sendale	Pauline of Ouborough	1926
Geri of Send	M	1925 Oct. 10	Cyclops of Sendale	Pauline of Ouborough	1926
Gaby of Send	F	1927 Mar. 24	Baldur Daheim of Send	Topsy of Cuddington	1927
Gilda of Send	F	1927 Mar. 24	Baldur Daheim of Send	Topsy of Cuddington	1927
Godwin of Send	M	1927 Mar. 24	Baldur Daheim of Send	Topsy of Cuddington	1927
Golem of Send	M	1927 Mar. 24	Baldur Daheim of Send	Topsy of Cuddington	1927
Gertrude of Send	F	1928 Sep. 16	Victor Gilli Illertal of Send		1930
Guido of Send	M	1929 May 9	Sultan Chartreuse of Send	Asta Galster of Send	1930
Gypsy of Send	F	1929 May 9	Sultan Chartreuse of Send	Asta Galster of Send	1930
Gillian of Send	F	1929 May 9	Sultan Chartreuse of Send	Asta Galster of Send	1930
Gert of Send	M	1929 May 9	Sultan Chartreuse of Send	Asta Galster of Send	1930
Genevieve of Send	F	1930 Feb. 28	Baldur Daheim of Send	Balaka of Send	1931
Gunar of Send	M	1931 June 18	Ramon of Send	Berthli of Send	1932
Gavin of Send	M	1931 June 18	Ramon of Send	Berthli of Send	1932
Griselda of Send	F	1930 Feb. 28	Baldur Daheim of Send	Balaka of Send	1932
Gritta of Send	F	1932 May 20	Tantalus of Send	Korane of Send	1932
Gugunco of Send	M	1931 Mar. 2	Bernard of Send	Corrine of Send	1932

Code: (IMP–Imported) (M–Male) (F–Female) (V–Von) (Ch.–Champion)

Name	Sex	Born	Sire	Dam	Year Registered at Kennel Club
Gwyneth of Send	F	1932 May 20	Tantalus of Send	Korane of Send	1933
Gethryn of Send	F	1931 Mar. 2	Bernard of Send	Corrine of Send	1933
Geoffrey of Send	M	1933 Mar. 14	Thor of Send	Ursula of Send	1933
Guardsman of Send	M	1933 Mar. 14	Thor of Send	Ursula of Send	1933
Gurth of Send	M	1933 Mar. 14	Thor of Send	Ursula of Send	1933
Gregor of Send	M	1933 June 28	Vincent of Send	Venus of Send	1933
Goth of Send	M	1931 June 18	Ramon of Send	Berthli of Send	1933
Gabrielle of Send	F	1931 Mar. 2	Bernard of Send	Corinne of Send	1934
Gaston of Send	M	1933 June 28	Vincent of Send	Venus of Send	1934
Gisella of Send	F	1933 Mar. 14	Thor of Send	Ursula of Send	1934
Gwynne of Send	F	1933 Mar. 14	Thor of Send	Ursula of Send	1934
Genita of Send	F	1933 Mar. 14	Thor of Send	Ursula of Send	1934
Gretel of Send	F	1933 Mar. 14	Thor of Send	Ursula of Send	1935
Ghita of Send	F	1935 Mar. 1	Juan of Send	Tansy of Send	1935
Gay of Send	F	1935 Mar. 1	Juan of Send	Tansy of Send	1936
Grania of Send	F	1935 Mar. 1	Juan of Send	Tansy of Send	1936
Gerard of Send	M	1935 Mar. 1	Juan of Send	Tansy of Send	1936
Grace of Send	F	1936 June 4	Laddie of Send	Stella of Send	1936
Gunner of Send	M	1936 June 4	Laddie of Send	Stella of Send	1937
Gonzalo of Send	M	1936 June 4	Laddie of Send	Stella of Send	1937
Godfrey of Send	M	1936 June 4	Laddie of Send	Stella of Send	1937
Gregory of Send	M	1936 June 4	Laddie of Send	Stella of Send	1937

Name	Sex	Date	Sire	Dam	Year
Gervaise of Send	M	1936 June 4	Laddie of Send	Stella of Send	1938
Gwenna of Send	F	1936 June 4	Laddie of Send	Stella of Send	1938

H

Name	Sex	Date	Sire	Dam	Year
Hedwigs Sonia of Send (IMP)	F	1921 May 20	Hedwigs Nestor	Aida	1926
Hedwigs v. Schloss Helmstad of Send (IMP)	F	1925 May 28	Albert v.d. Oldehove Hedwigs	Sonia of Send	1926
Hans Wartkopf of Send (IMP)	M	1927 Feb. 13	Dolf v.d. Saalburg	Danka v. Freigericht	1928
Hedwigs Marna of Send (IMP)	F	1924 Mar. 12	Saphir v. Lindenberg	Carin v. Teufels-Quelle	1928
Ch. Hermione of Send	F	1925 Oct. 16	Ch. Primley Pericles	Perpetua of Bellary	1926
Hilma of Send	F	1928 June 25	Dolf v.d. Saalburg	Kitty v. Birkenhof	1930
Hilary of Send	F	1929 May 9	Thor of Send	Omega of Send	1930
Haakon of Send	M	1931 Mar. 7	Sultan Chartreuse of Send	Lygia of Send	1931
Hannibal of Send	M	1925 Oct. 16	Primley Pericles	Perpetua of Bellary	1926
Hassan of Send	M	1925 Oct. 16	Primley Pericles	Perpetua of Bellary	1926
Hector of Send	M	1925 Oct. 16	Primley Pericles	Perpetua of Bellary	1926
Heda of Send	F	1925 Oct. 16	Primley Pericles	Perpetua of Bellary	1926
Hermann of Send	M	1925 Oct. 16	Primley Pericles	Perpetua of Bellary	1926
Hagan of Send	M	1927 Apr. 2	Bruno Rotenberg of Send	Rhoda of Sendale	1927
Hansel of Send	M	1927 Apr. 2	Bruno Rotenberg of Send	Rhoda of Sendale	1927
Hermes of Send	M	1927 Apr. 2	Bruno Rotenberg of Send	Rhoda of Sendale	1927
Hiawatha of Send	M	1927 Apr. 2	Bruno Rotenberg of Send	Rhoda of Sendale	1927
Herold of Send	M	1928 Apr. 1	Baldur Daheim of Send	Gilli Illertal of Sendale	1928
Helga of Send	F	1928 Apr. 1	Baldur Daheim of Send	Gilli Illertal of Sendale	1929
Herud of Send	M	1929 May 9	Thor of Send	Omega of Send	1930
Horus of Send	M	1930 Mar. 3	Baldur Daheim of Send	Wenonah of Send	1931

Code: (IMP-Imported) (M-Male) (F-Female) (V-Von) (Ch.-Champion)

Name	Sex	Born	Sire	Dam	Year Registered at Kennel Club
Hylma of Send	F	1931 Mar. 7	Sultan Chartreuse of Send	Lygia of Send	1933
Harald of Send	M	1933 Mar. 12	Ch. Lancelot of Send	Aprille of Send	1933
Horst of Send	M	1933 Mar. 12	Ch. Lancelot of Send	Aprille of Send	1933
Helen of Send	F	1933 Aug. 2	Thor of Send	Yucca of Send	1933
Hereward of Send	M	1933 Mar. 12	Ch. Lancelot of Send	Aprille of Send	1933
Harras of Send	M	1933 Aug. 2	Thor of Send	Yucca of Send	1933
Hasso of Send	M	1932 May 22	Ch. Lancelot of Send	Anette of Send	1934
Hawk of Send	M	1935 Mar. 2	Tantalus of Send	Sari of Send	1935
Hugo of Send	M	1933 Aug. 2	Tantalus of Send	Sari of Send	1935
Howard of Send	M	1936 June 4	Bernard of Send	Tansy of Send	1937
Hugh of Send	M	1936 June 4	Bernard of Send	Tansy of Send	1937
Hestor of Send	F	1936 June 4	Bernard of Send	Tansy of Send	1938
Honor of Send	F	1936 June 4	Bernard of Send	Tansy of Send	1939
I					
Iringa of Send (IMP)	M	1927 Oct. 4	Sultan Van Chartreuse	Minny	1928
Inigo of Wartkopf of Send (IMP)	M	1929 May 18	Cedric of Send	Aida Volbloed of Send	1930
Iver of Send	M	1935 Mar. 4	Ean of Send	Dorrine of Send	1936
Inga of Send	F	1930 Mar. 3	Ch. Lancelot of Send	Vera of Send	1932
Isolde of Send	F	1930 Mar. 3	Ch. Lancelot of Send	Vera of Send	1932
Ian of Send	M	1926 Jan. 18	Rupert of Sendale	Rufflyn of Send	1926
Ida of Send	F	1926 Jan. 18	Rupert of Sendale	Rufflyn of Send	1926
Ilka of Send	F	1926 Jan. 18	Rupert of Sendale	Rufflyn of Send	1926

Name	Sex	Date	Sire	Dam	Year
Inez of Send	F	1926 Jan. 18	Rupert of Sendale	Rufflyn of Send	1926
Ishbel of Send	F	1926 Jan. 18	Rupert of Sendale	Rufflyn of Send	1926
Isis of Send	F	1926 Jan. 18	Rupert of Sendale	Rufflyn of Send	1926
Istvan of Send	M	1927 Apr. 15	Ajax Lindenstadt of Send	Ermine of Send	1927
Ivan of Send	M	1927 Apr. 15	Ajax Lindenstadt of Send	Ermine of Send	1927
Inkas of Send	M	1928 Apr. 16	Baldur Daheim of Send	Aspe Amalienberg of Send	1929
Imogen of Send	F	1928 Sept. 19	Adonis of Send	Asta Galster of Send	1930
Imshi of Send	M	1929 May 18	Cedric of Send	Aida Volbloed of Send	1930
Irma of Send	F	1929 May 18	Cedric of Send	Aida Volbloed of Send	1930
Ivanhoe of Send	M	1929 May 18	Cedric of Send	Aida Volbloed of Send	1930
Iris of Send	F	1931 Mar. 11	Ch. Lancelot of Send	Niobe of Send	1931
Isko of Send	M	1931 June 30	Ch. Lancelot of Send	Safi of Send	1931
Ido of Send	M	1931 June 30	Ch. Lancelot of Send	Safi of Send	1932
Irene of Send	F	1931 June 30	Ch. Lancelot of Send	Safi of Send	1932
Isabella of Send	F	1931 Mar. 11	Ch. Lancelot of Send	Niobe of Send	1932
Ican of Send	M	1929 May 18	Cedric of Send	Aida Volbloed of Send	1932
Indra of Send	F	1933 Mar. 17	Bernard of Send	Zoe of Send	1933
Igor of Send	M	1933 Mar. 17	Bernard of Send	Zoe of Send	1933
Ilios of Send	M	1931 June 30	Ch. Lancelot of Send	Safi of Send	1933
Ilof of Send	M	1932 June 2	Thor of Send	Babette of Send	1933
Ivor of Send	M	1932 June 2	Thor of Send	Babette of Send	1933

J

Name	Sex	Date	Sire	Dam	Year
Jorg Osterholtz of Send	M	1924 Sept. 12	Herold Tipp	Topp Alma v.d. Laurereicke	1926
Ch. Joan of Send	F	1931 July 10	Ch. Midas of Send	Thea of Send	1933
Jane of Send	F	1926 Mar. 22	Wolfram of Sendale	Tricksey Link	1926

Code: (IMP–Imported) (M–Male) (F–Female) (V–Von) (Ch.–Champion)

Name	Sex	Born	Sire	Dam	Year Registered at Kennel Club
Judith of Send	F	1931 July 10	Ch. Midas of Send	Thea of Send	1932
Juan of Send	M	1931 July 10	Ch. Midas of Send	Thea of Send	1933
Jessica of Sendale	F	1925 Dec. 11	Cyclops of Sendale	Gretta of Lansmith	1927
Janet of Send	F	1927 May 21	Ador Viktoria of Send	Tricksey Link	1928
Julia of Send	F	1927 May 21	Ador Viktoria of Send	Tricksey Link	1928
Jupiter Apex of Send	M	1927 May 17	Kastor Klasserberg of Send	Cora	1928
Juno of Send	M	1928 Sept. 19	Achilles of Send	Dinah of Sendale	1929
Judy of Sendale	F	1925 Sept. 30	Magpie of Etive	Black Lady	1930
Janette of Send	F	1930 Feb. 20	Ch. Lancelot of Send	Rahie of Send	1930
Jason of Send	M	1930 Mar. 5	Akbar of Send	Babette of Send	1930
Jennifer of Send	F	1930 Feb. 20	Ch. Lancelot of Send	Rahie of Send	1930
Jervaise of Send	M	1930 Feb. 20	Ch. Lancelot of Send	Rahie of Send	1930
Joyce of Send	F	1930 Feb. 20	Ch. Lancelot of Send	Rahie of Send	1930
Julian of Send	M	1930 Mar. 5	Akbar of Send	Babette of Send	1930
Josette of Send	F	1929 June 2	Hans Wartkopf of Send	Hermione of Send	1930
Jester of Send	M	1930 Mar. 5	Akbar of Send	Babette of Send	1930
Jeffrey of Send	M	1931 July 10	Ch. Midas of Send	Thea of Send	1932
June of Send	F	1931 July 10	Ch. Midas of Send	Thea of Send	1932
Jasper of Send	M	1932 June 8	Thor of Send	Safi of Send	1932
Jervis of Send	M	1932 June 8	Thor of Send	Safi of Send	1932
Justin of Send	M	1932 June 8	Thor of Send	Safi of Send	1932
Jarrath of Send	M	1932 June 8	Thor of Send	Safi of Send	1932

Name	Sex	Date	Sire	Dam	Year
Josephine of Send	F	1931 July 10	Ch. Midas of Send	Thea of Send	1933
Juro of Send	M	1931 July 10	Ch. Midas of Send	Thea of Send	1933
Juanita of Send	F	1933 Mar. 19	Yule of Send	Alisa of Send	1933
Jessica of Send	F	1932 June 8	Thor of Send	Safi of Send	1933
Jude of Send	M	1933 Aug. 22	Thor of Send	Rita of Send	1933
Juana of Send	F	1933 Mar. 19	Yule of Send	Alisa of Send	1934
Jacqueline of Send	F	1931 July 10	Ch. Midas of Send	Thea of Send	1934
Jacquetta of Send	F	1933 Mar. 19	Yule of Send	Alisa of Send	1934
Jenny of Send	F	1931 July 10	Ch. Midas of Send	Thea of Send	1934
Jevan of Send	M	1933 Aug. 22	Thor of Send	Rita of Send	1934
Joletta of Send	F	1933 Mar. 9	Yule of Send	Alisa of Send	1934
Juletta of Send	F	1933 Aug. 22	Thor of Send	Rita of Send	1934
Junius of Send	M	1933 Aug. 22	Thor of Send	Rita of Send	1934
Judy of Send	F	1931 July 10	Ch. Midas of Send	Thea of Send	1934
Jack of Send	M	1935 Apr. 5	Ch. Lancelot of Send	Genita of Send	1936
James of Send	M	1936 June 6	Tantalus of Send	Faune of Send	1937
Janus of Send	M	1936 June 6	Tantalus of Send	Faune of Send	1937
Julius of Send	M	1936 June 6	Tantalus of Send	Faune of Send	1937
John of Send	M	1936 June 6	Tantalus of Send	Faune of Send	1937
Jonathon of Send	M	1936 June 6	Tantalus of Send	Faune of Send	1937
Jeromy of Send	M	1936 June 6	Tantalus of Send	Faune of Send	1937
Johann of Send	M	1936 June 6	Tantalus of Send	Faune of Send	1937
Jasmine of Send	F	1936 June 6	Tantalus of Send	Faune of Send	1937
Jewell of Send	F	1936 June 6	Tantalus of Send	Faune of Send	1938

Code: (IMP-Imported) (M-Male) (F-Female) (V-Von) (Ch.-Champion)

Name	Sex	Born	Sire	Dam	Year Registered at Kennel Club
K					
Kastor Klasserberg of Send (IMP)	M	1924 May 8	Nero v. Schiff Munster	Minka v. Schonbuch	1926
Karla Ottaburg of Send (IMP)					
Kitty v. Birkenhof of Send (IMP)	F	1926 Apr. 21	Attila Hexengold	Beate v. Wendenburg	1931
Korane of Send	F	1927 June 1	Egon Falkenhorst of Send	Toska Bohmerwald of Send	1928
Karieu of Dane Park (Late Sonja of Send)		1933 May 22	Godric of Send	Miranda of Send	
Karina of Dane Park (Late Karina of Send)	F	1934 Apr. 18	Bravado of Blendon	Judith of Send	1934
Karina of Send (see Karina of Dane Park)	F	1934 Apr. 18	Bravado of Blendon	Judith of Send	1934
Kavril of Dane Park (Late Avril of Send)	F	1933 June 9	Bernard of Send	Little Sister of Send	1934
Kenneth of Send	M	1926 Mar. 22	Robert of Send	Topsy of Cuddington	1926
Kitty of Send	F	1926 Mar. 22	Robert of Send	Topsy of Cuddington	1926
Karema of Send	F	1927 June 1	Egon Falkenhorst of Send	Tosko Bohmerwald of Send	1928
Karine of Send	F	1927 June 1	Egon Falkenhorst of Send	Tosko Bohmerwald of Send	1928
Katania of Send	F	1927 June 1	Egon Falkenhorst of Send	Tosko Bohmerwald of Send	1928
Kiki of Send	F	1927 June 1	Egon Falkenhorst of Send	Tosko Bohmerwald of Send	1928
Koos of Send	M	1927 June 1	Egon Falkenhorst of Send	Tosko Bohmerwald of Send	1928
Krishna of Send	M	1928 Apr. 21	Baldur Daheim of Send	Merrill of Cuddington	1929
Kama of Send	F	1928 Sept. 21	Uslus Volbloed of Send	Nancy of Send	1930
Klia of Send	F	1929 July 6	Jorg Osterholz of Send	Gilda of Send	1930

Name	Date	Sex	Sire	Dam	Year
Karel of Send	1930 Mar. 9	M	Akbar of Send	Neroli Camphausen of Send	1930
Khiva of Send	1930 Mar. 9	M	Akbar of Send	Neroli Camphausen of Send	1931
Kathryn of Send	1930 Mar. 9	F	Akbar of Send	Neroli Camphausen of Send	1931
Katja of Send	1931 Mar. 20	F	Sultan Chartreuse of Send	Lola of Sendale	1931
Karen of Send	1931 July 10	F	Ramon of Send	Fahme Ruhrtal of Send	1932
Kay of Send	1932 June 30	F	Thor of Send	Diana Niederaichbach of Send	1932
Korale of Send	1933 Mar. 19	F	Godric of Send	Amber of Send	1933
Katinka of Send	1933 Mar. 19	F	Godric of Send	Amber of Send	1934
Kara of Send	1928 Apr. 21	F	Baldur Daheim of Send	Merrel of Cuddington	1934
Kleeta of Send	1931 July 10	F	Ramon of Send Fahne	Ruhrtal of Send	1934
Karloo of Send	1934 Apr. 18	M	Bravado of Blendon	Judith of Send	1934
Karl of Send	1934 Apr. 18	M	Bravado of Blendon	Judith of Send	1934
Kerror of Send	1934 Apr. 18	M	Bravado of Blendon	Judith of Send	1935
Kyra of Send	1934 Apr. 18	F	Bravado of Blendon	Judith of Send	1935
Konrad of Send	1936 June 6	M	Ean of Send	Quixella of Send	1937
Kim of Send	1934 Apr. 18	M	Bravado of Blendon	Judity of Send	1938
L					
Little Sister of Send (IMP)	1928 June 18	F	Lloyd's Titan Boy	Etfa v.d. Saalburg	1931
Ch. Lancelot of Send	1928 May 13	M	Urlus Volbloed of Send	Alani of Sendale	1929
Lucifer of Send	1928 May 13	M	Urlus Volbloed of Send	Alani of Sendale	1929
Lola of Sendale	1925 July 3	F	Ch. Maurice of Cuddington	Tess of Rostrevor	1928
Lothar of Send	1931 Mar. 25	M	Eglon of Send	Rosalia of Send	1932
Lygia of Send	1928 May 13	F	Urlus Volbloed of Send	Alani of Sendale	1930
Lova of Send	1926 May 9	F	Wolfram of Sendale	Spring Mere Sally	1926
Lola of Send	1927 June 23	F	Egon Falkenhorst of Send	Hedwig Schloss Helmstad of Send	1928

Code: (IMP–Imported) (M–Male) (F–Female) (V–Von) (Ch.–Champion)

Name	Sex	Born	Sire	Dam	Year Registered at Kennel Club
Loreli of Send	F	1927 June 23	Egon Falkenhorst of Send	Hedwig Schloss Helmstad of Send	1928
Lorna of Send	F	1927 June 23	Egon Falkenhorst of Send	Hedwig Schloss Helmstad of Send	1928
Lucien of Send	M	1927 June 23	Egon Falkenhorst of Send	Hedwig Schloss Helmstad of Send	1928
Lucullus of Send	M	1927 June 23	Egon Falkenhorst of Send	Hedwig Schloss Helmstad of Send	1928
Ludwig of Send	M	1927 June 23	Egon Falkenhorst of Send	Hedwig Schloss Helmstad of Send	1928
Luigi of Send	M	1927 June 23	Egon Falkenhorst of Send	Hedwig Schloss Helmstad of Send	1928
Lycidas of Send	M	1927 June 23	Egon Falkenhorst of Send	Hedwig Schloss Helmstad of Send	1928
Londa of Send	F	1928 Oct. 5	Urlus Volbloed of Send	Enid of Send	1929
Leon of Send	M	1929 July 25	Wolfram of Sendale	Xenia of Send	1929
Leander of Send	M	1928 May 13	Urlus Volbloed of Send	Alani of Sendale	1930
Liane of Send	F	1928 May 13	Urlus Volbloed of Send	Alani of Sendale	1930
Lucia of Send	F	1928 May 13	Urlus Volbloed of Send	Alani of Sendale	1930
Lysander of Send	M	1930 Mar. 14	Fabian of Send	Freya of Send	1930
Lily of Send	F	1930 Mar. 14	Fabian of Send	Freya of Send	1930
Loyal of Send	M	1930 Mar. 14	Fabian of Send	Freya of Send	1930
Lydia of Send	F	1930 Mar. 14	Fabian of Send	Freya of Send	1930
Lucius of Send	M	1930 Mar. 14	Fabian of Send	Freya of Send	1930
Lisette of Send	F	1928 Oct. 5	Urlus Volbloed of Send	Enid of Send	1930
Lucie Volbloed of Send	F	1926 Apr. 15	Urlus Volbloed of Send	Asta v. Bernum	1931
Lucinda of Send	F	1930 Mar. 4	Fabian of Send	Freya of Send	1931
Lotte of Send	M	1931 July 16	Bernard of Send	Xcetyl of Send	1931
Lobengula of Send	M	1931 July 16	Bernard of Send	Xcetyl of Send	1932

Name	Sex	Birth	Sire	Dam	Year
Lois of Send	M	1931 July 16	Bernard of Send	Xcetyl of Send	1932
Lorontes of Send	M	1931 July 16	Bernard of Send	Xcetyl of Send	1932
Lilybet of Send	F	1931 July 16	Bernard of Send	Xcetyl of Send	1932
Locksley of Send	M	1931 Mar. 21	Eglon of Send	Rosalia of Send	1932
Loraine of Send	F	1931 Mar. 21	Eglon of Send	Rosalia of Send	1932
Larry of Send	M	1932 July 6	Cortes of Send	Sheba of Send	1932
Livia of Send	F	1928 Oct. 5	Urlus Volbloed of Send	Enid of Send	1933
Leal of Send	M	1933 Mar. 30	Thor of Send	Erna of Send	1933
Lados of Send	M	1933 Mar. 30	Thor of Send	Erna of Send	1933
Legacy of Send	M	1930 Mar. 14	Fabian of Send	Freya of Send	1933
Lorrell of Send	M	1933 Mar. 30	Thor of Send	Erna of Send	1934
Laddie of Send	M	1934 May 5	Ch. Ruffler of Ouborough	Ch. Ulana of Send	1935
Lilla of Send	F	1935 Apr. 16	Mark of Send	Soinita of Send	1935
Lorina of Send	F	1935 Apr. 16	Mark of Send	Soinita of Send	1936
Lahne of Send	F	1934 May 5	Ch. Ruffler of Ouborough	Ch. Ulana of Send	1936

M

Name	Sex	Birth	Sire	Dam	Year
Ch. Mavis of Send	F	1928 May 29	Urlus Volbloed of Send	Fahne Ruhrtal of Send	1929
Ch. Midas of Send	M	1928 May 29	Urlus Volbloed of Send	Fahne Ruhrtal of Send	1929
Mona of Send	F	1928 May 29	Urlus Volbloed of Send	Fahne Ruhrtal of Send	1929
Miranda of Send	F	1931 Apr. 8	Sultan Chartreuse of Send	Nancy of Send	1933
Martin of Sendale	M	1925 Feb. 9	Marcero of Walshale	Figular Model	1925
Marcus of Send	M	1926 May 9	Wolfram of Sendale	Pauline of Ouborough	1926
Max of Send	M	1926 May 9	Wolfram of Sendale	Pauline of Ouborough	1926
Mentor of Send	M	1926 May 9	Wolfram of Sendale	Pauline of Ouborough	1926
Magyar of Send	M	1927 June 29	Arco Romerturm of Send	Blanka Osterholtz of Send	1928

Code: (IMP-Imported) (M-Male) (F-Female) (V-Von) (Ch.-Champion)

Name	Sex	Born	Sire	Dam	Year Registered at Kennel Club
Margo of Send	F	1927 June 29	Arco Romerturm of Send	Blanka Osterholtz of Send	1928
Marie of Send	F	1927 June 29	Arco Romerturm of Send	Blanka Osterholtz of Send	1928
Marlin of Send	M	1927 June 29	Arco Romerturm of Send	Blanka Osterholtz of Send	1928
Melisande of Send	F	1927 June 29	Arco Romerturm of Send	Blanka Osterholtz of Send	1928
Mercedes of Send	F	1927 June 29	Arco Romerturm of Send	Blanka Osterholtz of Send	1928
Meteor of Send	M	1927 June 29	Arco Romerturm of Send	Blanka Osterholtz of Send	1928
Montezuma of Send	M	1927 June 29	Arco Romerturm of Send	Blanka Osterholtz of Send	1928
Mopo of Send	M	1927 June 29	Arco Romerturm of Send	Blanka Osterholtz of Send	1928
Magnus of Send	M	1928 May 29	Urlus Volbloed of Send	Fahne Ruhrtal of Send	1928
Malcolm of Send	M	1928 May 29	Urlus Volbloed of Send	Fahne Ruhrtal of Send	1928
Michael of Send	M	1928 May 29	Urlus Volbloed of Send	Fahne Ruhrtal of Send	1929
Minstrel of Send	M	1930 Mar. 13	Ch. Lancelot of Send	Anchusa of Send	1931
Marshall of Send	M	1930 Mar. 13	Ch. Lancelot of Send	Anchusa of Send	1931
Menteth of Send	M	1930 Mar. 13	Ch. Lancelot of Send	Anchusa of Send	1931
Megan of Send	F	1929 Jan. 15	Ador Viktoria of Send	Fahne Ruhrtal of Send	1931
Melissa of Send	F	1929 Jan. 15	Ador Viktoria of Send	Fahne Ruhrtal of Send	1931
Marko of Send	M	1931 Apr. 8	Sultan Chartreuse of Send	Nancy of Send	1931
Mutius of Send	M	1931 Apr. 8	Sultan Chartreuse of Send	Nancy of Send	1931
Marya of Send	F	1930 Mar. 13	Ch. Lancelot of Send	Anchusa of Send	1931
Markgraf of Send	M	1931 Apr. 8	Sultan Chartreuse of Send	Nancy of Send	1931
Mervyn of Send	M	1931 Apr. 8	Sultan Chartreuse of Send	Nancy of Send	1932
Marcia of Send	F	1931 Apr. 8	Sultan Chartreuse of Send	Nancy of Send	1932

Name	Sex	Date	Sire	Dam	Year
Meave of Send	F	1931 July 23	Rudolph of Send	Melissa of Send	1932
Mephisto of Send	M	1931 Apr. 8	Sultan Chartreuse of Send	Nancy of Send	1932
Mustapha of Send	M	1930 Mar. 13	Ch. Lancelot of Send	Anchusa of Send	1932
Minoru of Send	M	1931 Apr. 8	Sultan Chartreuse of Send	Nancy of Send	1932
Manfred of Send	M	1932 July 4	Bernard of Send	Bellona of Send	1932
Marina of Send	F	1931 July 23	Rudolph of Send	Melissa of Send	1932
Martyn of Send	M	1932 July 4	Bernard of Send	Bellona of Send	1933
Mohr of Send	F	1932 July 4	Bernard of Send	Bellona of Send	1933
Meredith of Send	M	1932 July 4	Bernard of Send	Bellona of Send	1933
Micah of Send	M	1932 July 4	Bernard of Send	Bellona of Send	1933
Miriam of Send	F	1932 July 18	Cortes of Send	Teresa of Send	1933
Macbeth of Send	M	1932 July 18	Cortes of Send	Teresa of Send	1933
Maximilian of Send	M	1932 July 18	Cortes of Send	Teresa of Send	1933
Morice of Send	M	1932 July 4	Bernard of Send	Bellona of Send	1933
Maurice of Send	M	1933 Mar. 29	Thor of Send	Danella of Send	1933
Manus of Send	M	1932 July 4	Bernard of Send	Bellona of Send	1933
Maris of Send	M	1933 Mar. 29	Thor of Send	Danella of Send	1933
Myrtle of Send	F	1932 July 18	Cortes of Send	Teresa of Send	1933
Mark of Send	M	1932 July 18	Cortes of Send	Teresa of Send	1933
Maid of Send	F	1932 July 18	Cortes of Send	Teresa of Send	1934
Myra of Send	F	1932 July 18	Cortes of Send	Teresa of Send	1934
Marion of Send	F	1933 Mar. 29	Thor of Send	Danella of Send	1934
Monica of Send	F	1932 July 18	Cortes of Send	Teresa of Send	1934
Madoc of Send	M	1934 July 5	Danilo of Send	Quella of Send	1934
Meg of Send	F	1934 July 5	Danilo of Send	Quella of Send	1934

Code: (IMP-Imported) (M-Male) (F-Female) (V-Von) (Ch.-Champion)

Name	Sex	Born	Sire	Dam	Year Registered at Kennel Club
Mougli of Send	M	1932 July 18	Cortes of Send	Teresa of Send	1935
Meta of Send	F	1932 July 18	Cortes of Send	Teresa of Send	1935
Marda of Send	F	1935 June 2	Rafe of Send	Umetta of Send	1936
Micha of Send	M	1936 June 10	Godric of Send	Judy of Send	1937
Miguel of Send	M	1936 June 10	Godric of Send	Judy of Send	1937
Mimi of Send	F	1936 June 10	Godric of Send	Judy of Send	1937
Matthew of Send	M	1936 June 10	Godric of Send	Judy of Send	1937
Miles of Send	M	1935 June 2	Rafe of Send	Umetta of Send	1937
Marcel of Send	M	1935 June 2	Rafe of Send	Umetta of Send	1938
N					
Nero Neroli Camphausen of Send (IMP)	F	1924 Nov. 3	Alexander v. Ferverturm	Merry	1926
Norga of Send (IMP)	F	1923 Dec. 18	Albert v.d. Oldehove	Suze	1926
Nomad of Send	M	1929 Jan. 19	Hans Wartkopf of Send	Norga of Send	1930
Nabob of Send	M	1926 Aug. 3	Acne Gaunt	Alani of Sendale	1926
Niobe of Send	F	1926 Aug. 3	Acne Gaunt	Alani of Sendale	1926
Nada of Send	M	1927 June 22	Boris of Send	Anneliese Rott of Send	1928
Nancy of Send	F	1926 Aug. 3	Acne Gaunt	Alani of Sendale	1926
Nigger of Send	M	1923 July 22	Professor of Falklands	Cora	1926
Natalie of Send	F	1926 Aug. 3	Acne Gaunt	Alani of Sendale	1926
Norseman of Send	M	1926 Aug. 3	Acne Gaunt	Alani of Sendale	1926
Nathan of Send	M	1927 June 22	Boris of Send	Anneliese Rott of Send	1928

Name	Sex	Date	Sire	Dam	Year
Nestor of Send	M	1927 June 22	Boris of Send	Anneliese Rott of Send	1928
Nigel of Send	M	1927 June 22	Boris of Send	Anneliese Rott of Send	1928
Nero of Send	M	1928 May 23	Baldur Daheim of Send	Ena of Send	1928
Neptune of Send	M	1928 May 23	Baldur Daheim of Send	Ena of Send	1929
Negus of Send	M	1929 Jan. 19	Hans Wartkopf of Send	Norga of Send	1930
Noel of Send	M	1929 Jan. 19	Hans Wartkopf of Send	Norga of Send	1930
Nitza of Send	F	1928 May 23	Baldur Daheim of Send	Ena of Send	1930
Naxos of Send	M	1930 Mar. 14	Akbar of Send	Gaby of Send	1930
Nerissa of Send	F	1929 Jan. 19	Hans Wartkopf of Send	Norga of Send	1930
Nina of Send	F	1930 Mar. 14	Akbar of Send	Gaby of Send	1930
Naomi of Send	F	1929 Jan. 19	Hans Wartkopf of Send	Norga of Send	1930
Nimrod of Send	M	1930 Mar. 13	Akbar of Send	Gaby of Send	1931
Noreen of Send	F	1929 Jan. 19	Hans Wartkopf of Send	Norga of Send	1932
Neil of Send	M	1931 Aug. 16	Norseman of Send	Genevieve of Send	1932
Nugget of Send	M	1931 Apr. 5	Sascha of Send	Blanka Usterholz of Send	1932
Norris of Send	M	1933 Apr. 27	Godric of Send	Ruth of Send	1933
Nanette of Send	F	1931 Aug. 16	Norseman of Send	Genevieve of Send	1933
Nadier of Send	M	1934 Aug. 4	Bravado of Blendon	Estelle of Send	1934
Nesta of Send	F	1934 Aug. 4	Bravado of Blendon	Estelle of Send	1935
Nieth of Send	M	1934 Aug. 4	Bravado of Blendon	Estelle of Send	1935
Norma of Send	F	1934 Aug. 4	Bravado of Blendon	Estelle of Send	1935
Nan of Send	F	1935 June 3	Tantalus of Send	Estelle of Send	1935
Nicko of Send	M	1935 June 3	Tantalus of Send	Estelle of Send	1936
Nino of Send	F	1935 June 3	Tantalus of Send	Estelle of Send	1936
Nedda of Send	F	1935 June 3	Tantalus of Send	Estelle of Send	1936

Code: (IMP-Imported) (M-Male) (F-Female) (V-Von) (Ch.-Champion)

Name	Sex	Born	Sire	Dam	Year Registered at Kennel Club
Neville of Send	M	1935 June 3	Tantalus of Send	Estelle of Send	1936
Nicolette of Send	F	1935 June 3	Tantalus of Send	Estelle of Send	1937
Nicola of Send	F	1935 June 3	Tantalus of Send	Estelle of Send	1937
Nolan of Send	M	1937 July 1	Tantalus of Send	Faune of Send	1938
Naylor of Send	M	1937 July 1	Tantalus of Send	Faune of Send	1938
Navarro of Send	M	1937 July 1	Tantalus of Send	Faune of Send	1938
Neal of Send	M	1937 July 1	Tantalus of Send	Faune of Send	1938
Neelia of Send	F	1937 July 1	Tantalus of Send	Faune of Send	1938
Norina of Send	F	1937 July 1	Tantalus of Send	Faune of Send	1938
Norman of Send	M	1937 July 1	Tantalus of Send	Faune of Send	1938
Nita of Send	F	1937 July 1	Tantalus of Send	Faune of Send	1938

O

Name	Sex	Born	Sire	Dam	Year Registered at Kennel Club
Omar of Send (IMP)	M	1926 July 7	Asko v.d. Rehhutte	Cilli v. Illertal	1926
Odin of Send	M	1927 July 22	Ador Viktoria of Send	Olga of Send	1928
Olga of Send	F	1925 Jan. 22	Marcus of Walsall	Springmere Sally	1925
Omega of Send	F	1927 July 22	Ador Viktoria of Send	Olga of Send	1928
Olaf of Send	M	1925 Jan. 22	Marcus of Walsall	Springmere Sally	1925
Olive of Send	F	1925 Jan. 22	Marcus of Walsall	Springmere Sally	1925
Odo of Send	F	1927 July 22	Ador Viktoria of Send	Olga of Send	1928
Opal of Send	F	1927 July 22	Ador Viktoria of Send	Olga of Send	1928
Orloff of Send	M	1928 June 8	Kastor Klasserburg of Send	Bonita of Send	1929
Oonagh of Send	F	1928 June 8	Kastor Klasserburg of Send	Bonita of Send	1929
Oranza of Send	F	1928 June 8	Kastor Klasserburg of Send	Bonita of Send	1929

Name	Sex	Date	Sire	Dam	Year
Othello of Send	M	1929 Feb. 7	Hans Wartkopf of Send	Neroli Camphausen of Send	1929
Oberon of Send	M	1929 Sept. 2	Sultan Chartreuse of Send	Neroli Camphausen of Send	1930
Ortho of Send	M	1929 Sept. 2	Sultan Chartreuse of Send	Neroli Camphausen of Send	1930
Orpheus of Send	M	1929 Sept. 2	Sultan Chartreuse of Send	Neroli Camphausen of Send	1930
Oswald of Send	M	1928 June 8	Kastor Klasserburg of Send	Bonita of Send	1930
Orlando of Send	M	1929 Sept. 2	Sultan Chartreuse of Send	Neroli Camphausen of Send	1930
Oliver of Send	M	1929 Jan. 25	Hans Wartkopf of Send	Neroli Camphausen of Send	1930
Ottokar of Send	M	1930 Mar. 9	Quintos of Send	Jane of Send	1930
Ouida of Send	F	1928 June 8	Kastor Klasserburg of Send	Bonita of Send	1930
Ophelia of Send	F	1928 June 8	Kastor Klasserburg of Send	Bonita of Send	1931
Odette of Send	F	1930 Mar. 21	Quintos of Send	Jane of Send	1931
Osric of Send	M	1929 Sept. 2	Sultan Chartreuse of Send	Neroli Camphausen of Send	1931
Owen of Send	M	1931 Aug. 23	Woden of Send	Karthryn of Send	1932
Orchid of Send	F	1933 May 2	Furst of Send	Hylma of Send	1933
Ormond of Send	M	1933 May 2	Furst of Send	Hylma of Send	1933

P

Name	Sex	Date	Sire	Dam	Year
Panther & Pegasus & Pennant of Send (Born Quarantine)	Males	1926 July 20	Arno v.d. Arendsberg	Adda v.d. Schole	1926
Pluto of Send	M	1928 July 27	Urlus Volbloed of Send	Norga of Send	1929
Pandora of Send	F	1928 June 7	Urlus Volbloed of Send	Norga of Send	1929
Patrick of Send	M	1923 July 22	Professor of Falklands	Cora	1925
Pixie of Send	M	1927 July 3	Baldur Daheim of Send	Dainah of Sendale	1928
Pollux of Send	M	1928 June 7	Urlus Volbloed of Send	Norga of Send	1929
Pandor of Send	M	1928 June 7	Urlus Volbloed of Send	Norga of Send	1930
Pat of Send	M	1929 Sept. 7	Falstaff of Send	Rowena of Send	1930

Code: (IMP-Imported) (M-Male) (F-Female) (V-Von) (Ch.-Champion)

Name	Sex	Born	Sire	Dam	Year Registered at Kennel Club
Pam of Send	F	1929 Sep. 7	Falstaff of Send	Rowena of Send	1930
Pedro of Send	M	1929 Sept. 7	Falstaff of Send	Rowena of Send	1930
Perseus of Send	M	1929 Sept. 7	Falstaff of Send	Rowena of Send	1930
Peter of Send	M	1929 Sept. 7	Falstaff of Send	Rowena of Send	1930
Pascha of Send	M	1930 Mar. 28	Akbar of Send	Dinah of Sendale	1930
Pilot of Send	M	1930 Mar. 28	Akbar of Send	Dinah of Sendale	1930
Parsival of Send	M	1931 Apr. 15	Cortes of Send	Carla Ottoberg of Send	1932
Pauline of Send	F	1931 Apr. 15	Cortes of Send	Carla Ottoberg of Send	1932
Paulette of Send	F	1931 Apr. 15	Cortes of Send	Carla Ottoberg of Send	1932
Paul of Send	M	1931 Apr. 15	Cortes of Send	Carla Ottoberg of Send	1932
Plutus of Send	M	1931 Apr. 15	Cortes of Send	Carla Ottoberg of Send	1932
Panza of Send	M	1932 Aug. 3	Roland of Send	Benita of Send	1933
Portia of Send	F	1931 Apr. 15	Cortes of Send	Carla Ottoberg of Send	1933
Psyche of Send	F	1931 Apr. 15	Cortes of Send	Carla Ottoberg of Send	1933
Priam of Send	M	1932 Aug. 3	Roland of Send	Benita of Send	1933
Pryde of Send	F	1932 Aug. 3	Roland of Send	Benita of Send	1933
Pippa of Send	F	1929 Jan. 27	Urlus Volbloed of Send	Blanka Osterholz of Send	1933
Paula of Send	F	1933 May 7	Bernard of Send	Fahne Ruhrtal of Send	1933
Pancho of Send	M	1933 May 7	Bernard of Send	Fahne Ruhrtal of Send	1933
Puma of Send	M	1933 May 7	Bernard of Send	Fahne Ruhrtal of Send	1933
Patsy of Send	F	1932 Aug. 3	Roland of Send	Benita of Send	1934
Peri of Send	F	1932 Aug. 3	Roland of Send	Benita of Send 1	1935

Name	Sex	Date	Sire	Dam	Year
Pompey of Send	M	1934 Aug. 12	Godric of Send	Sari of Send	1935
Punch of Send	M	1934 Aug. 12	Godric of Send	Sari of Send	1935
Pola of Send	F	1934 Aug. 12	Godric of Send	Sari of Send	1935
Pietro of Send	M	1935 June 13	Godric of Send	Judy of Send	1936
Philemon of Send	M	1935 June 13	Godric of Send	Judy of Send	1936
Phillip of Send	M	1935 June 13	Godric of Send	Judy of Send	1936
Petal of Send	F	1935 June 13	Godric of Send	Judy of Send	1936
Perivil of Send	M	1935 June 13	Godric of Send	Judy of Send	1937
Philo of Send	M	1935 June 13	Godric of Send	Judy of Send	1937
Peril of Send	F	1935 June 13	Godric of Send	Judy of Send	1937
Pirate of Send	M	1935 June 13	Godric of Send	Judy of Send	1938
Patricia of Send	F	1939 Mar. 2	Sylvius of Send	Lia of Ouborough	1939
Prudence of Send	F	1939 Mar. 2	Sylvius of Send	Lia of Ouborough	1939
Q					
Quella of Send	F	1930 May 2	Woden of Send	Renee of Send	1933
Quintas of Send	M	1927 Apr. 21	Ador Viktoria of Send	Pauline of Ouborough	1928
Quita of Send	F	1929 Sept. 17	Falstaff of Send	Norga of Send	1930
Quentin of Send	M	1929 Feb. 1	Hans Wartkopf of Send	Rhoda of Sendale	1930
Quest of Send	F	1929 Feb. 1	Hans Wartkopf of Send	Rhoda of Sendale	1930
Quex of Send	M	1929 Sept. 17	Falstaff of Send	Norga of Send	1930
Quix of Send	M	1929 Sept. 17	Falstaff of Send	Norga of Send	1930
Queros of Send	M	1929 Sept. 17	Falstaff of Send	Norga of Send	1930
Quester of Send	M	1929 Sept. 17	Falstaff of Send	Norga of Send	1930
Quigor of Send	M	1929 Sept. 17	Falstaff of Send	Norga of Send	1930
Quince of Send	M	1929 Sept. 17	Falstaff of Send	Norga of Send	1930

Code: (IMP.-Imported) (M-Male) (F-Female) (V-Von) (Ch.-Champion)

Name	Sex	Born	Sire	Dam	Year Registered at Kennel Club
Quinita of Send	F	1929 Sept. 17	Falstaff of Send	Norga of Send	1930
Quispah of Send	M	1929 Sept. 17	Falstaff of Send	Norga of Send	1930
Quain of Send	M	1931 Aug. 24	Springmere Cedric	Danella of Send	1932
Queenie of Send	F	1929 Feb. 1	Hans Wartkopf of Send	Rhoda of Send	1932
Quixo of Send	M	1932 Aug. 11	Yule of Send	Genevieve of Send	1932
Questa of Send	F	1932 Aug. 11	Yule of Send	Genevieve of Send	1933
Quodo of Send	F	1932 Aug. 11	Yule of Send	Genevieve of Send	1933
Quail of Send	M	1932 Aug. 11	Yule of Send	Genevieve of Send	1933
Qixella of Send	F	1931 Aug. 4	Springmere Cedric	Danella of Send	1933
Quintess of Send	F	1932 Aug. 11	Yule of Send	Genevieve of Send	1933
R					
Rowena of Send (IMP)	F	1926 May 27	Nero v. Schiff Munster	Affra C. Schonbuch	1927
Roxana of Send (IMP)	F	1926 May 27	Nero v. Schiff Munster	Affra C. Schonbuch	1927
Rani v. Weisenau of Send (IMP)	F	1926 June 22	Bosco v.d. Saalburg	Fackel Hansa	1928
Ch. Ramon of Send	M	1929 Sept. 20	Ch. Midas of Send	Rosalia of Send	1930
Rhanva of Send	F	1929 Feb. 20	Ch. Midas of Send	Rosalia of Send	1930
Ch. Rahie of Send	F	1928 June 13	Adonis of Send	Aida Volbloed of Send	1929
Rosina of Send	F	1929 Sept. 20	Ch. Midas of Send	Rosalia of Send	1930
Rupert of Sendale	M	1924 Sept. 12	Rolf of Ouborough	Sheelah of Powes	1925
Ravina of Send	F	1929 Feb. 20	Ch. Midas of Send	Rosalia of Send	1930
Rosalia of Send	F	1927 Oct. 27	Sultan Chartreuse of Send	Kitty	1930
Ch. Ramon of Send	M	1929 Feb. 20	Ch. Midas of Send	Rosalia of Send	1930

Name	Sex	Birth Date	Sire	Dam	Year
Rafe of Send	M	1931 Aug. 23	Thor of Send	Erma of Send	1932
Renee of Send	F	1928 June 13	Adonis of Send	Aida Volbloed of Send	1929
Rita of Sendale	F	1924 Sept. 12	Rolf of Ouborough	Sheelah of Powis	1925
Rhoda of Sendale	F	1925 Aug. 25	Valrola of Ouborough	Sheba of Ouborough	1926
Robert of Send	M	1923 Sept. 9	Magpie of Etive	Springmere Sally	1926
Ranee of Send (IMP)	F	1926 May 27	Nero v.s. Schiff	Affra v. Schonbuch	1927
Ra of Send	M	1927 Aug. 24	Kastor Klasserburg of Send	Brenda of Send	1928
Rames of Send	M	1927 Aug. 24	Kastor Klasserburg of Send	Brenda of Send	1928
Raoul of Send	M	1927 Aug. 24	Kastor Klasserburg of Send	Brenda of Send	1928
Rima of Send	F	1927 Aug. 24	Kastor Klasserburg of Send	Brenda of Send	1928
Rosamund of Send	F	1927 Aug. 24	Kastor Klasserburg of Send	Brenda of Send	1928
Robin of Send	M	1929 July 30	Springmere Cedric	Babette of Send	1929
Ralph of Sendale	M	1929 July 29	Adonis of Send	Blue Beth of Blendon	1930
Roger of Send	M	929 Feb. 1	Adonis of Send	Blue Beth of Blendon	1930
Roland of Send	M	1929 Sept. 20	Ch. Midas of Send	Rosalia of Send	1930
Radames of Send	M	1929 Feb. 7	Ador Victoria of Send	Anchusa of Send	1930
Rita of Send	F	1929 Feb. 7	Ador Victoria of Send	Anchusa of Send	1930
Rudolph of Send	M	1929 Feb. 7	Ador Victoria of Send	Anchusa of Send	1930
Rinaldo of Send	M	1929 July 19	Adonis of Send	Blue Beth of Blendon	1930
Ria of Send	F	1929 July 19	Adonis of Send	Blue Beth of Blendon	1930
Ravenna of Send	F	1929 Sept. 20	Ch. Midas of Send	Rosalia of Send	1930
Rizzo of Send	M	1930 May 11	Ch. Lancelot of Send	Rosalia of Send	1931
Rosel of Send	F	1930 Sept. 7	Eglon of Send	Ula of Send	1931
Ranus of Send	M	1930 May 11	Ch. Lancelot of Send	Rosalia of Send	1931
Rimini of Send	F	1929 July 19	Adonis of Send	Blue Beth of Blendon	1931

Code: (IMP-Imported) (M-Male) (F-Female) (V-Von) (Ch.-Champion)

Name	Sex	Born	Sire	Dam	Year Registered at Kennel Club
Rosita of Send	F	1928 June 13	Adonis of Send	Aida Volbloed of Send	1931
Roquette of Send	F	1931 Aug. 23	Thor of Send	Erna of Send	1932
Ruth of Send	F	1931 Apr. 22	Elch Edler v.d. Saalburg	Little Sister of Send	1933
Ragnar of Send	M	1932 Aug. 13	Bernard of Send	Berthli of Send	1933
Rex of Send	M	1933 May 14	Thor of Send	Diana Niederaichbach of Send	1933
Ronald of Send	M	1933 May 14	Thor of Send	Diana Niederaichbach of Send	1933
Rolph of Send	M	1931 Aug. 23	Thor of Send	Erna of Send	1933
Rufus of Send	M	1932 Aug. 13	Bernard of Send	Berthli of Send	1934
Rena of Send	F	1932 Aug. 13	Bernard of Send	Berthli of Send	1934
Rhona of Send	F	1933 May 14	Thor of Send	Diana Niederaichbach of Send	1934
Rhouma of Send	F	1934 Aug. 13	Ch. Danilo of Send	Roquette of Send	1934
Rispah of Send	F	1930 May 11	Ch. Lancelot of Send	Rosalia of Send	1935
Ryan of Send	M	1934 Aug. 13	Ch. Danilo of Send	Roquette of Send	1935
Remus of Send	M	1935 June 18	Springmere Sergius	Serena of Sen	1936
Rosenda of Send	F	1934 Aug. 13	Ch. Danilo of Send	Roquette of Send	1936
Randolph of Send	M	1935 June 18	Springmere Sergius	Serena of Send	1936
Rezia of Send	F	1935 June 18	Springmere Sergius	Serena of Send	1936
Rosette of Send	F	1935 June 18	Springmere Sergius	Serena of Send	1936
Rip of Send	M	1935 June 18	Springmere Sergius	Serena of Send	1937
S					
Sonia of Send	F	1931 Apr. 26	Bernard of Send	Teresa of Send	1932
Sultan Chartreuse of Send	M	1926 May 12	Urlus Volbloed of Send	Myrrah	1930

Name	Sex	Date	Sire	Dam	Year
Sheba of Send	F	1929 Feb. 23	Hans Wartkopf of Send	Carla Ottoberg of Send	1930
Sascha of Send	M	1929 Feb. 23	Hans Wartkopf of Send	Carla Ottoberg of Send	1930
Sohrab of Send	M	1931 Apr. 26	Bernard of Send	Teresa of Send	1932
Sybil of Send	F	1929 Feb. 23	Hans Wartkopf of Send	Carla Oterberg of Send	1930
Sonja of Send	F	1933 May 22	Godric of Send	Miranda of Send	1934
(See Karieu of Dane Park)					
Safi of Send	F	1927 Aug. 29	Ador Viktoria of Send	Topsy of Cuddingham	1929
Sibell of Send	F	1927 Aug. 29	Ador Viktoria of Send	Topsy of Cuddingham	1929
Siward of Send	M	1928 June 15	Baldur Daheim of Send	Topsy of Cuddingham	1929
Sebastian of Send	M	1929 Feb. 23	Hans Wartkopf of Send	Carla Oterberg of Send	1930
Shah of Send	M	1929 Feb. 23	Hans Wartkopf of Send	Carla Oterberg of Send	1930
Sheila of Send	F	1929 Feb. 23	Hans Wartkopf of Send	Carla Oterberg of Send	1930
Sylvia of Send	F	1929 Feb. 23	Hans Wartkopf of Send	Carla Oterberg of Send	1930
Sirocco of Send	M	1927 Aug. 29	Ador Viktoria of Send	Topsy of Cuddington	1928
Serena of Send	F	1928 June 15	Baldur Daheim of Send	Topsy of Cuddington	1931
Stella of Send	F	1931 Apr. 26	Bernard of Send	Teresa of Send	1932
Stephen of Send	M	1931 Aug. 28	Ch. Lancelot of Send	Omega of Send	1932
Siefried of Send	M	1931 Apr. 26	Bernard of Send	Teresa of Send	1932
Sharon of Send	M	1931 Aug. 28	Ch. Lancelot of Send	Omega of Send	1932
Suzanna of Send	F	1932 Aug. 16	Yule of Send	Serena of Send	1932
Saturn of Send	M	1932 Aug. 16	Yule of Send	Serena of Send	1932
Suza of Send	F	1921 Apr. 26	Bernard of Send	Teresa of Send	1933
Shawn of Send	M	1933 May 22	Godric of Send	Miranda of Send	1933
Susanne of Send	F	1933 May 22	Godric of Send	Miranda of Send	1933
Soinita of Send	F	1933 May 22	Godric of Send	Miranda of Send	1934

Code: (IMP-Imported) (M-Male) (F-Female) (V-Von) (Ch.-Champion)

Name	Sex	Born	Sire	Dam	Year Registered at Kennel Club
Sorrell of Send	F	1933 May 22	Godric of Send	Miranda of Send	1934
Susan of Send	F	1932 Aug. 16	Yule of Send	Serena of Send	1934
Samson of Send	M	1933 May 22	Godric of Send	Miranda of Send	1934
Sirdar of Send	M	1933 May 22	Godric of Send	Miranda of Send	1935
Sylvius of Send	M	1935 July 18	Mark of Send	Elise of Send	1936
Storm of Send	M	1935 June 18	Mark of Send	Elise of Send	1936
Shane of Send	M	1935 July 18	Mark of Send	Elise of Send	1937
Sapper of Send	M	1935 July 18	Mark of Send	Elise of Send	1937
Shamus of Send	M	1935 July 18	Mark of Send	Elise of Send	1938
Singora of Send	M	1938 Jan. 26	Zingaro of Sudbury	My Queen	1938
T					
Tekla Rotenburg of Send (IMP)	F	1923 Aug. 5	Adonis v.d. Wilhelmsburg	Tekla v. Schonbuch	1926
Toska Bohmerwald of Send (IMP)	F	1922 July 4	Famulus Hansa	Eva v.d. Wartau	1926
Tantalus of Send	M	1929 Feb. 21	Eglon of Send	Lucie of Axwell	1930
Tessa of Send	F	1929 Feb. 21	Eglon of Send	Lucie of Axwell	1929
Thor of Send	M	1927 Aug. 27	Baldur Daheim of Send	Jane of Send	1928
Tansy of Send	F	1929 Feb. 21	Eglon of Send	Lucie of Axwell	1930
Teresa of Send	F	1929 Feb. 21	Eglon of Send	Lucie of Axwell	1930
Thea of Send	F	1929 Feb. 21	Eglon of Send	Lucie of Axwell	1930
Twala of Send	M	1927 Aug. 27	Baldur Daheim of Send	Jane of Send	1928
Tony of Send	M	1928 June 22	Fra of Send	Blanka of Send	1928
Titus of Send	M	1928 June 22	Fra of Send	Blanka of Send	1929

Name	Sex	Date	Sire	Dam	Year
Tasso of Send	M	1928 June 22	Fra of Send	Blanka of Send	1929
Tartar of Send	M	1928 June 22	Fra of Send	Blanka of Send	1929
Tilla of Send	F	1928 June 22	Fra of Send	Blanka of Send	1930
Togo of Send	M	1929 Nov. 1	Ch. Lancelot of Send	Opal of Send	1930
Tarquin of Send	M	1929 Feb. 21	Eglon of Send	Lucie of Axwell	1930
Tarzan of Send	M	1929 Nov. 1	Ch. Lancelot of Send	Opal of Send	1931
Tiger of Send	M	1932 Aug. 28	Bernard of Send	Thea of Send	1932
Thora of Send	F	1932 Aug. 28	Bernard of Send	Thea of Send	1933
Thelma of Send	F	1932 Aug. 28	Bernard of Send	Thea of Send	1934
Tonie of Send	F	1933 May 23	Pixie of Send	Vivia of Send	1934
Tonio of Send	M	1934 Sept. 15	Juan of Send	Kleeta of Send	1934
Tim of Send	M	1934 Sept. 15	Juan of Send	Kleeta of Send	1935
Truant of Send	M	1935 Aug. 15	Tantalus of Send	Meta of Send	1939
Tanis of Send	F	1935 Aug. 15	Tantalus of Send	Meta of Send	1939

U

Name	Sex	Date	Sire	Dam	Year
Urlus Volbloed of Send (IMP)	M	1923 June 12	Hedwigs Nestor	Hedwigs Niza	1927
Ch. Ulana of Send	F	1928 July 2	Urlus Volbloed of Send	Electra of Send	1929
Ula of Send	F	1928 July 2	Urlus Volbloed of Send	Electra of Send	1930
Ulysses of Send	M	1928 June 2	Urlus Volbloed of Send	Electra of Send	1929
Uhlan of Send	M	1929 Nov. 7	Ch. Lancelot of Send	Bella Forstenriederquelle of Send	1930
Ulva of Send	F	1929 Mar. 8	Kastor Klasserberg of Send	Gaby of Send	1930
Umetta of Send	F	1930 Oct. 9	Thor of Send	Danner of Elverland	1931
Udo of Send	M	1931 Sept. 6	Roland of Send	Hermione of Send	1932
Una of Send	F	1930 Oct. 9	Thor of Send	Danners of Elverland	1932
Uncas of Send	M	1929 Nov. 7	Ch. Lancelot of Send	Bella Forstenriederquelle of Send	1932

Code: (IMP–Imported) (M–Male) (F–Female) (V–Von) (Ch.–Champion)

Name	Sex	Born	Sire	Dam	Year Registered at Kennel Club
Ulfrick of Send	M	1932 Aug. 26	Yule of Send	Balaka of Send	1932
Uno of Send	M	1932 Aug. 26	Yule of Send	Balaka of Send	1933
Ufa of Send	F	1930 Oct. 9	Thor of Send	Danner of Elverland	1933
Ursula of Send	F	1929 Nov. 7	Ch. Lancelot of Send	Bella Forstenriederquelle of Send	1933
Ulick of Send	M	1936 Feb. 9	Tantalus of Send	Lahne of Send	1936
V					
Vivienne of Send		1931 Apr. 29	Bernard of Send	Bellona of Send	1931
Vera of Send	F	1928 July 5	Baldur Daheim of Send	Babette of Send	1930
Verinda of Send	F	1931 Apr. 29	Bernard of Send	Bellona of Send	1932
Valerie of Send	F	1927 Aug. 31	Primley Quintus	Cilli Illertal of Send	1928
Velma of Send	F	1927 Aug. 31	Primley Quintus	Cilli Illertal of Send	1928
Veronica of Send	F	1927 Aug. 31	Primley Quintus	Cilli Illertal of Send	1928
Vesta of Send	F	1927 Aug. 31	Primley Quintus	Cilli Illertal of Send	1928
Villette of Send	F	1927 Aug. 31	Primley Quintus	Cilli Illertal of Send	1928
Volga of Send	M	1927 Aug. 31	Primley Quintus	Cilli Illertal of Send	1928
Voltaire of Send	M	1927 Aug. 31	Primley Quintus	Cilli Illertal of Send	1928
Vosper of Send	M	1927 Aug. 31	Primley Quintus	Cilli Illertal of Send	1928
Vulture of Send	F	1927 Aug. 31	Primley Quintus	Cilli Illertal of Send	1928
Vandyke of Send	M	1928 July 5	Baldur Daheim of Send	Babette of Send	1929
Victor of Send	M	1929 Mar. 11	Hagen of Send	Hedwig Schloss Helmstad of Send	1930
Vanessa of Send	F	1929	Hedwig Schloss Helmstad of Send	Hagen of Send	1930

Name	Sex	Date	Sire	Dam	Year
Valjean of Send	M	1931 Apr. 29	Bernard of Send	Bellona of Send	1931
Vida of Send	F	1931 Feb. 8	Thor of Send	Vera of Send	1931
Violetta of Send	F	1931 Apr. 29	Bernard of Send	Bellona of Send	1931
Vixen of Send	F	1931 Apr. 29	Bernard of Send	Bellona of Send	1931
Valhall of Send	M	1931 Apr. 29	Bernard of Send	Bellona of Send	1932
Vasco of Send	M	1931 Apr. 29	Bernard of Send	Bellona of Send	1932
Val of Send	M	1931 Sept. 2	Thor of Send	Anette of Send	1932
Vanda of Send	F	1929 Mar. 11	Hagan of Send	Hedwig Schloss Helmstad of Send	1932
Viking of Send	M	1931 Sept. 2	Thor of Send	Anette of Send	1933
Vivia of Send	F	1931 Feb. 8	Thor of Send	Vera of Send	1933
Venus of Send	F	1931 Sept. 2	Thor of Send	Anette of Send	1933
Vicar of Send	M	1931 Apr. 29	Bernard of Send	Bellon of Send	1933
Vanora of Send	F	1933 June 3	Thor of Send	Quella of Send	1933
Vincent of Send	M	1931 Feb. 8	Thor of Send	Vera of Send	1933
Vulstan of Send	M	1933 June 3	Thor of Send	Quella of Send	1933
Vilma of Send	F	1933 June 3	Thor of Send	Quella of Send	1933
Vandal of Send	M	1933 June 3	Thor of Send	Quella of Send	1933
Vance of Send	M	1933 June 3	Thor of Send	Quella of Send	1933
Volkmar of Send	M	1933 June 3	Thor of Send	Quella of Send	1934
Vanra of Send	F	1932 Sept. 3	Roland of Send	Mona of Send	1934
Vido of Send	M	1933 June 3	Thor of Send	Quella of Send	1934
Vamar of Send	M	1933 June 3	Thor of Send	Quella of Send	1934
Vaughan of Send	M	1934 Sep. 29	Thor of Send	Aphrodite of Send	1935
Vanity of Send	F	1931 Apr. 29	Bernard of Send	Bellona of Send	1935

Code: (IMP-Imported) (M-Male) (F-Female) (V-Von) (Ch.-Champion)

Name	Sex	Born	Sire	Dam	Year Registered at Kennel Club
W					
Ch. Wolfram of Sendale	M	1923 Aug. 19	Magpie of Etive	Bess of Ouborough	1930
Ch. Wotan of Send	F	1930 Jan. 6	Ch. Lancelot of Send	Eunice of Send	1930
Wendla of Send	F	1930 Jan. 6	Ch. Lancelot of Send	Eunice of Send	1930
Woden of Send	M	1928 July 8	Norseman of Send	Neroli Camphausen of Send	1930
Wanda of Send	F	1927 Sep. 12	Ador Viktoria of Send	Chloe of Send	1928
Wykon of Send	M	1928 July 8	Norseman of Send	Neroli Camphausen of Send	1929
Wendy of Send	F	1928 July 8	Norseman of Send	Neroli Camphausen of Send	1929
Wasil of Send	M	1928 July 8	Norseman of Send	Neroli Camphausen of Send	1929
Wenonah of Send	F	1928 July 8	Norseman of Send	Neroli Camphausen of Send	1930
Wompa of Send	M	1929 Mar. 17	Jorg Osterholz of Send	Xyla of Send	1930
Wenzel of Send	M	1929 Mar. 17	Jorg Osterholz of Send	Xyla of Send	1930
Wellyn of Send	M	1930 Jan. 6	Ch. Lancelot of Send	Eunice of Send	1931
Wimibald of Send	F	1931 Feb. 9	Thor of Send	Donna of Send	1931
Wizard of Send	M	1931 Apr. 29	Egbert of Send	Ophelia of Send	1932
Winifred of Send	F	1931 Sept. 9	Yule of Send	Odette of Send	1932
Wanzella of Send	F	1932 Aug. 31	Furst of Send	Sheilah of Send	1932
Weland of Send	M	1932 Aug. 31	Furst of Send	Sheilah of Send	1933
Welga of Send	F	1932 Aug. 31	urst of Send	Sheilah of Send	1933
Wilfroy of Send	M	1932 Aug. 31	Furst of Send	Sheilah of Send	1933
Winnie of Send	F	1932 Aug. 31	Furst of Send	Sheilah of Send	1933
Winifried of Send	F	1930 Jan. 6	Ch. Lancelot of Send	Eunice of Send	1934
Willette of Send	F	1934 Oct. 11	Rafe of Send	Umetta of Send	1935

Name	Sex	Date	Sire	Dam	Year
Wilma of Send	F	934 Oct. 11	Rafe of Send	Umetta of Send	1935
X					
Xenia of Send	F	1927 Sept. 17	Baldur Daheim of Send	Elaine of Send	1928
Xerces of Send	M	1927 Sept. 17	Baldur Daheim of Send	Elaine of Send	1928
Xyla of Send	F	1927 Sept. 17	Baldur Daheim of Send	Elaine of Send	1928
Xoctyl of Send	F	1928 July 19	Egon Falkenhorst of Send	Anneliese Rott of Send	1929
Xander of Send	M	1929 Mar. 22	Thor of Send	Lorna of Send	1929
Xaver of Send	M	1929 Mar. 22	Thor of Send	Lorna of Send	1930
Xaron of Send	M	1929 Mar. 22	Thor of Send	Lorna of Send	1930
Xenon of Send	M	1930 Jan. 3	Wolfram of Sendale	Julia of Send	1930
Xandra of Send	F	1930 Jan. 3	Wolfram of Sendale	Julia of Send	1931
Y					
Yak of Send	M	1927 Oct. 4	Burggraf Falkenhorst of Send	Bonita of Send	1928
Yasmin of Send	M	1927 Oct. 4	Burggraf Falkenhorst of Send	Bonita of Send	1928
Yogi of Send	M	1927 Oct. 4	Burggraf Falkenhorst of Send	Bonita of Send	1928
Yole of Send	M	1927 Oct. 4	Burggraf Falkenhorst of Send	Bonita of Send	1928
Yolonde of Send	M	1927 Oct. 4	Burggraf Falkenhorst of Send	Bonita of Send	1928
Ypselt of Send	F	1927 Oct. 4	Burggraf Falkenhorst of Send	Bonita of Send	1928
Ypsilanti of Send	M	1927 Oct. 4	Burggraf Falkenhorst of Send	Bonita of Send	1928
Yukon of Send	M	1927 Oct. 4	Burggraf Falkenhorst of Send	Bonita of Send	1928
Yuma of Send	F	1927 Oct. 4	Burggraf Falkenhorst of Send	Bonita of Send	1928
Yvette of Send	F	1927 Oct. 4	Burggraf Falkenhorst of Send	Bonita of Send	1928
Yvonne of Send (IMP)	F	1927 Oct. 4	Sultan Van Chartreuse	Minny	1928
Yoskyl of Send	M	1928 July 19	Egon Falkenhorst of Send	Anneliese Rott of Send	1929
Yen of Send	M	1930 Jan. 9	Akbar of Send	Omega of Send	1930

Code: (IMP-Imported) (M-Male) (F-Female) (V-Von) (Ch.-Champion)

Name	Sex	Born	Sire	Dam	Year Registered at Kennel Club
Yao of Send	M	1930 Jan. 9	Akbar of Send	Omega of Send	1930
Yeo of Send	M	1930 Jan. 9	Akbar of Send	Omega of Send	1931
Yucca of Send	F	1930 Jan. 9	Akbar of Send	Omega of Send	1933
Z					
Zorro of Send	M	1931 Feb. 10	Eglon of Send	Ch. Ulana of Send	1931
Zoola of Send	M	1931 Feb. 19	Eglon of Send	Ch. Ulana of Send	1932
Zena of Send	F	1931 Feb. 19	Eglon of Send	Ch. Ulana of Send	1932
Ziska of Send	F	1931 Feb. 19	Eglon of Send	Ch. Ulana of Send	1932
Zikali of Send	M	1927 Oct. 15	Donar Falkenhorst of Send	Fahne Ruhrtal of Send	1928
Zello of Send	M	1929 Mar. 26	Hans Wartkopf of Send	Toska Bohmerwald of Send	1929
Zelba of Send	F	1929 Mar. 26	Hans Wartkopf of Send	Toska Bohmerwald of Send	1930
Zenno of Send	M	1930 Jan. 29	Egbert of Send	Fay of Send	1930
Zampa of Send	F	1930 Jan. 29	Egbert of Send	Fay of Send	1930
Zarina of Send	F	1930 Jan. 29	Egbert of Send	Fay of Send	1930
Zertina of Send	F	1930 Jan. 29	Egbert of Send	Fay of Send	1930
Zsupan of Send	M	1930 Jan. 29	Egbert of Send	Fay of Send	1931
Zachem of Send	M	1931 May 14	Guido of Send	Enid of Send	1932
Zaza of Send	F	1931 Feb. 19	Eglon of Send	Ch. Ulana of Send	1932
Zorn of Send	M	1931 May 14	Guido of Send	Enid of Send	1932
Zoos of Send	M	1931 Oct. 3	Furst of Send	Casilda of Send	1932
Zelia of Send	F	1931 May 14	Guido of Send	Enid of Send	1932
Zillah of Send	F	1931 Feb. 19	Guido of Send	Enid of Send	1932

Name	Sex	Date	Sire	Dam	Year
Zarga of Send	M	1931 Feb. 19	Guido of Send	Enid of Send	1932
Zarna of Send	F	1932 Sept. 2	Ch. Lancelot of Send	Aprille of Send	1933
Zenith of Send	M	1932 Sept. 2	Ch. Lancelot of Send	Aprille of Send	1933
Zurga of Send	M	1932 Sept. 2	Ch. Lancelot of Send	Aprille of Send	1933
Zanga of Send	F	1932 Sept. 2	Ch. Lancelot of Send	Aprille of Send	1933
Zoe of Send	F	1930 Jan. 29	Egbert of Send	Fay of Send	1933
Zamia of Send	F	1931 May 14	Guido of Send	Enid of Send	1933
Zaros of Send	M	1931 Oct. 3	Furst of Send	Casilda of Send	1933
Zona of Send	F	1933 June 9	Thor of Send	Livia of Send	1934
Zontex of Send	M	1933 June 9	Thor of Send	Livia of Send	1934

Code: (IMP-Imported) (M-Male) (F-Female) (V-Von) (Ch.-Champion)

How to order additional copies of

The Danes of Send Manor

BY ROBERT HEAL

Please copy the form below and telephone,
fax, write or email us at the address shown.
We welcome payment via money order,
bank draft or credit card.
If using a credit card, please do not forget to
include the expiry date and cardholder's name.

The Danes of Send Manor

6 x 9, hardcover, 320 pp, over 180 B&W photographs.
ISBN 1-55046-355-1

$34.95 CDN / $25.95 US / £17 UK
Plus shipping and handling of $5 CDN / $4 US / £5 UK
Please add $10 CDN for all other international shipping.
credit card orders will be billed in Canadian dollars.

Name _____

Address _____

_____

POSTAL CODE / ZIP

TELEPHONE   FAX   EMAIL

CREDIT CARD #   EXPIRY   ❏   ❏
                                        VISA   MASTERCARD

NAME OF CARDHOLDER

www.bostonmillspress.com

THE BOSTON MILLS PRESS
132 Main Street, Erin, Ontario, Canada N0B 1T0
Telephone 519-833-2407 Fax 519-833-2195